WEST ACADEMIC PUBLISHING'S LAW SCHOOL ADVISORY BOARD

SALES AND LEASES OF GOODS

IN A NUTSHELL®

FIFTH EDITION

ANNE LAWTON
Professor of Law Emerita
Michigan State University College of Law

WEST ACADEMIC PUBLISHING

860 Blue Gentian Road, Suite 350
Eagan, MN 55121
1-877-888-1330

Printed in the United States of America

ISBN: 978-1-68561-113-2

Dedicated to the memory of my good friends
Judy Barrett and Camille Kelley, R.S.M.

OUTLINE

TABLE OF CASES

References are to Pages

TABLE OF REFERENCES TO UCC PROVISIONS AND COMMENTS

References are to Pages

SALES AND LEASES OF GOODS

IN A NUTSHELL®

FIFTH EDITION

INTRODUCTION

A. BACKGROUND

This Nutshell covers revised Article 1, original Article 2, and original Article 2A of the Uniform Commercial Code ("UCC"). It is not intended to serve as a study guide of common law contracts or secured transactions.[1] There is some discussion of common law rules and the distinction between a secured sale and a lease, but such discussion is limited to comparisons with Article 2's and Article 2A's provisions.

Article 1, which last was revised in 2001, contains definitions, principles of interpretation, and general rules that apply throughout the various Articles of the UCC. All fifty states, the District of Columbia, and the U.S. Virgin Islands have enacted revised Article 1. For the enactment history, *see* https://www.uniformlaws.org/committees/community-home?communitykey=53650937-4723-4bc4-9a81-fa609b431933.

Article 2 provides the rules for sales of goods. In 1951, the National Conference of Commissioners on Uniform State Laws (NCCUSL) and the American

---

1 This Nutshell also does not cover the amendments to the UCC, including changes to Articles 1, 2, and 2A, that the Uniform Law Commission approved and recommended for adoption in July of 2022. The amendments were drafted to accommodate emerging technologies. As of the drafting of this Nutshell, no state has adopted the 2022 amendments. For the text and status of the 2022 amendments, *see* https://www.uniformlaws.org/committees/community-home?CommunityKey=1457c422-ddb7-40b0-8c76-39a1991651ac.

Law Institute (ALI) approved the original Uniform Commercial Code, of which Article 2 was a part. In the early aughts, the NCCUSL and the ALI both approved amendments to Article 2. Not a single jurisdiction adopted the Article 2 amendments. In 2011, the Article 2 amendments were withdrawn. For a brief history of the UCC project, including Article 2, *see* https://www.uniformlaws.org/acts/ucc. Therefore, this Nutshell only covers the provisions of the original Article 2. The original Article 2 applies in forty-nine states (the exception being Louisiana), the District of Columbia, Guam, the Northern Mariana Islands, and the U.S. Virgin Islands.

Article 2A provides the rules for leases of personal property. The current version, covered in this Nutshell, was added to the UCC in 1987 and amended in 1990. In 2003, the NCCUSL and ALI approved amendments to Article 2A, but no state adopted those amendments. Therefore, in 2011, the 2003 amendments were withdrawn. With the exception of Louisiana, every state, as well as the District of Columbia and the U.S. Virgin Islands, has adopted the 1987 version of Article 2A, as amended in 1990. For the map of jurisdictions that have adopted Article 2A, *see* https://www.uniformlaws.org/committees/community-home?CommunityKey=16b9e44b-f2c5-4210-99c3-78e7d3fe985f.

B. OUTLINE OF ARTICLE 2

Article 2 is divided into seven parts, which cover different aspects of the contract for sale of goods, e.g., definitions, formation, remedies. Each part contains a number of different sections. The citation for any Article 2 section follows this format: § 2–xxx. The "2" refers to Article 2. The "xxx" is the three-digit section number within any particular part. Thus, § 2–103 is in Part 1 of Article 2, § 2–203 is in Part 2, § 2–303 is in Part 3, and so on.

Part 1 of Article 2 contains a number of definitional sections, including the all-important § 2–105, which defines the term *goods*. In Part 2, you will find sections on form, formation, and readjustment of contract, including the UCC's provisions on the Statute of Frauds (§ 2–201), the parol evidence rule (§ 2–202), and the Battle of the Forms (§ 2–207). Part 3 contains the gap fillers, e.g., open price term at § 2–305, various warranties and warranty-related provisions (§ 2–312 through § 2–318), and various shipping terms, e.g., § 2–319. Part 4 of Article 2 is the shortest with only three sections (§ 2–401 through § 2–403) that deal with issues related to title and good faith purchasers.

Part 5 of Article 2 contains provisions on performance of the parties' agreement. Sections include the seller's right to cure in certain circumstances (§ 2–508), rules on risk of loss (§ 2–509 and § 2–510), and the buyer's right to inspect the goods (§ 2–513). Part 6 provides the rules on breach, repudiation, and excuse. Section 2–601 articulates the perfect tender rule, which is a change from the common law's substantial performance rule. Sections 2–602 and § 2–606 describe the conduct that constitutes rejection and acceptance of goods, respectively, while § 2–608 provides the requirements for revocation of acceptance. Part 6 also contains provisions on anticipatory repudiation (§ 2–610 and § 2–611), adequate assurance (§ 2–609), and excuse of performance, such as impracticability (§ 2–615).

Finally, Part 7 of Article 2 deals with remedies for breach of contract. The index of seller's remedies can be found at § 2–703 and the basic formulae for seller's damages based on resale, market price, lost volume sales, and the price are found at §§ 2–706, 2–708(1), 2–708(2), and 2–709, respectively. Section 2–711 is the index section for buyer's remedies. The formulae for damages based on cover, market, and breach of warranty are located at §§ 2–712, 2–713, and 2–714, respectively. Other provisions on the buyer's right to specific performance, contractual liquidated damages clauses, and contractual limitations on remedies are found at §§ 2–716, 2–718, and 2–719, respectively.

C. OUTLINE OF ARTICLE 2A

Article 2A is divided into five parts. As is evident from Article 2A's Official Comments, many of the provisions of Article 2A are modeled on sections of Article 2. *See, e.g.*, UCC § 2A–201, Comment: Changes (stating that the Statute of Frauds provision for leases is "modeled on Section 2–201, with changes to reflect the differences between a lease contract and a contract for the sale of goods").

Part 1 of Article 2A contains general provisions, including definitions. Part 2 covers formation and construction of the lease contract. It includes provisions on the Statute of Frauds, the parol evidence rule, formation, firm offers, modification, warranties, risk of loss, and casualty to identified goods. Part 3's provisions cover the effect of the lease contract and include sections on subleases, priority of liens, and the rights of the lessor and lessee when the leased goods become fixtures or accessions. (The Nutshell does not cover several sections that are modeled on provisions of Article 9. *See, e.g.*, UCC §§ 2A–306, 2A–309. Any detailed discussion of Article 9 is beyond the scope of this study guide.) Part 4 deals with performance issues: repudiation, substituted performance, and excuse of performance. It includes provisions on adequate assurance of performance, anticipatory repudiation, substituted performance, and excuse of performance. Finally, Part 5 covers default and is broken into three subparts. Part A contains general provisions, including sections on liquidation of damages, while the lessee's and the lessor's remedy provisions are found in Parts B and C, respectively.

CHAPTER 1

WHICH LAW GOVERNS?

A. DOES ARTICLE 2 APPLY?

There are several categories of transactions to which Article 2 does not apply. *See infra* Flowchart #1 and Diagram #1.

First, Article 2 does not apply to "any transaction . . . intended to operate only as a security transaction." UCC § 2–102. Suppose you apply for a loan at Local Bank, which wants collateral to secure your promise to repay the loan. You grant Local Bank a security interest in a valuable painting that you own. This is a secured transaction governed by Article 9, not Article 2, of the UCC. Suppose, however, that you buy a car from Car Dealer. You finance the purchase through Car Dealer. You sign a valid security agreement granting Car Dealer a security interest in the financed vehicle. This is a secured sale governed by both Article 2 and Article 9. Article 2 applies to the sale of the vehicle, e.g., warranties and remedies, while Article 9 applies to the security aspect of the transaction, e.g., perfection and priority of Car Dealer's interest in the vehicle.

Second, Article 2A, not Article 2, applies to leases of personal property. Suppose Acme enters into a contract with CopyCo for a copy machine that Acme plans to use in its business. Depending on the terms of the contract, that transaction may be a secured sale, or it may be a lease. If it is a secured sale, then Article 2 applies to the sale aspects of the transaction while Article 9 applies to the security aspects. If the transaction is a lease, then Article 2A applies. *See infra* § B of this Chapter for a detailed discussion of the tests used to determine whether a transaction is a sale or a lease.

Third, the Convention on Contracts for the International Sale of Goods (CISG) governs certain contracts for the sale of goods between parties that have their places of business in different Contracting States. *See* CISG Art. 1(1). The United States is a signatory to the CISG, albeit with certain reservations. Thus, if Company A has its place of business in New York and Company B's place of business is located in a different Contracting State, then the CISG *may* apply to a contract between the parties for the sale of goods. The CISG excludes certain sales from its coverage. *See, e.g.*, CISG Art. 2. Moreover, the parties may opt out of the CISG and provide that the UCC governs their contract. *See* CISG Art. 6.

Fourth, Article 2 does not apply to sales of real property or to contracts for services. Instead, common law rules govern these transactions. Suppose you are in the market to buy a house. You hire a real estate broker who finds you the perfect house. You make an offer on that house, which the seller accepts. Common law rules apply to both your contract with the real estate broker for her services and your contract to buy the house from the seller. *See infra* § A.3 of this Chapter on how to determine whether Article 2 or common law rules apply to hybrid transactions.

To what, then, does Article 2 apply? To "transactions in goods." UCC § 2–102. The ensuing sections discuss (1) the UCC's definition of goods, (2) whether the UCC applies to goods severed from realty, (3) how courts decide whether Article 2 applies to hybrid transactions, e.g., a sale of goods *and* services, and (4) what constitutes a contract for sale versus a transaction.

1. DEFINITION OF GOODS: § 2–105

The UCC defines goods as "all things (including specially manufactured goods) which are movable at the time of identification to the contract for sale." UCC § 2–105(1). Notice that specially manufactured goods are included in the UCC's definition. For example, if Acme Corporation contracts with Omega Company to manufacture a machine to Acme's specifications, that machine is a good. While certain hybrid transactions may fall outside the purview of Article 2, it is important to recognize that the production of goods involves services. The mere fact that some service is involved in manufacturing a good does not mean that Article 2 does not apply.

What does it mean that the good is "movable at the time of identification to the contract for sale"? If you purchase a coat off the rack at a retail store, identification occurs when the contract is made for purchase of the coat. At that time, the coat is movable and, thus, is a good. *See* UCC §§ 2–105, 501(1)(a). Suppose, however, that Acme Corporation places an order for 1,000 widgets from Omega Company. Assume that the widgets do not exist at the time that

Omega accepts Acme's offer for the purchase of 1,000 widgets. In this example, the widgets are "future goods" because they do not yet exist. Nonetheless, Article 2 applies to this contract for sale. *See* UCC § 2–105(2). When Omega produces the widgets and ships, marks, or otherwise designates that the widgets are for the Acme contract, identification occurs. UCC § 2–501(1)(b). At that time, the widgets are movable and, thus, are goods.

Goods also include the "unborn young of animals and growing crops and other identified things attached to realty." UCC § 2–105(1). *See infra* § A.2 on the rules for "other identified things attached to realty" that are to be severed. Identification for the unborn young of animals occurs at the time of conception if the animals are to be born within twelve months of the parties' contract. UCC § 2–501(1)(c). As for crops, identification happens when the crops are planted if the crops "are to be harvested within the year or within the next normal harvest season after contracting, whichever is longer." UCC § 2–501(1)(c); *see* UCC § 2–501, Comment ¶ 6.

Money is not a good if it is the parties' medium of exchange. In the example above in which Acme buys 1,000 widgets from Omega, the money that Acme pays for the widgets is not a good. But if Acme were to purchase foreign currency from Omega, then the currency is considered a good. *See* UCC § 2–105, Comment ¶ 1. Investment securities also are not goods. Article 8, not Article 2, of the UCC provides the relevant rules for investment securities. Finally, a chose in action—what the UCC calls a thing in action—is not a good. UCC § 2–105(1).

2. GOODS SEVERED FROM REALTY: § 2–107

The UCC provides specific rules for things to be severed from the land. Article 2 applies to a contract for the sale of minerals, oil, or gas to be removed from the land *only* if the minerals, oil, or gas "are to be severed by the seller." UCC § 2–107(1). For example, if Land Owner makes a contract with Acme in which Acme is to extract minerals from Land Owner's land, then Article 2 does not apply to this transaction. Instead, common law rules governing contracts for land apply. *See* UCC § 2–107, Comment ¶ 1. The same rule applies to a contract for the sale of a structure or its materials to be removed from the land. UCC § 2–107(1). Suppose Omega owns and operates a private railroad for moving timber. Acme and Omega enter into a contract in which Acme agrees to remove a section of the rail line affixed to Omega's land and buy the rails, ties, and other salvageable materials. Removal does not harm the land. Article 2 does not apply to the contract. The railroad is a structure affixed to the land and the buyer Acme, not the seller Omega, effected the severance of the rail line. *See* Condon Bros., Inc. v. Simpson Timber Co., 966 P.2d 355 (Wash. Ct. App. 1998).

For *other* things attached to the land, the determination of whether Article 2 applies turns on whether severance from the land can be accomplished "without material harm." UCC § 2–

107(2). It matters not whether the buyer or the seller effects the severance. A contract to cut timber also is a contract for the sale of goods regardless of whether the buyer or seller of the timber severs it from the land. UCC § 2–107(2).

When deciding whether a contract involves the sale of a good, be careful not to use § 2–107 to override the rule in § 2–105. If the thing is movable at the time of identification to the contract, it is a good under § 2–105, even if that good later is attached to realty. *See, e.g.,* The Timken Co. v. MTS Systems Corp., 539 F. Supp. 3d 770 (N.D. Ohio 2021) (rejecting argument that § 2–107(2) controls analysis of whether test system was a good and noting "focus [under Ohio law] on identification of merchandise to the contract to determine movability"). Suppose you purchase materials from Home Depot to build a deck onto the back of your home. The contract is for materials alone, not for construction of the deck itself by Home Depot. The contract with Home Depot to purchase the deck materials involves the sale of goods even though you intend to attach the deck to your house and anchor it into the real property behind your home. In other words, "the fact that goods are installed so that they are no longer movable does not remove the transaction from Article 2 so long as the goods were movable at the time of identification." 2 Anderson U.C.C. § 2–105:36 (3d ed.). At the time that you made the contract with Home Depot, the deck materials were movable and, thus, were goods. UCC §§ 2–105(1), 2–501(1)(a).

3. HYBRID TRANSACTIONS

For many transactions, determining whether Article 2 applies is easy. For example, if you buy a car sitting on Car Dealer's lot, the contract that you sign for purchase of the vehicle is a contract for the sale of a good. While production of the car involved substantial labor inputs, your contract is for the final product—the vehicle. When you entered into the contract, identification occurred and at that time the vehicle was movable. *See* UCC §§ 2–105(1), 2–501(1)(a). Thus, Article 2 applies.

What happens, however, if the parties' contract calls for the provision of both goods and services? For such hybrid transactions, a majority of courts use the predominant purpose or predominant factor test to determine Article 2's applicability to the transaction. The predominant purpose test asks whether a transaction's "predominant factor, [its] thrust, [its] purpose, reasonably stated, is the rendition of service, with goods incidentally involved (e.g., contract with artist for painting) or is a transaction of sale, with labor incidentally involved (e.g., installation of a heater in a bathroom." Bonebrake v. Cox, 499 F.2d 951 (8th Cir. 1974).

Courts examine several factors in determining a contract's predominant purpose: (1) the contract's language; (2) the business of the seller; (3) the reason the parties made the contract; and (4) the amounts paid for the goods versus the services. Audio Visual Artistry v. Tanzer, 403 S.W.3d 789 (Tenn. Ct. App. 2012). In *Tanzer,* the court held that Article 2 applied to the sale and installation of a smart home system by Audio Visual Artistry (AVA). The court first noted that the language of the parties' contract indicated that the contract was for a sale of goods. The contract referred to Tanzer as a "purchaser", which the court said "connote[d] a sale of goods contract." *Id.* at 800. The contract also used various other terms peculiar to the sale of goods, such as "equipment," "delivered equipment," "delivery of goods," "pre-paid goods," "product", and "electronic hardware." *Id.*

Second, AVA was in the business of designing and selling home theater, music, and phone/intercom systems. AVA did not manufacture such systems but rather sold products from various manufacturers. The court pointed out that AVA's " 'design' role" was limited to determining what the customer wanted and which systems would work to connect the various system components. Thus, the court concluded that "installation and service" were "incidental to the overarching purpose of [AVA's] business, which [was] to sell 'smart home' components." *Id* at 803.

Third, "the final product" for which Tanzer had bargained was electronic equipment. In other words, the reason Tanzer made the contract was to obtain the equipment, not the services provided by AVA. In fact, AVA ordered the required equipment from the manufacturer and installed it; AVA did not build the equipment at Tanzer's home. In addition, Tanzer was willing to return some of the equipment, which "support[ed] a finding that it had not become a permanent improvement to his realty." *Id.* Finally, the cost of the equipment was $56,375 of the total $71,915 contract price. By comparison, the cost of labor and service was $9,880 or less than 14% of the total contract price.

In Kaitz v. Landscape Creations, Inc., 2000 Mass. App. Div. 140 (Mass. Dist. Ct. 2000), the court held that Article 2 did not apply to a contract for landscape services. While the trees, plants, and shrubs that Landscape Creations provided as part of its landscaping service were goods, the predominant purpose of the transaction was the provision of services. First, the project's scope was "extensive," extending over a period of months. A sale of trees, plants, and shrubs would not take several months to complete. Second, the project was "labor intensive" with Landscape Creations developing "a landscape design, grading the soil, [and] preparing and mulching plant beds." *Id.* at 141. Third, Landscape Creations was not a nursery that only sold trees, plants, and shrubs. Instead, it was a landscaping company that provided a "full range of services" to customers. Thus, the "main thrust" of the contract was "the design, layout, grading and beautification" of Kaitz's property with the purchase of trees, plants, and shrubs as incidental to the provision of services. *Id.*

Why does it matter whether Article 2 or common law rules apply? The applicable rules under Article 2 and the common law differ in some important respects. For example, unless disclaimed, the implied warranty of merchantability applies to the sale of a good by a merchant. *See* UCC § 2–314. In addition, the statute of limitations for filing suit may vary. The UCC has a four-year statute of limitations. *See* UCC

§ 2–725. The decision in *Kaitz* illustrates what is at stake. *Kaitz* involved an appeal from dismissal of the case based on the statute of limitations. The lower court had applied the UCC's four-year limitations period and concluded that Kaitz's complaint was untimely. The appeals court reversed the dismissal after finding that the contract was one for services to which a six-year statute of limitations applied.

4. TRANSACTIONS AND CONTRACTS FOR SALE

Article 2 applies to sales of goods. A sale is the "passing of title from the seller to the buyer for a price." UCC § 2–106(1). A contract for sale "includes both a present sale of goods and a contract to sell goods at a future time." UCC § 2–106(1). Goods that do not exist at the time of contract formation are "future goods." UCC § 2–105(2). The parties may form a contract for the purchase and sale of future goods, and such a contract is a contract for sale. UCC § 2–105(2); *see* UCC § 2–105, Comment ¶ 2.

But Article 2 covers not just sales of goods. It applies to "transactions in goods." UCC § 2–102. What is a transaction in goods? The UCC does not define the word "transaction" but "[o]bviously 'transactions in goods'—the scope of [A]rticle 2—is broader than 'sales.' " Mieske v. Bartell Drug Co., 593 P.2d 1308 (Wash. 1979). For example, in Kaspers v. Howmedica Osteonics Corp., 2015 WL 12085853 (W.D. Wash. 2015), the court held that Article 2 applied to implied warranty claims against a company's product even though there was no contract for sale of the product. *Kaspers* involved a human clinical trial of CerviCore Invertebral Disc as part of Howmedica's efforts to obtain pre-market approval for CerviCore from the FDA. Howmedica wanted to market CerviCore as an alternative to disc surgery for patients with herniated or degenerated cervical discs. Kaspers was one of four hundred participants in the CerviCore clinical trial. After surgical implantation of CerviCore, Kaspers experienced various injuries that she alleged resulted from Howmedica's product. Kaspers filed a multi-count complaint against Howmedica, which included claims for breach of implied warranty. Howmedica argued that Article 2 did not apply to Kaspers's warranty claims because Howmedica did not sell CerviCore to Kaspers. The court rejected Howmedica's argument and explained that Article 2 applies to "transactions in goods", not merely sales of goods. "Ms. Kaspers provided consideration by participating in the human clinical trial, and in return Howmedica provided her with the CerviCore—this constitutes a transaction in goods." *Kaspers,* 2015 WL at *10. Thus, the court concluded that Article 2 applied to Kaspers's implied warranty claims against Howmedica.

FLOWCHART #1: DOES ARTICLE 2 APPLY?

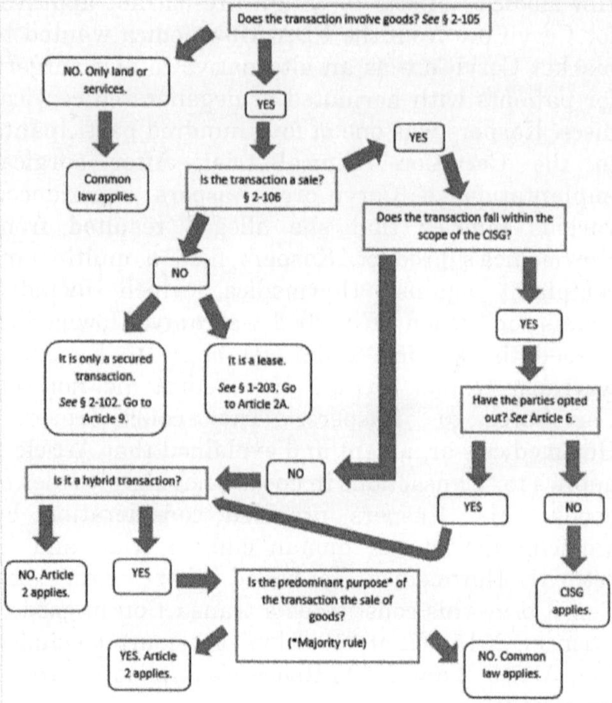

DIAGRAM #1: RELATIONSHIP AMONG ARTICLES 2, 2A AND 9

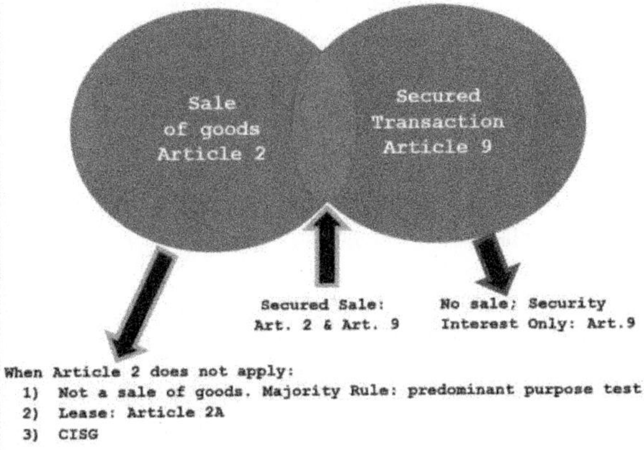

B. DOES ARTICLE 2A APPLY?

Recall the transaction described in § A above involving Acme and CopyCo. If the transaction is a secured sale, then Article 2 applies to the sale aspects of the transaction, e.g., warranties, remedies for breach. But if the transaction is a lease, then Article 2A applies. *See* UCC § 2A–102 (stating that Article 2A "applies to any transaction, regardless of form, that creates a lease").

Why does it matter? Article 1's definitions and "principles of construction and interpretation" apply to Article 2A. UCC § 2A–103(4). More importantly, Article 2 is the statutory analogue for Article 2A.

> Many of the provisions of [Article 2] were carried over, changed to reflect differences in style, leasing terminology or leasing practices. Thus,

the official comments to those sections of Article 2 whose provisions were carried over are incorporated by reference in Article 2A, as well; further, any case law interpreting those provisions should be viewed as persuasive but not binding on a court when deciding a similar issue with respect to leases.

UCC § 2A–101, Comment: Relationship of Article 2A to Other Articles.

TABLE #1: ARTICLE 2 AND ARTICLE 2A: COMPARISON OF STATUTORY SECTIONS

Column A contains the Article 2A provision and Column B lists the statutory analogue in Article 2. A "yes" in Column C means that there is substantive commentary for the Article 2A provision that is additional to the Official Comment for the similar Article 2 provision. Article 1 and Article 9 statutory analogues are omitted from the table, but you can find them at the start of the Official Comment under Uniform Statutory Source for each Article 2A provision.

A Article 2A	B Article 2	C Official Comment
Part 1. General Provisions		
§ 2A-108 (Unconscionability)	§ 2-302	Yes
Part 2. Formation and Construction		
§ 2A-201(Statute of Frauds)	§ 2-201	Yes
§ 2A-202 (Parol Evidence Rule)	§ 2-202	Yes
§ 2A-203 (Seals Inoperative)	§ 2-203	No
§ 2A-204 (Formation in General)	§ 2-204	No
§ 2A-205 (Firm Offers)	§ 2-205	No
§ 2A-206 (Offer and Acceptance)	§ 2-206(1), (2)	No
§ 2A-208 (Modification)	§ 2-209	Yes
§ 2A-210 (Express Warranties)	§ 2-313	Yes
§ 2A-211 (Warranties against Infringement)	§ 2-312	Yes
§ 2A-212 (Implied Warranty of Merchantability)	§ 2-314	No

A Article 2A	B Article 2	C Official Comment
§ 2A-213 (Implied Fitness Warranty)	§ 2-315	No
§2A-214 (Exclusion/Modification of Warranties)	§ 2-316, § 2-312(2)	Yes
§ 2A-215 (Cumulation/Conflict of Warranties)	§ 2-317	No
§ 2A-216 (Third-Party Beneficiaries)	§ 2-318	Yes
§ 2A-217 (Identification)	§ 2-501	Yes
§ 2A-218 (Insurance and Proceeds)	§ 2-501	Yes
§ 2A-219 (Risk of Loss)	§ 2-509	Yes
§ 2A-220 (Effect of Default on Risk of Loss)	§ 2-510	Yes
§ 2A-221 (Casualty to Identified Goods)	§ 2-613	Yes
Part 3. Effect of Lease Contract		
§ 2A-303 (Delegation of Performance; Transfer of Rights)	§ 2-210	Yes
§ 2A-304 (Subsequent Lease of Goods by Lessor)	§ 2-403	Yes
§ 2A-305 (Lessee Sale or Sublease of Goods)	§ 2-403	Yes
§ 2A-308 (Special Rights of Creditors)	§ 2-402(2), 3(b)	Yes
Part 4. Performance: Repudiated, Substituted, Excused		
§ 2A-401 (Adequate Assurance)	§ 2-609	No
§ 2A-402 (Anticipatory Repudiation)	§ 2-610	No
§ 2A-403 (Retraction of Anticipatory Repudiation)	§ 2-611	No
§ 2A-404 (Substituted Performance)	§ 2-614	No
§ 2A-405 (Excused Performance)	§ 2-615	No
§ 2A-406 (Procedure on Excused Performance)	§ 2-616(1), (2)	Yes
Part 5A. Default in General		
§ 2A-503 (Modification/Impairment of Rights/Remedies)	§§ 2-719, 2-701	Yes
§ 2A-504 (Liquidation of Damages)	§ 2-718(1)-(3), § 2-719(2)	Yes
§ 2A-505 (Cancellation, Termination, Rescission)	§ 2-106(3), (4), §§ 2-720, 2-721	No
§ 2A-506 (Statute of Limitations)	§ 2-725	Yes
§ 2A-507 (Market Rent: Time and Place)	§§ 2-723, 2-724	No
Part 5B. Default by Lessor (Lessee Remedies)		
§ 2A-508 (Lessee's Remedies)	§§ 2-711, 2-717	Yes
§ 2A-509 (Improper Delivery; Rightful Rejection)	§ 2-601, § 2-602(1)	No
§ 2A-510 (Installment Lease Contract)	§ 2-612	No
§ 2A-511 (Merchant Lessee's Duties as to Rightfully Rejected Goods)	§ 2-603, § 706(5)	Yes
§ 2A-512 (Lessee's Duties Rightfully Rejected Goods)	§ 2-602(2)(b), (c), § 2-604	Yes
§ 2A-513 (Cure)	§ 2-508	No
§ 2A-514 (Waiver of Lessee's Objections)	§ 2-605	No
§ 2A -515 (Acceptance of Goods)	§ 2-606	Yes
§ 2A-516 (Effect of Acceptance; Default Notice; Burden of Establishing Default; Notice of Claim)	§ 2-607	Yes
§ 2A-517 (Revocation of Acceptance of Goods)	§ 2-608	Yes
§ 2A-518 (Cover)	§ 2-712	Yes
§ 2A-519 (Market Rent Damages; Breach of Warranty)	§§ 2-713, 2-714	Yes
§ 2A-520 (Incidental & Consequential Damages)	§ 2-715	Yes
§ 2A-521 (Specific Performance or Replevin)	§ 2-716	Yes
§ 2A-522 (Rights to Goods on Lessor's Insolvency)	§ 2-502	No

A Article 2A	B Article 2	C Official Comment
Part 5C. Default by Lessee (Lessor Remedies)		
§ 2A-523 (Lessor's Remedies)	§ 2-703	Yes
§ 2A-524 (Right to Identify Goods to Lease Contract)	§ 2-704	Yes
§ 2A-525 (Right to Possession of Goods)	§ 2-702(1)	Yes
§ 2A-526 (Stoppage of Delivery in Transit or Otherwise)	§ 2-705	No
§ 2A-527 (Rights to Dispose of Goods)	§ 2-706(1), (5), (6)	Yes
§ 2A-528 (Damages: Non-Acceptance, Failure to Pay, Repudiation, Other Default)	§ 2-708	Yes
§ 2A-529 (Action for Rent)	§ 2-709	Yes
§ 2A-530 (Incidental Damages)	§ 2-710	No
§ 2A-531 (Standing to Sue Third Parties for Injury to Goods)	§ 2-722	No

Let's return to our earlier question: Does it really matter whether a transaction is a sale or a lease?

The short answer is "yes". It matters in bankruptcy. *See, e.g., In re* Price, 577 B.R. 643 (Bankr. E.D. N.C. 2017) (listing differences between a lease and a secured transaction in Chapter 13 bankruptcy case). Suppose Acme files for relief under Chapter 11 of the Bankruptcy Code with the intent to reorganize its business. Acme wants to keep the copy machine it obtained from CopyCo. If the transaction is a lease, that means that Acme must assume the lease and cure certain defaults prior to assumption. *See* 11 U.S.C. § 365. Acme cannot keep the copy machine without assuming the lease because a lease transfers the right to possess and use the goods, but does not transfer ownership, as in a sale. *See* UCC § 2A–103(1)(j). By assuming the lease, Acme assumes the obligations under the lease that the parties entered into prior to bankruptcy. *See, e.g., In re* Double G Trucking of the Arklatex, Inc., 432 B.R. 789 (Bankr. W.D. Ark. 2010) (stating that if agreement was a lease, then debtor had to either reject the lease and "relinquish the property or assume the lease, cure any default, and perform under the lease terms in accordance with 11 U.S.C. § 365").

If the court determines that the transaction is a sale with CopyCo taking a security interest in the machine, then CopyCo's interest is subject to the bankruptcy trustee's strong arm powers. *See* 11 U.S.C. § 544. Thus, if CopyCo failed to file a UCC-1 or financing statement to perfect its security interest in the machine, then the trustee may avoid CopyCo's security interest in bankruptcy. *See* UCC § 9–505, Comment ¶ 2 (stating the creditor may make a precautionary UCC-1 filing if it is uncertain whether the transaction is a sale or lease). CopyCo then ends up as an unsecured creditor in Acme's bankruptcy case. Acme retains the copy machine because Acme, not CopyCo, owns the machine. CopyCo merely held a security interest in the machine.

Notwithstanding similarities between many provisions of Article 2 and Article 2A, the difference between a lease and a secured sale is an important one. How, then, do you determine whether the law governing the transaction is Article 2 or Article 2A? The next section of the Nutshell explores that question with a discussion both of § 1–203's bright-line test and the economic realities test that courts use when the bright-line test does not produce a clear answer as to whether the parties' transaction is a lease or a secured sale. This portion of the Nutshell then concludes with a brief discussion of finance leases and consumer leases, for which Article 2A provides special rules.

1. BRIGHT-LINE TEST

Section 1–203 creates a "bright-line" test for determining whether a transaction denominated as a lease is not a lease but rather a disguised secured sale. The test in § 1–203(b) "focus[es] on economics, not the intent of the parties." UCC § 1–203, Comment ¶ 2. A transaction in the form of a lease is a secured sale if the lessee cannot terminate the "lease" *and*

1. the lease term equals or exceeds the good's remaining economic life; *or*
2. the lessee must renew the lease for the good's remaining economic life or is bound by the lease to become the good's owner; *or*
3. the lessee has the option to renew the lease for the remaining economic life of the goods for no additional or for nominal consideration; *or*
4. the lessee has the option to own the goods for no additional or for nominal consideration.

UCC § 1–203(b). In other words, if the lease cannot be terminated and one of the four conditions listed above is satisfied, then the analysis ends. *See, e.g., In re* Price, 577 B.R. 643 (Bankr. E.D. N.C. 2017) (stating that "if the criteria of the Bright-Line Test are satisfied, then the lease is classified as a security agreement as a matter of law"). The transaction is a secured sale regardless of whether the agreement is called a lease.

Suppose you enter into what is termed a "lease agreement" with Big Auto Company (BAC). The agreement provides that you cannot terminate the lease, which runs for 36 months. The vehicle is new and has an economic life at the start of the lease of 12 years. The agreement provides you with the option to own the vehicle at the end of 36 months by paying $1. This transaction is a secured sale. You cannot terminate the lease and you can own a new car for $1, a nominal amount, at the end of 36 months. *See, e.g., In re* Price, 577 B.R. at 655 (holding that leases were disguised secured sales because lessee could not terminate and had purchase option of " 'nominal additional consideration' of one dollar" at end of the leases' terms); *In re* Southeastern Materials, Inc., 433 B.R. 177 (Bankr. M.D. N.C. 2010) (holding that lease that lessee could not terminate and that gave lessee option to buy equipment at lease end for $1—"clearly a nominal value"—was not a lease but rather "created a security interest as a matter of law").

What if the payment at the end of 36 months is $100? Is that amount considered nominal? "The test is whether 'the option price is so low that the lessee will certainly exercise it and will, in all plausible circumstances, leave no meaningful reversion for the lessor.' " *In re* Bailey, 326 B.R. 156 (Bankr. W.D. Ark. 2005) (quoting White & Summers, 4 Uniform Commercial Code § 30–3 at 33 (5th ed. 2002)). Returning to the transaction with BAC described above, the car would have nine years of economic life remaining, which is a meaningful reversion, at the time you would exercise the option to purchase. The likelihood that you would pass on buying the car for an additional $100 is incredibly slim. "In other words, if only a fool would fail to exercise the option, the option price is considered nominal and the transaction revealed to be a disguised sale." *Bailey,* 326 B.R. at 163. Therefore, the transaction in this example is a disguised sale and not a lease. *Cf. In re* Wells, 2015 Bankr. LEXIS 2041 (Bankr. N.D. Ala. 2015) (finding that option to buy vehicle was not nominal, regardless of whether the amount represented 20% of the car's original value or 38.8% of its value at buyout).

What if the option to purchase requires you to pay the fair market value of the vehicle? The additional consideration that you must pay to own the car is not nominal if the lease agreement provides for payment of "the fair market value of the goods determined at the time the option is to be performed." UCC § 1–203(d)(2); *see* Gilbraltar Financial Corporation v. Prestige Equipment Corporation, 949 N.E.2d 314 (Ind. 2011) (citing to § 1–203(d)(2) and holding that because purchase option price was stated as "fair market value" the consideration was not nominal).

Suppose Acme signs a contract called "Lease Agreement" for a piece of equipment for its business. The equipment at the inception of the Lease Agreement has an economic life of 15 years. The Lease Agreement cannot be terminated. The lease term is 5 years and requires Acme to pay any taxes on the equipment, to insure the equipment, and to pay for the equipment's service and maintenance. The Lease Agreement also states that Acme, as lessee, assumes the risk of loss for the equipment. Does the fact that Acme must pay taxes, insurance, for service and maintenance, and assumes the risk of loss mean that the transaction is a disguised sale? Not necessarily. This transaction is a "net lease"—"a type of lease in which 'the lessee assumes all risk of loss and pays all taxes, insurance, maintenance, and the like.' " *In re* Double G Trucking of the Arklatex, Inc., 432 B.R. 789 (Bankr. W.D. Ark. 2010). Section 1–203(c) provides that "a transaction in the form of a lease does not create a security interest merely because" the lessee must pay taxes, insurance, and for service and maintenance, or the lessee assumes the risk of loss for the good. UCC § 1–203(c)(2), (3).

Suppose Acme signs an agreement with Commercial Car Company (CCC) for a vehicle that Acme intends to use in its business. The contract is called "Lease Agreement". CCC's cost for the vehicle is $60,000 but Acme's rental payments under the agreement total $65,000. Is this transaction a disguised sale? Not necessarily. This agreement is a full payout lease, in which the present value of the payments made by the lessee are "substantially equal to or [ ] greater than the fair market value of the goods." UCC § 1–203(c)(1); *see In re Double G Trucking,* 432 B.R. at 799 (stating that with a full payout lease the lessee's payment equals or exceeds the " 'lessor's cost of the goods or their fair market value' ").

While the UCC provides that a lease is not a secured sale merely because it is a full payout lease, why would Acme (or any lessee) enter into such an agreement?

> First, the lessor and lessee might be controlled by the same party and the lease might be a device for shifting income from one to the other. Second, there may be unique tax benefits to be gained by the lessee. . . . Of course, the lessee might be making payments to the lessor to enjoy certain other benefits of the lease such as the avoidance of debt limitations in other loan documents or the avoidance of state and local personal property taxes. . . . The end result is that the lessee realizes a valuable benefit which, when offset against the payments to the lessor, means the net amount the lessee is paying to the lessor is not equal to or greater than the fair market value of the goods.

In re Gateway Ethanol, LLC, 415 B.R. 486 (Bankr. D. Kan. 2009) (quoting 4 Wright & Summers, § 30–3(c)(2)).

If the lessee has the right to terminate the lease, does that mean that the agreement is *not* a secured sale but is truly a lease? Again, not necessarily. For example, in *In re* Cherry, 2012 WL 3252231 (Bankr. N.D. Ala. 2012), the debtor, prior to bankruptcy, had signed an agreement to "lease" a car from Access Automotive. The agreement provided the lessee with the right to terminate prior to the end of the lease term but only upon payment of a "substantial charge" that varied depending on when the lessee terminated. The earlier the termination, the greater the charge. The agreement also provided that upon termination the debtor had to pay both an early termination fee and "all outstanding payments due." Given that the "substantial charge" varied based on when termination occurred—higher for early termination—the bankruptcy court interpreted the phrase "all outstanding payments due" to mean all lease payments remaining on the lease at the time of termination. The court concluded that while the debtor could terminate the lease, she could not terminate her *obligations* under the lease. Therefore, the contract was not a true lease but rather an agreement intended as security. *See also* Automotive Leasing Specialists, LLC v. Little, 392 B.R. 222 (W.D. La. 2008).

2. ECONOMIC REALITIES TEST

What happens if the court cannot determine whether the transaction is a lease or a disguised sale based on the bright-line test? The fact that the transaction does not fit cleanly into § 1–203(b) does not mean that the transaction is a lease. Instead, the court must look to the economic realities of the transaction. The crux of the analysis is whether the lessor retains a meaningful reversionary interest in the good that is the subject of the parties' agreement. *See, e.g.,* Gibraltar Financial Corporation v. Prestige Equipment Corporation, 949 N.E.2d 314 (Ind. 2011) (stating that for most courts and commentators the "principal inquiry" in determining the economic reality of a transaction is " 'whether the lessor retains a meaningful reversionary interest in the goods' "). In other words, when the parties enter into the lease, what are the chances that at the end of that lease the lessor will get back a good with meaningful economic life? If the lessee has an option to purchase and "the lessee's only economically sensible option is to exercise the option, then the agreement will be considered to create a security interest." *In re* Lash, 2010 WL 5141760 (Bankr. M.D. N.C. 2010).

Suppose Acme enters into a contract with EquipCo to lease five pieces of equipment for five years. During the five-year term, Acme cannot terminate the agreement. The equipment, at the inception of the lease, has an economic life of 20 years. The agreement provides Acme with a choice. It can purchase the equipment for $1 million at the end of the original 5-year lease term, or it can renew the lease for another five years during which time it will make rental payments to EquipCo totaling $2 million. While the parties' agreement cannot be terminated, the option to purchase the equipment is not nominal. Therefore, the bright-line test is not satisfied. But what is the likelihood that Acme will renew the lease and pay $2 million for the next five years when it can pay $1 million at the end of the original lease term and own equipment with 15 years left of meaningful economic life? *See* American President Lines v. Lykes Brothers Steamship Company (*In re* Lykes Brothers Steamship Company), 196 B.R. 574 (Bankr. M.D. Fla. 1996) (holding that agreement was a secured sale, noting that it "made no sense" for the debtor, at the end of the original lease term, to rent vessels for an additional five years at a total rental of $91 million when it could buy those vessels at the end of the original lease term for $44.4 million).

3. FINANCE LEASE

Certain provisions of Article 2A except finance leases from their coverage. *See, e.g.*, §§ 2A–212 (merchantability warranty), 2A–213 (fitness warranty), 2A–219 (risk of loss). The reasons for these exceptions are explored in the section of the Nutshell covering the particular Article 2A provision. The discussion here is limited to answering the following question: what is a finance lease?

There are three statutory requirements for a finance lease. First, in a finance lease, the lessor "does not select, manufacture, or supply the goods." UCC § 2A–103(1)(g)(i). Second, the "lessor acquires the goods or the right to possession and use of the goods in connection with the lease." UCC § 2A–103(1)(g)(ii). Finally, to qualify as a finance lease, one of the following four conditions must be satisfied.

a. Before the lessee signs the lease contract, the lessee receives a copy of the contract under which the lessor either acquired the good or the right to possess and use the good [hereinafter *Lessor/Supplier Contract*]. UCC § 2A–103(1)(g)(iii)(A); *or*

b. A condition to the lease agreement's effectiveness is the lessee's approval of the *Lessor/Supplier Contract*. UCC § 2A–103(1)(g)(iii)(B); *or*

c. Before the lessee signs the lease contract, the lessee receives "an accurate and complete statement" of the promises, warranties, warranty disclaimers, limitations or modifications of remedies, and liquidated damages in the *Lessor/ Supplier Contract*. UCC § 2A–103(1)(g)(iii)(C); *or*

d. Before the lessee signs the lease contract, the lessor, except in the case of a consumer lease, informs the lessee in writing (i) of the identity of the supplier, unless the lessee selected the supplier and directed the lessor to obtain the good from the supplier; (ii) that the lessee is entitled to the promises and warranties provided by the supplier to the lessor pursuant to the *Lessor/Supplier Contract; and* (iii) that the lessee may communicate with the supplier and receive "an accurate and complete statement" of the promises, warranties, warranty disclaimers, limitations or modifications of remedies, and liquidated damages in the *Lessor/Supplier Contract*. UCC § 2A–103(1)(g)(iii)(D).

If the transaction does not satisfy the three statutory requirements for a finance lease, the lessor and lessee nonetheless may agree to treat their agreement as a finance lease. *See* UCC § 2A–103, Comment ¶ (g) (stating that "[i]f a transaction does not qualify as a finance lease, the parties may achieve the same result by agreement").

Notice that a finance lease involves three parties: (1) the supplier or supplier/manufacturer of the good; (2) the lessor; and (3) the lessee. In a finance lease, the supplier supplies the good to the lessee pursuant to the lessee's specifications. The lessor is not involved in the selection, production, or supply of the good. For that reason, the lessor in a finance lease is "releas[ed] . . . from most of its traditional liability." UCC § 2A–103, Comment ¶ (g). The lessor's role is to "finance[ ] the lessee's right to use of the property." 4C Anderson U.C.C. § 2A–103:18 (3d ed.). The lessee generally relies on the supplier's warranties and promises, which explains the four alternatives under § 2A–103(1)(g)(iii)—all aimed at ensuring that the lessee, prior to signing the lease contract with the lessor, is aware of the terms of the contract between the supplier and the lessor.

Construction Resources Group, LLC v. Element Financial Corporation, 2017 WL 2266894 (W.D. Okla. 2017) is a good case to use to work through the statutory requirements of a finance lease. *See* Diagram #2: CRG Case. Construction Resources Group (CRG) contracted to excavate a lake and needed a wheel loader for the excavation work. CRG decided on a wheel loader manufactured by Doosan but did not have sufficient cash flow to purchase the wheel loader. Instead, CRG financed the equipment through Element Financial. Element and H&E Equipment, an authorized Doosan dealer, entered into a contract in which Element purchased the wheel loader from H&E. Element paid the full purchase price for the wheel loader and then leased it to CRG pursuant to a lease agreement (Element

Lease) for a monthly payment with an option to purchase at the end of the Element Lease term.

As the district court explained, this transaction met the first two requirements for a finance lease. CRG selected the wheel loader, not Element. Element neither manufactured nor supplied the equipment. Doosan manufactured the wheel loader and H&E, Doosan's authorized dealer, supplied it. *See* UCC § 2A–103(1)(g)(i). Element purchased the wheel loader in order to lease it to CRG; thus, its acquisition was "in connection with the lease." UCC § 2A–103(1)(g)(ii). The problem was with the third requirement for a finance lease. CRG did not receive a copy of the H&E/Element agreement prior to signing the Element Lease and CRG's approval of the H&E/Element Agreement was not a condition to the effectiveness of the Element Lease. *See* UCC § 2A–103(1)(g)(iii)(A), (B). In addition, no evidence was presented to satisfy § 2A–103(1)(g)(iii)(D). But Element argued that the Element Lease disclaimed all warranties, thereby satisfying § 2A–103(1)(g)(iii)(C). As the district court correctly explained, however, the definition of a finance lease required an accurate and complete statement of the manufacturer Doosan's warranties. The disclaimer of warranties by Element in the Element Lease did not satisfy the statutory alternative at § 2A–103(1)(g)(iii)(C). Therefore, the court found that the Element Lease did not satisfy the statutory definition of a finance lease.

But the Element Lease contained the following language: "THIS LEASE IS A 'FINANCE LEASE' AS

DEFINED IN ARTICLE 2A OF THE UNIFORM COMMERCIAL CODE." Because the lessor and lessee can agree to treat their agreement as a finance lease, the court held that the Element Lease was a finance lease. *See* UCC § 2A–103, Comment ¶ (g).

DIAGRAM #2: CRG CASE

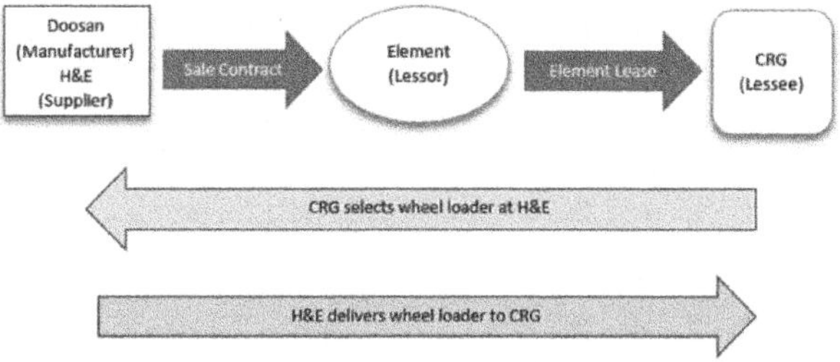

4. CONSUMER LEASE

Identifying a lease as a consumer lease is important for at least two reasons. First, Article 2A provides certain protections for lessees in consumer leases. For example, if the choice of law provided for in the lease agreement is a jurisdiction different from the jurisdiction of the lessee's residence or where the goods are to be used, then that choice-of-law provision in the lease is not enforceable. UCC § 2A–106(1). Similarly, a choice-of-forum provision in a lease is not enforceable if the forum selected is one that "would not otherwise have jurisdiction over the lessee." UCC § 2A–106(2). These statutory protections address the drafters' concerns that a lessor would induce a consumer lessee to agree to the law of a jurisdiction with "little effective consumer protection" or to an inconvenient forum for litigation. UCC § 2A–106, Comment: Purposes.

Second, a consumer lease subject to Article 2A is subject to a state's consumer protection statutes, whether in existence at the time of Article 2A's enactment or enacted afterward. UCC § 2A–104(1)(c); *see* UCC § 2A–104, Comment ¶ 2. Thus, if a state adopts the Uniform Consumer Credit Code (UCCC), the UCCC "prevails over" Article 2A, in the event of a conflict between the two. UCC § 2A–104, Comment ¶ 2. The same holds true for a conflict between Article 2A and a "final consumer protection decision" of the state, but only for decisions that predate Article 2A's effective date. UCC § 2A–104(1)(c).

To qualify as a consumer lease, a transaction must satisfy several statutory requirements. First, the lessor must be "regularly engaged in the business of leasing or selling." UCC § 2A–103(1)(e). Second, the lessee must be an individual, not an artificial entity, like a corporation. *Id.* Third, the individual must lease the goods "primarily for a personal, family, or household purpose." *Id.* The uniform version of Article 2A left it to the individual states to decide whether to limit the definition to leases with total payments, excluding option payments to buy or renew the lease, below a certain amount of money. *See* UCC § 2A–103, Comment ¶ (e). For example, Vermont's definition of consumer lease contains no monetary limitation. *See* 9A VT. STAT. ANN. § 2A–103(1)(e) (2021). Consumer leases with small and very large total payments qualify. Michigan, however, restricts its definition to consumer leases with total payments, excluding purchase and renewal options, of $25,000 or less. *See* MICH. COMP. LAWS SERV. § 440.2803(1)(e) (2022). Alabama's definition also contains a monetary limit, but it is substantially higher than that of Michigan's –$100,000. *See* ALA. CODE § 7–2A–103(1)(e) (2022).

C. SUMMARY

Article 2 applies to "transactions in goods," which includes sales of goods. It does not apply to (1) transactions intended only to operate as security for a loan or extension of credit; (2) leases; (3) certain international sales covered by the CISG; or (4) contracts for land or services, to which common law rules apply.

A majority of courts use the predominant purpose test to determine whether Article 2 or common law rules apply to hybrid transactions, e.g., a sale of goods and services. Of course, if the UCC and common law rules are the same, there is no need to determine whether the predominant thrust of the contract is the provision of goods or services. In many cases, however, the rules vary, e.g., different statutes of limitations, and, therefore, such an analysis is necessary. Bear in mind that even if the transaction in question does not involve the sale of goods, a court nonetheless may apply Article 2's rules by analogy "to fill a gap in the common law." Shikwan Sung v. Hamilton, 676 F. Supp.2d 990 (D. Haw. 2009); *see* Brewer v. Poole Construction Co., 49 U.C.C. Rep. Serv. 2d (Callaghan) 1045 (Mass. Super. Ct. 2001) (stating that "[c]xclusion from Article 2, however, does not preclude the application by analogy of its policies and principles to the common law").

Article 2A applies to any transaction that creates a lease. Many provisions of Article 2A are modeled on Article 2, but the difference between a lease and a secured sale is important in other contexts, for example in bankruptcy. Section 1–203 sets forth a bright-line test for determining whether a transaction constitutes a lease or a secured sale. If a transaction satisfies the bright-line test, then it is a secured sale, not a lease. But the analysis does not end simply because a transaction does not satisfy the bright-line test. Instead, courts look to the economic realities of the transaction to decide whether it is a lease or a secured sale.

CHAPTER 2
CONTRACT FORMATION

A. SALES

Article 2's rules on contract formation are quite liberal. A contract for the sale of goods may be formed in "any manner sufficient to show agreement," including by the conduct of the parties. UCC § 2–204(1). It is not necessary to identify the exact moment of contract formation in order to have an agreement sufficient to constitute a contract. UCC § 2–204(2). Moreover, the fact that the parties leave open a term or terms does not mean that the contract fails for indefiniteness if the parties intended to form a contract and there is a "reasonably certain basis for giving a remedy." UCC § 2–204(3); *see* UCC § 2–311(1) (providing that a contract is valid even though it leaves to one party to specify certain particulars of performance; that party must act in good faith and in accordance with commercial standards). The UCC contains provisions that fill in the gaps left open by the contracting parties. *See, e.g.,* UCC § 2–305 (price), UCC § 2–308 (place for delivery), § 2–309 (time for shipment or delivery). Of course, the more terms left open, the more likely it is that the parties did not intend to conclude a contract for sale. Moreover, despite Article 2's liberal formation rules, the parties will not form a contract without a quantity unless their agreement constitutes a requirements or output contract. *See infra* § A.3 of this Chapter. While a market price exists for goods sold, there is no such thing as a "market quantity."

The basic elements of a contract are the same under the UCC as under the common law: (1) offer; (2) acceptance; and (3) consideration. Common law rules supplement the provisions of Article 2 unless some provision of Article 2 displaces the common law rule. *See* UCC § 1–103(b). The following sections of the Nutshell examine those provisions of Article 2 that displace certain common law rules on offer, acceptance, and consideration.

1. OFFER

Typically, at common law, an offeree must provide consideration in order to keep an offer open. Otherwise, the offeror is free to revoke the offer at any time. Section 2–205 of the UCC, however, provides that certain offers by merchants, called "firm offers," are irrevocable even though the offeree does not provide consideration to keep the offer open. The firm offer is a statutorily created option contract.

> An offer by a merchant to buy or sell goods in a signed writing which by its terms gives assurance that it will be held open is not revocable for lack of consideration, during the time stated or if no time is stated for a reasonable time, but in no event may such period of irrevocability exceed three months; but any such term of assurance on a form supplied by the offeree must be separately signed by the offeror.

UCC § 2–205. Several requirements must be satisfied to create a firm offer. First, the party making the offer must be a merchant. Second, the offer must be in a signed writing. Third, the offer, by its terms, must give assurance that it will remain open.

A merchant is a person with "specialized knowledge as to the goods, specialized knowledge as to business practices, or specialized knowledge as to both." UCC § 2–104, Comment ¶ 2. But a party not acting in his or her mercantile capacity does not qualify as a merchant. *See id.* For example, suppose Neighbor owns a restaurant. Neighbor wants to sell the barbecue grill he uses at home. You are interested in purchasing the grill but want time to consider the purchase. Neighbor signs a piece of paper stating that that he will sell you the grill for $100 and will hold open the offer for 5 days. Two days later, Neighbor sells the grill to someone else. Neighbor's offer was not a firm offer because Neighbor was not acting in his mercantile capacity; he offered to sell an item from his home. Because you did not provide Neighbor with consideration, e.g., $5, to keep the offer open, Neighbor was free to revoke the offer at any time.

A signed writing need not be a formal document. The UCC defines a "writing" to include "printing, typewriting, or any other intentional reduction to tangible form." UCC § 1–201(b)(43). A signature includes "any symbol executed or adopted with present intention to adopt or accept a writing." UCC § 1–201(b)(37). Thus, a court may decide that an offer on a merchant's letterhead may constitute a "signed writing." *See* UCC § 1–201(b)(37), Comment ¶ 37 (stating that the signature in "appropriate cases may be found in a billhead or letterhead").

Finally, the merchant's offer must give assurance that it will remain open. It is important to distinguish between a deadline in an offer and an assurance that an offer will remain open. Suppose Coyote Corporation wants to buy anvils from Acme Company. Acme quotes Coyote a price but Coyote wants time to think about the offer. In a signed writing, the sales agent for Acme states: "Acme Company offers to sell 100 anvils to Coyote for $10 per anvil. Coyote must accept this offer no later than the close of business Friday." This is not a firm offer, because Acme does not promise to keep the offer open until Friday; it merely states a deadline for accepting the offer. Acme would have made a firm offer had the second sentence stated: "Acme will hold open this offer until the close of business on Friday."

2. ACCEPTANCE: § 2–206 AND § 2–207

Unless the terms of an offer or the circumstances surrounding its making unambiguously indicate to the contrary, an offeree may accept an offer in "any manner and by any medium reasonable in the circumstances." UCC § 2–206(1)(a). Thus, an offeree may accept by email an offer sent by snail mail. A seller who receives an order for prompt or current shipment of goods may accept either by a prompt promise to ship or by promptly shipping the goods ordered. UCC § 2–206(1)(b). If the buyer places an order for prompt shipment of blue widgets and the seller ships green widgets, the parties have a contract—for blue widgets—and the seller is in breach. *See* UCC § 2–206(1)(b), Comment ¶ 4. If the seller does not have blue widgets and instead ships green widgets with a seasonable notification to the buyer that the shipment is an accommodation, then the shipment is not an acceptance. UCC § 2–206(1)(b). The parties do not have a contract until the buyer accepts the shipment of green widgets. Then, the contract is one for green, not blue, widgets.

At common law, any change to the offer by the offeree constituted a counteroffer. This mirror image rule requires that the "acceptance" mirror the terms of the offer. Suppose Acme orders 1000 blue widgets from Omega for a price of $1 per widget with delivery to occur no later than February 10. Omega sends Acme an acknowledgment of its order, agreeing to the price, quantity, type of good, and delivery date. But Omega's acknowledgment form contains a disclaimer of all warranties. If the common law rule applied, Omega's acknowledgment would not be an acceptance of Acme's offer because it added a disclaimer of warranties. If Acme did not read the acknowledgment and later accepted the blue widgets sent by Omega, the parties would have a contract on Omega's terms—no warranties. Omega's acknowledgment was the "last shot" and, thus, controlled the terms of the parties' agreement.

Section 2–207 of the UCC changes the mirror image rule. The basic framework of § 2–207 is as follows:

- § 2–207(1) answers the question: Do the parties have a contract based on their writings?
- § 2–207(2) answers the question: If the parties have a contract based on their writings, what are the terms of that contract?
- § 2–207(3) answers two questions: If the parties do not have a contract on the writings, did they form a contract based on their conduct? If so, what are the terms of that contract?

The ensuing discussion explains Article 2's answers to the questions posed above.

a. Do the Parties Have a Contract Based on Their Writings?

Section 2–207 provides as follows.

> A definite and seasonable expression of acceptance or a written confirmation which is sent within a reasonable time operates as an acceptance even though it states terms additional to or different from those offered or agreed upon, unless acceptance is expressly made conditional on assent to the additional or different terms.

UCC § 2–207(1). Notice that § 2–207(1) addresses two types of writings. The first is the written confirmation of an existing agreement, such as a contract formed orally between the parties. The second is typified by the exchange of offer and acknowledgment forms, which is why § 2–207 is often referred to as "the Battle of the Forms" provision of Article 2. *See* UCC § 2–207, Comment ¶ 1. It may be helpful to follow along on Flowchart #2 as you read the following analysis of § 2–207(1).

The first question to ask with a § 2–207 problem is whether the writing is a confirmation of an existing oral agreement *or* a purchase order. If the former, then there is no further analysis required under § 2–207(1). Remember that you use subsection (1) to determine whether the parties have formed a contract. If the writing is a confirmatory memorandum of an existing oral contract, the parties have a contract. Thus, subsection (1) is not needed. For confirmatory memoranda of existing contracts, the analysis proceeds to subsection (2) to determine the terms of the parties' agreement. (Yes, § 2–207(1) does say "a written confirmation . . . operates as an acceptance" but this is unartful drafting. How can a confirmation of a contract operate as an acceptance?)

If the writings involve a purchase order and an acknowledgment, then § 2–207(1) applies. Some courts hold that § 2–207 applies only when there are two forms. *See* ProCD, Inc. v. Zeidenberg, 86 F.3d 1447 (7th Cir. 1996) (stating that case involved "only one form; [thus] UCC § 2–207 [was] irrelevant"). Yet nothing in the language of § 2–207 requires two forms. Klocek v. Gateway, Inc., 104 F. Supp.2d 1332 (D. Kan. 2000) (stating that while § 2–207 disputes often involve a "battle of forms," nothing in § 2–207's "language precludes application in a case which involves only one form"). When conducting a § 2–207 analysis, keep in mind that the majority of courts treat the buyer's purchase order as the offer and the seller's acknowledgment as the potential acceptance of that offer. *But see* Hill v. Gateway 2000, Inc., 105 F.3d 1147 (7th Cir. 1997) (finding that consumer buyers were bound to arbitrate dispute because seller Gateway's form containing arbitration was the offer that buyers accepted).

Determining whether the acknowledgment constitutes an acceptance of the buyer's offer requires an answer to the following three questions. First, is the acknowledgment definite? Second, is the acknowledgment seasonable? Finally, is the acknowledgment expressly conditional? If the acknowledgment is definite, seasonable, and *not* expressly conditional, then the parties formed a contract on their writings.

1) Is the Acknowledgment Definite?

The UCC does not define the term "definite." If the acknowledgment changes certain "dickered terms," such as decreasing the quantity of goods ordered or changing the goods themselves, e.g., stating it will deliver A2 widgets when the buyer ordered A1 widgets, then it is not definite. If the acknowledgment is not definite, then it is not an acceptance. No contract is formed on the basis of the parties' exchange of a purchase order and an acknowledgment. But the parties still may form a contract based on their conduct. Thus, even if there is no further exchange of communications, be sure to look to § 2–207(3) in the case of a non-definite acknowledgment.

Be careful not to define the term "definite" too broadly. The drafters of § 2–207 sought to change the common law mirror image rule. The more changes that render an acknowledgment non-definite, the fewer contracts that are formed. The end result is a movement back toward the mirror image rule with additions or deletions to the "accepting" document rendering it a counteroffer rather than an acceptance.

2) Is the Acknowledgment Seasonable?

Section 1–205 of the UCC provides that "[a]n action is taken seasonably if it is taken at or within the time agreed or, if no time is agreed, at or within a reasonable time." UCC § 1–205(b). What does it mean to say that the acknowledgment is seasonable? It means that the acknowledgment was sent to the buyer within a reasonable time of the seller receiving the buyer's offer. What constitutes a reasonable time is a question of fact. The parties' prior course of dealing and course of performance, if any, as well as trade usage are relevant to the question of reasonableness. UCC § 1–205, Comment ¶ 2. If the acknowledgment is not seasonable, then it is *not* an acceptance of the buyer's offer. The parties, of course, still may form a contract based on their conduct. *See* UCC § 2–207(3).

3) Is the Acknowledgment Expressly Conditional?

In its acknowledgment, the seller may state that its acceptance is expressly made conditional on the buyer's agreement to the additional or different terms in the acknowledgment. An expressly conditional acknowledgment is *not* an acceptance. If the parties exchange no further communications, there is no contract based on the purchase order and the acknowledgment. The parties still may form a contract based on their conduct, however. *See* UCC § 2–207(3).

One question that has arisen is what words the acknowledgment must use in order to qualify as "expressly conditional?" Courts have "interpret[ed] narrowly the 'expressly made conditional' language of § 2–207(1)'s second clause." Option Wireless, Ltd. v. OpenPeak, Inc., 2012 WL 6045936 (S.D. Fla. 2012) Of course, the safest route for the seller is to simply track the language of § 2–207(1) and state that its acknowledgment is "expressly made conditional on [buyer's] assent to the additional or different terms." *See* PCS Nitrogen Fertilizer, LP v. Christy Refractories, LLC, 225 F.3d 974 (8th Cir. 1999) (noting that "an acceptance which precisely follows § 2–207(1) clearly forestalls contract formation"). The language of the acknowledgment form need not mimic that of § 2–207(1). Nonetheless, it must communicate unequivocally that the seller's "willingness to enter into a bargain [is] conditioned on the [buyer's] 'assent' to additional or different terms." Gardner Zemke Co. v. Dunham Bush, Inc.

850 P.2d 319 (N.M. 1993). Thus, an acknowledgment providing that acceptance of the buyer's order was "subject to" additional or different terms on the acknowledgment form did not suffice to make the acknowledgment expressly conditional on the buyer's "*assent* to those terms." Dorton v. Collins & Aikman Corp., 453 F.2d 1161 (6th Cir. 1972) (emphasis in original). A statement in a seller invoice requiring the buyer to "contest any unwelcome terms" within 14 calendar days or else "The Buyer shall be deemed to have accepted the terms of any invoice" also did not make the seller's acceptance expressly conditional on buyer's assent to the additional or different terms. *Option Wireless,* 2012 WL 6045936, at **20–21.

4) Summary

If the seller's acknowledgment is definite, seasonable, and *not* expressly conditional, then the parties formed a contract with the exchange of their purchase order and acknowledgment forms. Section 2–207(2) then determines whether the additional (or different) terms in the acknowledgment are part of the parties' agreement. If the acknowledgment is not definite or not seasonable, or is expressly conditional, then the parties did not form a contract on the writings. The parties still may form a contract based on their conduct. That analysis, however, proceeds under § 2–207(3), not § 2–207(2).

FLOWCHART #2: SECTION 2–207(1)

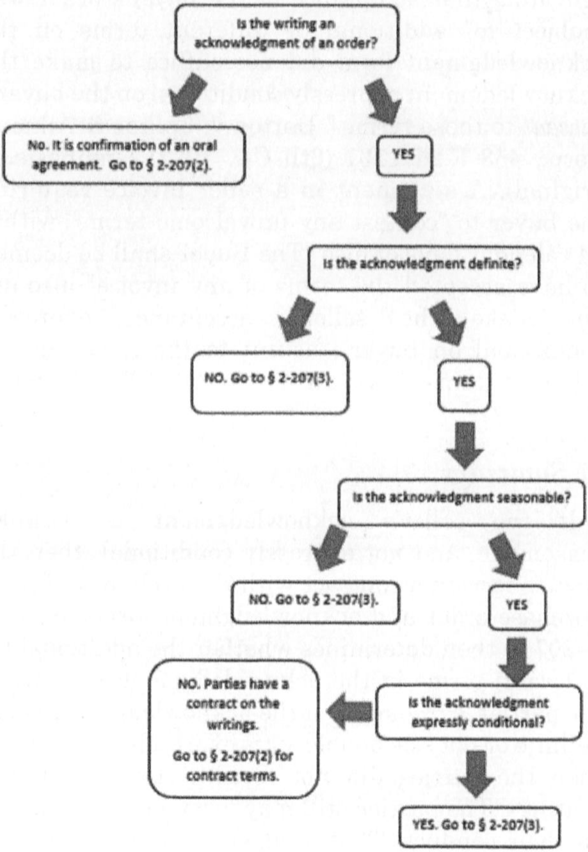

b. What Are the Terms of the Contract?

Recall that if the parties make an oral contract and one or both send a confirmation of that oral agreement, there is nothing to analyze under § 2–

207(1). Instead, the analysis proceeds right to § 2–207(2). Section 2–207(2), then, applies to both confirmations and contracts formed by the parties' exchange of a purchase order and an acknowledgment. You may find it helpful to follow along on Flowchart #3 as you read the analysis of § 2–207(2) in this part of the Nutshell.

Unlike § 2–207(1), which mentions additional *or* different terms, § 2–207(2)'s language is limited to additional terms. Yet, Comment ¶ 3 to § 2–207 states: "Whether or not additional or different terms will become part of the agreement depends upon the provisions of subsection (2)." Thus, the first question to answer is whether § 2–207(2) applies to different terms. Courts have adopted three different approaches to different terms. *See* Daitom, Inc. v. Pennwalt Corp., 741 F.2d 1569 (10th Cir. 1984) (describing three approaches). The majority of courts apply what they call the "knock-out" rule to different terms. For example, if Firm A's purchase order provides that the buyer is entitled to all implied warranties under the UCC, but Company B's acknowledgment properly disclaims all implied warranties, those two conflicting terms knock each other out. The end result in this case favors Firm A, the buyer; unless disclaimed, an implied warranty of merchantability applies to the sale of goods by a merchant like Company B. *See* UCC § 2–314.

If the term in the acknowledgment is an additional, not a different term, then the next question to ask is whether both parties to the transaction are merchants. Recall that § 2–104(1) defines the term "merchant." A merchant is a person with specialized knowledge of (1) the goods; (2) business practices; or (3) the goods and business practices. In other words, for purposes of § 2–207(2), "almost every person in business" operating in her mercantile capacity qualifies as a "merchant." UCC § 2–104, Comment ¶ 2.

If both parties are merchants, additional terms are part of the parties' contract unless:

(a) the offer expressly limits acceptance to the terms of the offer;

(b) they materially alter it; or

(c) notification of objection to them has already been given or is given within a reasonable time after notice of them is received.

UCC § 2–207(2). Section 2–207(2)(a) through (c) are *exceptions* to the general rule that as between merchants, additional terms become part of the parties' agreement. Consider the following example as a way to understand how these exceptions work. Rubble Company sends a purchase order to buy granite from Flintstone Corporation. Flintstone's acknowledgment contains boilerplate on the back that requires the parties to submit all disputes to binding arbitration.

Suppose Rubble's purchase order form provides that it is "expressly limited" to its terms. While the default rule for a transaction between merchants is that an additional term becomes part of the parties' agreement, one exception is for offers that are expressly limited to their terms. Because Rubble's offer was expressly limited to its terms, binding arbitration is not part of the parties' contract. UCC § 2–207(2)(a). Notice that this exception to the general default rule does not apply to confirmations. The reason is that a contract already exists. It makes no sense to talk about an *expressly limited offer* when the question is whether a term or terms in a writing or memorandum confirming the parties' *existing contract* is part of that contract.

Be careful *not* to confuse expressly conditional with expressly limited. The words "expressly conditional" apply to *acknowledgments or acceptances* and preclude formation of a contract on the basis of the parties' writings. The words "expressly limited" appear in § 2–207(2)(a) and apply to *offers*. Section 2–207(2) provides the rules for determining which terms are part of the parties' agreement, *not* whether the parties formed an agreement.

Suppose Rubble's purchase order does not contain any "expressly limited" language but when Barney, the president of Rubble Company, receives and reads the acknowledgment, he dashes off an email to Fred of Flintstone Corporation stating that Rubble does not agree to submit disputes to binding arbitration. Once again, binding arbitration is not part of the parties' agreement. Barney provided "notification of objection" to the binding arbitration term "within a reasonable time" after receiving notice of the term. UCC § 2–207(2)(c). Article 2 does not require the objection to be in writing, but it is wise to do so.

Suppose, once again, that Rubble's purchase order does not say it is "expressly limited". In addition, Barney neither reads Flintstone's acknowledgment form nor objects to anything in it. Nonetheless, binding arbitration will not be a term in the parties' agreement if it constitutes a material alteration. *See* UCC § 2–207(2)(b). What is a material alteration? The first thing to realize is that Article 2 does not define "material alteration." Comment ¶¶ 4 and 5 to § 2–207 provide examples of terms that normally do (Comment ¶ 4) and do not (Comment ¶ 5) materially alter the contract. But the terms in many contracts fall outside those listed in Comment ¶¶ 4 and 5. What happens then? Most courts ask whether the additional term results in surprise or hardship. *But see* Union Carbide Corp. v. Oscar Mayer Foods Corp., 947 F.2d 1333 (7th Cir. 1991) (concluding that hardship is a "consequence, not a criterion" of material alteration because a party cannot "walk away from a contract" simply because its "performance turns out to be a hardship for you").

The parties' course of performance and course of dealing, as well as the usage of trade are relevant to determine whether the additional term constitutes a surprise and, hence, a material alteration. *See* UCC § 1–303. For example, if binding arbitration is common in Rubble's and Flintstone's industry, then it is not a surprise. *See* Bayway Refining Co. v. Oxygenated Marketing & Trading A.G., 215 F.3d 219 (2d Cir. 2000) (finding that "compelling proof that shifting tax liability to a buyer is the custom and practice in the petroleum industry" meant that additional term in seller's confirmatory fax that allocated liability to buyer for excise tax was not a surprise).

But what if Flintstone argues that Rubble and Flintstone had done business on numerous prior occasions and that every Flintstone acknowledgment contained the exact same binding arbitration provision? Does the mere exchange of forms with boilerplate language constitute a course of dealing that negates Rubble's claim of surprise? The courts are split on the question. *See* 1 Corbin on Contracts § 3.37(3)(D). But it is hard to understand how the mere exchange of forms, which courts and commentators alike recognize often are not read, qualifies as a "sequence of conduct . . . between the parties . . . that is fairly to be regarded as establishing *a common basis of understanding* for interpreting their expressions and other conduct." UCC § 1–303(b) (emphasis added).

The discussion to this point has dealt with transactions between two merchants. What if neither party is a merchant or if the transaction is between a consumer and a merchant? In such a case, the additional term in the acknowledgment is a "proposal[ ] for addition to the contract." UCC § 2–207(2). Suppose Sam Seller puts an ad in the local paper to sell his car. Ben Buyer stops by to examine the car. He and Sam talk terms, come to an agreement, and shake hands on the deal. They agree that Ben will return on the weekend with the money for the car. Ben asks Sam for his email address and later that night sends Sam an email confirming the sale of the car. Ben's email correctly describes the terms of the sale—the car, the price, the date for exchange of the car and the money. But it also states: "Sam Seller agrees to detail the car before Ben Buyer picks up the car on Saturday." The parties formed an oral contract for the purchase and sale of the car; the email is a written confirmation of that contract. The confirmation, however, adds a term to which the parties did not agree. Because Sam and Ben are not merchants, that term about detailing is only a proposal. Sam must agree to the proposal for it to become part of the contract. Sam must expressly agree to the new term; silence on his part does not constitute assent.

FLOWCHART #3: SECTION 2–207(2)

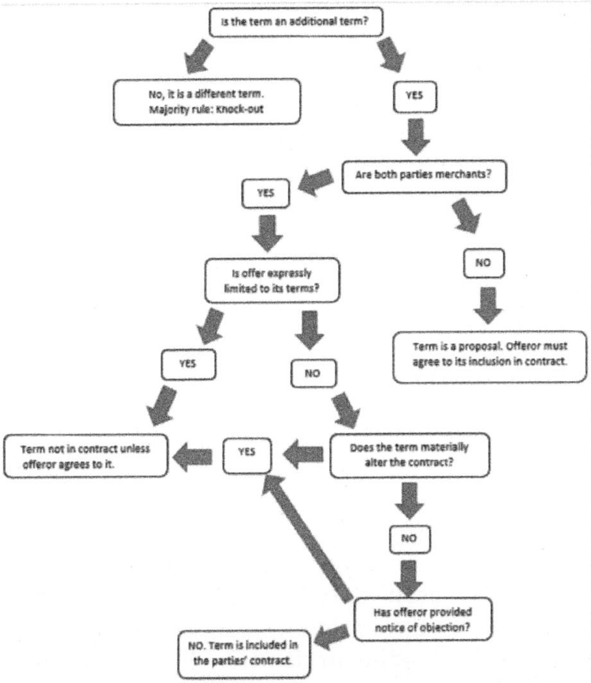

c. Did the Parties Form a Contract Based on Their Conduct?

Before exploring the rule at § 2–207(3), a note of caution is in order. Do not apply § 2–207(3) to a written confirmation of an existing oral contract. If the parties already have a contract, albeit an oral one, then there is no need to determine whether the parties formed a contract based on their conduct.

Suppose Rubble sends Flintstone a purchase order for granite and Flintstone sends an acknowledgment form that agrees to the basic terms, e.g., quantity and price, but contains boilerplate on the reverse that requires the parties to submit all disputes to binding arbitration. Flintstone's acknowledgment also states in bold on the front that its acceptance is expressly made conditional on the buyer's assent to the additional and different terms on the reverse side of the form. The expressly conditional acknowledgment is not an acceptance of Rubble's offer. If the parties communicate no further with one another, then there is no contract based on the purchase order and acknowledgment.

But suppose Rubble does not read the terms on the reverse of Flintstone's acknowledgment. Flintstone sends the granite to Rubble Company, which accepts and subsequently pays for the goods. Rubble Company later complains to Flintstone about the quality of the granite. If the two firms are unable to resolve the dispute on their own, must Rubble submit the dispute to binding arbitration? The short answer is "no." The parties did not form a contract on the basis of Rubble's purchase order and Flintstone's acknowledgment because the acknowledgment was expressly conditional. But Flintstone shipped the goods and Rubble Company accepted and paid for them. Thus, the parties formed a contract based on their conduct. Section 2–207(3) provides that in such a case, the terms of the parties' contract are those "on which the writings of the parties agree, together with any supplementary terms incorporated under any other [UCC] provisions." UCC § 2–207(3). Binding arbitration was a term *only* on Flintstone's form. Thus, binding arbitration is not part of the parties' contract.

Contrast the result if the common law rule applied. By adding binding arbitration to its acknowledgment, Flintstone created a counteroffer. When Flintstone shipped the goods to Barney, Barney accepted the terms of Flintstone's counteroffer. Thus, under the common law rule, binding arbitration would become part of the parties' agreement.

3. CONSIDERATION

Article 2 contains three provisions that affect, in some way, the common law requirement of consideration. The first is Article 2's firm offer rule discussed *supra* § A.1 of this Chapter. At common law, an offeror could revoke an offer unsupported by consideration. Section 2–205, however, makes irrevocable a merchant's signed written offer that provides assurance it will remain open even though the offeree provides no consideration.

The second is § 2–209 on contract modifications. A modification to a contract is a contract and, thus, at common law typically required consideration. A modification to a contract for the sale of goods, however, "needs no consideration to be binding." UCC § 2–209(1). The modification must be made in good faith. "[E]xtortion of a 'modification' without legitimate commercial reason is ineffective as a violation of the duty of good faith." UCC § 2–209, Comment ¶ 2. The UCC's definition of good faith contains both a subjective—"honesty in fact"—and an objective—"observance of reasonable commercial standards of fair dealing"—standard. UCC § 1–201(b)(20).

Suppose Seller and Buyer enter into a contract for Good X, which Seller manufactures. The market price of one component of Good X subsequently increases substantially. Seller asks Buyer to increase the contract price to account for the increased cost of production of Good X. Buyer agrees. The modification is binding without consideration. Seller did not extort the price increase, e.g., by refusing to deliver without it. Moreover, Seller did not request a modification simply because it later regretted the terms to which it had originally agreed. The market price increase is "an objectively demonstrable reason for seeking a modification." UCC § 2–209, Comment ¶ 2; *see, e.g.*, Weisberg v. Handy & Harman, 747 F.2d 416 (7th Cir. 1984) (stating that "[a] precipitous change in market prices satisfies the requirement of good faith found in § 2–209"); Man Industries India Ltd. v. Midcontinent Express Pipeline, LLC, 407 S.W.3d 342 (Tex. App. 2013) (affirming trial court finding that modification was sought in good faith even though party seeking modification based on dramatic price increase faced only a reduction in profit and not a loss on the contract). *Cf.* RESTATEMENT (SECOND) OF CONTRACTS § 89(a) (providing that a modification of a contract "not fully performed on either side is binding" without consideration "if the modification is fair and equitable in view of circumstances not anticipated by the parties when the contract was made").

The third provision is § 2–306 on output and requirements contracts. An output contract is one in which the seller agrees to sell all its output to a particular buyer; under a requirements contract, the buyer agrees to purchase all its requirements from a particular seller. UCC § 2–306(1). At common law, such contracts were considered illusory and, thus, failed for lack of consideration. The absence of a specific quantity meant that the seller in an output contract could decide to sell nothing and the buyer in a requirements contract could decide to buy nothing. Article 2, however, imposes an obligation of good faith on the seller's and buyer's conduct.

> [T]he party who will determine quantity is required to operate the plant or conduct his business in good faith and according to commercial standards of fair dealing in the trade so that his output or requirements will approximate a reasonably foreseeable figure.

UCC § 2–306, Comment ¶ 2. The good faith requirement means that the failure of a buyer to order any product from the seller under the terms of a requirements contract constitutes bad faith on the buyer's part. The buyer's bad faith, in turn, is a breach of the parties' agreement. *See* Structural Polymer Group, Ltd. v. Zoltek Corp., 543 F.3d 987 (8th Cir. 2008) (explaining that if buyer under requirements contract failed to buy any product, seller could allege bad faith and that "assertion of bad faith" [ ] is an argument that [buyer] *breached* the agreement, not that the agreement lacked mutuality or consideration") (emphasis in original). Thus, neither an output nor a requirements contract fails for consideration.

B. LEASES

With the exception of § 2–207 on the Battle of the Forms, the contract formation provisions of Article 2—§§ 2–204, 2–205, 2–206, and 2–209[1]—were carried over to Article 2A. The Official Comments for sections of Article 2 carried over to Article 2A are "incorporated by reference in Article 2A" and, thus, are relevant to understanding the similar Article 2A provision. UCC § 2A–101, Comment: Relationship of Article 2A to Other Articles. This is particularly important for those provisions of Article 2A, e.g., §§ 2A–204 and 2A–205, that have no additional substantive commentary. *See supra* Table #1. Also, judicial decisions interpreting Article 2 sections carried over to Article 2A are persuasive, although not binding, on a court dealing with similar issues that have arisen under lease contracts. *See* UCC § 2A–101, Comment: Relationship of Article 2A to Other Articles.

With the exception of minor word or phrasing changes, e.g., "even though" becomes "although", and changes to terminology, e.g., replacing "contract for sale of goods" with "lease contract", the language of § 2A–204 on formation in general and § 2A–205 on firm offers by merchants is identical to that of §§ 2–204 and 2–205 of Article 2. Apart from minor word changes, e.g., "shall" becomes "must", formatting

---

[1] Section 1–303 of revised Article 1 has replaced § 2–208 of Article 2.

differences, and terminology changes, e.g., "contract" to "lease contract", § 2A–206(1) and (2) are identical to § 2–206(1)(a) and (c). Section 2–206(1)(b) on orders to buy goods for prompt or current shipment is not relevant to formation of a lease contract and, thus, was deleted from § 2A–206.

There is no counterpart in Article 2A to § 2–207, the UCC's Battle of the Forms provision. The reason is simple. Lease contracts are not formed through the exchange of purchase order and acknowledgment forms.

Finally, as with a contract for the sale of goods, no consideration is needed to modify a lease contract. UCC § 2A–208(1); *cf.* UCC § 2–209(1). Apart from the writing requirement of § 2–209(3), the remaining subsections of § 2–209 were carried over to Article 2A with only changes to terminology. The Official Comment explains the reason for the omission of the writing requirement.

> This provision was not incorporated as it is unfair to allow an oral modification to make the entire lease contract unenforceable, e.g., if the modification takes it a few dollars over the dollar limit. At the same time, the problem could not be solved by providing that the lease contract would still be enforceable in its premodification state (if it then satisfied the statute of frauds) since in some cases that might be worse than no enforcement at all. Resolution of the issue is left to the courts based on the facts of each case.

UCC § 2A–208, Comment: Purposes. Be careful interpreting the absence of a specific writing requirement in § 2A–208. Article 2A contains a Statute of Frauds provision. *See infra* Chapter 3, § B. The drafters did not intend all lease modifications to be enforceable notwithstanding the parties' failure to memorialize the modification in writing. Instead, they left it to the courts to determine based on the facts of each case whether an oral modification to a lease contract is enforceable.

CHAPTER 3
STATUTE OF FRAUDS

A. SALES: INTRODUCTION TO § 2–201

When talking about the Statute of Frauds, it is important to distinguish between two terms: void and unenforceable. A "void contract" means there is no contract. Thus, the phrase "void contract" is an oxymoron. But a contract that is unenforceable because of the Statute of Frauds is not void. There is a contract, but it may be unenforceable based on the absence of a writing.

The Statute of Frauds requires certain contracts to be in a writing signed by the party against whom enforcement is sought. At common law, for example, contracts for the sale of land must be in writing. Article 2 has its own Statute of Frauds, which provides as follows:

> Except as otherwise provided in this section a contract for the sale of goods for the price of $500 or more is not enforceable by way of action or defense unless there is some writing sufficient to indicate that a contract for sale has been made between the parties and signed by the party against whom enforcement is sought or by his authorized agent or broker. A writing is not insufficient because it omits or incorrectly states a term agreed upon but the contract is not enforceable under this paragraph beyond the quantity of goods shown in such writing.

UCC § 2–201(1). Thus, if Buyer and Seller enter into an oral contract for the purchase and sale of 400 widgets at a price of $400, the contract is enforceable notwithstanding the fact that it is oral and not written. But for contracts for sale with a price (not value) of $500 or more, § 2–201 requires some writing, which, at a minimum, "evidence[s] a contract for the sale of goods," is "signed" by the party against whom enforcement is sought, and states a quantity. UCC § 2–201, Comment ¶ 1.

The UCC's writing requirement is liberal. A writing includes "printing, typewriting, or any other intentional reduction to tangible form." UCC § 1–201(b)(43). A signature may be "any symbol executed or adopted with present intention to adopt or accept a writing." UCC § 1–201(b)(37). The symbol need not be written; it can be printed or stamped. Initials or a thumbprint may suffice. UCC § 1–201, Comment ¶ 37. A note sent on firm letterhead may satisfy the requirement that the writing be signed. *Id.*

Suppose Astro Enterprises sues Spacely Space Sprockets, claiming that Spacely had breached a contract to deliver 2,000 sprockets (a good) at a price of $10 per sprocket for a total contract price of $20,000. Astro alleges that its agent contacted George Jetson, Spacely's sales manager, and that the parties formed a contract for the sprockets over the phone. There is no written evidence of the deal, and Spacely raises the Statute of Frauds as a defense. The contract is unenforceable because the price exceeds $500, and Astro has no writing signed by Jetson or any other agent of Spacely Space Sprockets.

Suppose, however, that after hanging up with Astro's purchasing agent, Jetson sent a confirmation of the oral agreement to Astro. The confirmation is on Spacely letterhead and Jetson, as agent for Spacely, signed the confirmation, which stated the terms, including the quantity of sprockets, to which the parties had agreed over the phone. In this scenario, Spacely will lose on its Statute of Frauds defense. Astro has a writing indicating that a contract was formed, Jetson, as an authorized agent of Spacely, signed the confirmation on behalf of the firm, and the firm's letterhead also constitutes a signature. Finally, the confirmation provides the quantity.

Suppose the confirmation stated the quantity as 200, rather than 2,000, sprockets? The contract is still within the Statute of Frauds because 200 sprockets at $10 per item equals $2,000. If Spacely delivers 200 sprockets and Astro sues for breach of contract, Astro is out of luck. The only writing evidencing a contract and signed by Jetson is one that specifies the quantity as 200 sprockets. Section 2–201 expressly states that the contract is enforceable even if terms are stated incorrectly but the contract is not enforceable beyond the quantity stated in the writing. In other words, Astro has no claim for breach of contract based on its assertion that the parties actually formed a contract for 2,000 sprockets.

Even if the writing requirement of § 2–201(1) is not satisfied, a contract nonetheless may be enforceable if a party satisfies one of § 2–201's exceptions. There are four statutory exceptions: (1) the merchants' exception; (2) the specially manufactured goods exception; (3) the admission exception; and (4) the part performance exception. UCC § 2–201(2), (3)(a)–(c). While not provided for by the statute, some courts also recognize an estoppel exception.

1. THE MERCHANTS' EXCEPTION

In order to understand the merchants' exception, return to the example above in which Jetson sends a signed confirmation to Astro that provides that the parties had formed a contract over the phone for the purchase and sale of 2,000 sprockets at a price of $10 per item. Spacely makes a timely delivery of the sprockets, but Astro refuses them claiming that the parties had no contract. If Spacely sues Astro for breach, Astro will raise the Statute of Frauds as a defense because Spacely has no writing signed by *Astro*. Thus, the rule at § 2–201(1) is not satisfied. But the merchants' exception at § 2–201(2) provides that in certain circumstances a merchant, like Spacely, may satisfy the Statute of Frauds with a confirmatory memo that it signed and sent.

> Between merchants if within a reasonable time a writing in confirmation of the contract and sufficient against the sender is received and the party receiving it has reason to know its contents, it satisfies the requirements of subsection (1) against such party unless written notice of objection to its contents is given within 10 days.

UCC § 2–201(2). In our hypothetical, both Astro and Spacely are merchants. *See* UCC § 2–104(1). Jetson, on behalf of Spacely, signed and sent to Astro's offices a confirmation of the alleged oral contract on Spacely letterhead. Because Jetson signed the memo and it appeared on Spacely letterhead, it is sufficient against Spacely, the sender. Astro had reason to know of the memo's contents because it received the memo at its office. *Cf.* Lindell v. Belville, 848 F.2d 192 (6th Cir. 1988) (rejecting merchant Deal's argument that his bank's wire instructions accompanying money wire to merchant Belville satisfied § 2–201(2), explaining that Belville had "no reason to know of the contents of this internal bank document"). Yet, Astro failed to object in writing to the existence of the contract within 10 days of receiving Spacely's memo. Therefore, even though no one at Astro signed the Spacely memo, it nonetheless satisfies the Statute of Frauds.

Bear in mind that the fact that Astro loses on its Statute of Frauds defense does not mean that Spacely prevails on the question of whether the parties formed a contract. Astro's failure to respond to Spacely's confirmatory memorandum "take[s] away" Astro's "defense of the Statute of Frauds; the burden of persuading the trier of fact that a contract was in fact made orally prior to the written confirmation is unaffected." UCC § 2–201, Comment ¶ 3.

Recall that § 2–207 also applies to confirmatory memoranda. *See supra* Chapter 2, § A.2. If the case involves an oral contract in which one party sends a memo in confirmation of the parties' agreement, that memo may add or change terms to which the parties orally agreed. With one exception, § 2–207(2) governs whether additional or different terms in confirmatory memoranda become part of the parties' agreement. The exception is quantity. If the confirmatory memo satisfies either § 2–201(1) or (2), the quantity in that memo controls. Neither party can introduce evidence that the parties agreed to a different quantity. *See* § 2–207, Comment ¶ 6 (stating that "[t]he written confirmation is also subject to Section 2–201").

2. THE SPECIALLY MANUFACTURED GOODS EXCEPTION

The specially manufactured goods exception is another exception to the requirement that a contract for the sale of goods with a price of $500 or more be in writing. The contract is enforceable even without satisfying § 2–201(1)'s writing requirement

> if the goods are to be specially manufactured for the buyer and are not suitable for sale to others in the ordinary course of the seller's business and the seller, before notice of repudiation is received and under circumstances which reasonably indicate that the goods are for the buyer, has made either a substantial beginning of their manufacture or commitments for their procurement[.]

UCC § 2–201(3)(a). The party seeking to invoke this exception must prove four elements. First, the goods must be specially made for the buyer. Second, the goods cannot be suitable for sale in the ordinary course of the seller's business. Third, before the seller receives notice of repudiation by the buyer, the seller either must have substantially begun producing the goods or made a commitment to procure them. Finally, the seller's action in beginning production or making a commitment for the goods must be under circumstances reasonably indicating that the goods are for the buyer.

Suppose Spacely Space Sprockets makes an oral contract with Paper Works to produce 500 calendars that carry the Spacely name and logo, and photos of various Spacely products for each calendar month. The contract price is $5,000. Paper Works is in the business of producing paper products, including calendars, brochures, journals, and letterhead.

The calendars are goods specially made for the buyer Spacely. "In determining whether goods are specially manufactured, courts have traditionally looked to the goods themselves. . . . 'to the nature of the particular goods in question and not to whether the goods were made in an unusual, as opposed to the regular, business operation or manufacturing process of the seller.' " Webcor Packaging Corp. v. Autozone, Inc. 158 F.3d 354 (6th Cir. 1998). The calendars satisfy this requirement. Spacely's logo appears on the product and each month of the calendar is a photo of a different Spacely product. These same facts also mean that if Paper Works produces the calendars, it will be unable to resell them in the ordinary course of its business. Goods "imprinted or stamped with the buyer's name is a strong factor in concluding that the goods are not resellable in the ordinary course of the seller's business." 2 Anderson U.C.C. § 2–201:309 (3d ed.).

Not only would the calendars bear Spacely's name and logo, but each month also would feature a different Spacely product. The calendars would be so specialized that only Spacely would want them.

The third and fourth requirements of the specially manufactured goods exception depend on what steps, if any, Paper Works has taken in the production process. Suppose Spacely contacts Paper Works by phone and cancels the order before Paper Works produces a single calendar. Even though the calendars were to be specially made for Spacely, production has not yet begun. Thus, the exception does not apply, and Paper Works cannot use the specially manufactured goods exception to enforce the contract with Spacely.

What if at the time that Spacely cancels the contract Paper Works has ordered reams of glossy paper for the calendar photos but has not yet produced a single calendar? Is ordering reams of glossy paper a substantial beginning of production under circumstances that reasonably indicate the goods are for the buyer? No. To begin with, Paper Works has not begun production of the calendars. It only has ordered materials necessary for production of the goods and those materials are not unique to the Spacely contract. Paper Works is a company that deals in paper. Ordering reams of glossy photo paper does not reasonably indicate that the glossy paper is for Spacely's calendars. Paper Works can use that paper for other production jobs. Therefore, Paper Works cannot use the specially manufactured goods exception to enforce the contract with Spacely.

What if at the time that Spacely cancels the contract Paper Works has completed production of 250 of the 500 calendars? Assume that Spacely has not begun production of the remaining 250 calendars. There is an enforceable contract for 250, not 500, calendars. Remember that the purpose of § 2–201(1)'s writing requirement is to evidence formation of a contract; the contract is not enforceable beyond the quantity stated in the writing. Similarly, the quantity enforceable under the specially manufactured goods exception is the quantity that Paper Works produced because that quantity evidences a contract for 250 calendars. Any amount in excess of that quantity requires the parties to testify as to the quantity term of their oral contract, thereby undermining the reason for the Statute of Frauds in the first instance. *See* EMSG Systems Division, Inc. v. Miltope Corporation, 1998 WL 1095078 (E.D. N.C. 1998) (emphasis in original) (holding that oral contract for 6,000 circuit boards was not enforceable under the specially manufactured goods exception beyond the 1,000 circuit boards produced and noting that "those 1,000 sets are *not* sufficient to except an additional 5,000 sets, which were never actually produced, from the writing requirement of § 7–2–201").

3. THE ADMISSION EXCEPTION

The admission exception to the Statute of Frauds provides that a contract that does not satisfy § 2–201(1) nonetheless is enforceable "if the party against whom enforcement is sought admits in his pleading, testimony or otherwise in court that a contract for sale was made." UCC § 2–201(3)(b). The contract, however, is enforceable only to the "quantity of goods admitted." *Id.*

The exception does not require the party against whom enforcement is sought to utter the phrase: "We made an oral contract." Nor must the statement spell out all the particulars of the contractual arrangement. Instead, if the party's words reasonably lead to the conclusion that the parties formed a contract, then the admission exception applies. For example, in Wehry v. Daniels, 784 N.E.2d 532 (Ind. Ct. App. 2003), Daniels, who sold Formula One memorabilia, sued Wehry for breach of an oral contract to purchase a 1985 Aryton Senna helmet. When asked during cross-examination whether he had told Daniels to order the helmet for him, Wehry replied: "At Seventeen ($1700.00) Eighteen Hundred Dollars ($1800.00) yes." *Id.* at 534. Daniels claimed the price was $2,750. The court held that Wehry's statement that he had placed the order for the helmet constituted an admission even though there was no agreement on price. Thus, the contract was enforceable. *See also* Jones v. Baran Co., LLC, 660 S.E.2d 420 (Ga. Ct. App. 2008) (holding that even though parties disagreed over contract terms, admission exception applied because dealer had admitted in its answer to the complaint that it had made a contract with customer Jones and dealer's representative had testified at a deposition that the parties had entered into a contract).

A party's belief that he is not contractually bound until he signs a written agreement does not preclude his statements from constituting an admission. For example, in St. Francis Mercantile Equity Exchange v. Newton, 996 P.2d 365 (Kan. Ct. App. 2000), Newton, a farmer, entered into an oral contract with the Exchange to sell corn. Newton did not deliver the corn believing that he was not bound because the contract was oral. Newton admitted in a deposition that he had agreed to sell 40,000 bushels of corn at a specified price to the Exchange. The court found that even though Newton testified at trial that he was not obligated to deliver the corn until he signed a written contract, "his deposition testimony indicated there was a meeting of the minds concerning the quantity, price, and place of delivery." *Id.* at 370. Therefore, Newton's deposition statement constituted an admission for purposes of § 2–201(3)(b) and the Statute of Frauds did not preclude recovery by the Exchange.

At what point does litigation end if the party against whom enforcement is sought denies the existence of a contract? Suppose Acme contends that it made an oral contract with Omega for 10,000 widgets at a price of $1.00 per widget. When Omega does not deliver the widgets, Acme files suit against Omega for breach of contract. Omega files an answer to Acme's complaint denying the existence of a contract between the parties and raising the Statute of Frauds as an affirmative defense. Omega files a motion for judgment on the pleadings. These are basically the facts of Triangle Marketing, Inc. v. Action Industries, Inc., 630 F. Supp. 1578 (N.D. Ill. 1986). The *Triangle* court granted the motion for judgment on the pleadings and dismissed the breach-of-contract lawsuit. The court explained that the defendant had "answered and denied the existence of a contract." In such a case, "Section 2–201(3)(b) does not create an affirmative right for plaintiff to badger defendant through discovery and trial simply because of the possibility of obtaining an admission some time before proofs are closed." *Id.* at 1583.

DF Activities Corp. v. Brown, 851 F.2d 920 (7th Cir. 1988) also involved a motion to dismiss a suit for breach of contract. DF filed suit against Brown for breach of a contract to sell a chair designed by Frank Lloyd Wright. Brown filed a motion to dismiss the lawsuit; she attached an affidavit to the motion in which she denied making any contract with DF for the chair. The Seventh Circuit noted how some courts, such as the *Triangle* court, "allow the judicial-admission exception to be defeated by the defendant's simple denial, in a pleading, that there was a contract." *Id.* at 923. The court explained that if there were only a denial in a pleading, as in *Triangle,* the possibility existed that the defendant might admit in a deposition, for example, that a contract existed. "But where as in this case the defendant swears in an affidavit that there was no contract, we see no point in keeping the lawsuit alive." Therefore, the Seventh Circuit affirmed the trial court's dismissal of the lawsuit. *Id.* at 922.

Courts disagree on where to draw the line in terms of ending litigation in which the party against whom enforcement is sought denies the existence of a contract. There are arguments on each side. The defendant should not have to face protracted litigation simply so the plaintiff can attempt to extract an admission in a deposition or at trial. But, as Judge Flaum in his dissent in *Brown* explained: "The testimonial admissions provision would be virtually meaningless if a district court could never exercise its discretion to permit additional discovery in the face of a defendant's sworn denial in an affidavit." *Brown*, 851 F.2d at 926 (Flaum, J., dissenting).

4. THE PART PERFORMANCE EXCEPTION

An oral contract is enforceable "with respect to goods for which payment has been made and accepted or which have been received and accepted (Section 2–606)." UCC § 2–201(3)(c). The contract is enforceable only to the extent of the part performance, however.

Suppose Buyer claims that it made an oral contract with Seller for the purchase and sale of 10,000 widgets at a price of $5 per widget. Buyer paid Seller $5,000 as a deposit on the purchase. Seller does not deliver any widgets to Buyer and Buyer sues Seller for breach of contract. The court will enforce the contract up to 1000 widgets. The contract is for divisible units (each widget). The seller's acceptance of $5,000 evidences a contract for 1,000 widgets ($5,000/$5 per widget = 1,000 widgets). *See* UCC § 2–201, Comment ¶ 2 (stating that "the seller can be forced to deliver an apportionable part of the goods"). Unfortunately for Buyer, however, there is no writing evidencing a contract for 10,000 widgets and Seller's accepting payment for $5,000 worth of widgets does nothing more than evidence a deal for 1,000 widgets.

What if the good is not divisible? Suppose Fred Flintstone owns a used car that he wants to sell. Barney Rubble, his neighbor, offers to buy the car for $3,000. Fred accepts the offer, but Barney asks whether Fred can wait until the following Monday (it is Thursday night) for full payment. Fred agrees and Barney gives Fred a deposit of $300–10% of the car's purchase price. Fred cashes Barney's check but reconsiders selling the car for only $3,000. When Barney shows up with the remaining $2,700 on Monday, Fred tells Barney he no longer wants to sell the car so cheaply. Barney sues Fred for breach of contract and Fred asserts the Statute of Frauds as a defense. The part performance exception applies. The Statute of Frauds is not a bar to enforcement of the parties' oral agreement. A car cannot be broken up into divisible units; thus, Barney's partial payment evidences a contract for the entire car. *See* Paloukos v. Intermountain Chevrolet Co., 588 P.2d 939 (Idaho 1978) (noting that the majority of courts have held that "part payment for a non-divisible unit, such as an automobile, permits the party under [§ 2–207(3)(c)] to prove and recover in full on the oral contract").

5. PROMISSORY ESTOPPEL

Section 2–201 contains four exceptions to the requirement that a contract for sale of goods of $500 or more be in writing. Suppose Acme makes an oral contract with Omega. Acme relies on the existence of the contract to its detriment but there is no writing evidencing the agreement, and none of the exceptions at § 2–201(2) or (3) apply. Can Acme use promissory estoppel as an exception to Article 2's Statute of Frauds?

Section 2–201 begins: "Except as otherwise provided in this section." That language suggests that no exceptions to § 2–201 exist beyond those specifically provided for in § 2–201(2) and § 2–201(3)(a)–(c). The drafters of revised Article 2 deleted the "except" clause from § 2–201(1). They did so to make clear that the "statutory exceptions to subsection (1) [did] not preclude the possibility that a promisor [would] be estopped to raise the statute-of-frauds defense in appropriate cases." UCC revised § 2–201, Comment ¶ 2. No jurisdiction, however, has adopted the revised Article 2.

While the courts are divided on the question, "[a] majority of jurisdictions have adopted the rule that promissory estoppel may remove an oral contract from the requirements of the UCC statute of frauds." S&P Brake Supply, Inc. v. STEMCO LP, 385 P.3d 567 (Mont. 2016). These courts often look to § 1–103(b), which provides that unless displaced by particular provisions of the UCC, principles of common law and equity, including the law of estoppel, supplement the UCC's provisions. UCC § 1–103(b); *see* UCC § 1–103, Comment ¶ 3. "[B]ecause promissory estoppel is not explicitly displaced by any particular provision of the UCC, § 1–103 allows for promissory estoppel to supplement the UCC statute of frauds." *STEMCO,* 385 P.3d at 574.

B. LEASES: § 2A–201

Section 2A–201 is similar, but not identical, to Article 2's provision on the Statute of Frauds. First, while § 2–201 applies to any sale of goods with a price of $500 or more, § 2A–201 applies to any lease contract in which total payments, excluding payments for purchase or renewal options, are $1,000 or more. *Compare* UCC § 2A–201(1)(a) *with* UCC § 2–201(1).

Second, the writing not only must be signed by the party against whom enforcement is sought and be sufficient to indicate a lease contract was made but also must "describe the goods leased and the lease term." UCC § 2A–201(1)(b); *see* UCC § 2A–201, Comment: Changes (noting addition of requirement describing leased goods and lease term). The description of the leased goods or of the lease term suffices "if it reasonably identifies what is described." UCC § 2A–201(2).

Third, unlike § 2–201, § 2A–201 contains no merchants' exception. *See supra* § A.1. of this Chapter. The drafters did not include this exception because "the number of such transactions involving leases, as opposed to sales, was thought to be modest." UCC § 2A–201, Comment: Purposes.

Fourth, there are three exceptions to the basic writing requirement of § 2A–201(1): specially manufactured goods, admissions, and part performance. Section § 2A–201(4)(a) provides a specially manufactured goods exception. While similar to Article 2's specially manufactured goods exception, "[t]he Article 2A provision goes further than the terms of the sales provision in that it explicitly covers goods to be specially obtained for the lessee as well as those to be specially manufactured." 3 Hawkland UCC Series § 2A–201:3.

Section 2A–201(4)(b)'s admission exception is the same (with terminology changes, e.g., lease contract for contract for sale) as § 2–201's similarly named exception. *Compare* UCC § 2A–201(4)(b) *with* § 2–201(3)(b); *see* Performance Machinery Company v. Yellowstone Mountain Club, LLC, 169 P.3d 394 (Mont. 2007) (holding that parties had a binding and enforceable lease agreement based on admissions in the answer and at trial by the party against whom enforcement was sought).

Section 2A–201's part performance exception differs from § 2–201's exception. Section 2–201(3)(c) applies to goods that were received and accepted *and* to goods for which payment was made and accepted. UCC § 2–201(3)(c). Section 2A–201's part performance exception applies *only* with respect to goods received and accepted by the lessee. UCC § 2A–201(4)(c). The reason for not including the payment piece of the exception is that payment under a lease contract differs fundamentally from payment under a contract for the sale of goods.

> Unlike a buyer in a sales transaction, the lessee does not tender payment in full for goods delivered but only payment of rent for one or

more months. It was decided that, as a matter of policy, this act of payment is not a sufficient substitute for the required memorandum.

UCC § 2A–201, Comment: Purposes.

Finally, § 2A–201 contains a provision articulating the rules for determining the term of a lease found enforceable under one of the three exceptions to the writing requirement set forth at § 2A–201(4). The lease term for such a lease is (1) the term specified in a writing signed by the party against whom enforcement is sought; (2) the lease term admitted by the party against whom enforcement is sought; or (3) a "reasonable lease term." UCC § 2A–201(5); *see* UCC § 2A–201, Comment: Purposes (stating that subsection (5) establishes the criteria for supplying an omitted lease term). Bear in mind that subsection (5)'s criteria for determining the lease term apply to lease contracts "referred to in subsection (4)", which means that the lease is enforceable *not* by satisfying § 2A–201's writing requirement, but by satisfying one of the *exceptions* to that requirement. *See* UCC § 2A–201(4) & (5).

CHAPTER 4

PAROL EVIDENCE RULE AND INTERPRETATION

A. INTRODUCTION

Chapter 2 of the Nutshell covers contract formation issues. Chapter 3 on the Statute of Frauds discusses the requirement that certain contracts for the sale of goods be in writing in order to be enforceable. The parol evidence rule, discussed in this Chapter, applies once you have concluded that the parties have an enforceable, written contract. The parol evidence rule applies to a writing by the parties intended to be either the final or the complete and exclusive statement of the terms of their agreement.

Contrary to its name, the parol evidence rule is *not* a rule of evidence.

> The parol evidence rule, as is now universally recognized, is not a rule of evidence but is one of substantive law. It does not exclude evidence for any of the reasons ordinarily requiring exclusion, based on the probative value of such evidence or the policy of its admission. The rule as applied to contracts is simply that as a matter of substantive law, a certain act, the act of embodying the complete terms of an agreement in a writing (the "integration"), *becomes the contract of the parties*. The point then is, not how the agreement is to be proved, because as a matter of law the writing is the agreement.

> Extrinsic evidence is excluded because it cannot serve to prove what the agreement was, this being determined as a matter of law to be the writing itself. The rule comes into operation when there is a single and final memorial of the understanding of the parties. When that takes place, prior and contemporaneous negotiations, oral or written, are excluded; or, as it is sometimes said, the written memorial supersedes these prior or contemporaneous negotiations.

In re Estate of Gaines, 100 P.2d 1055 (Cal. 1940) (emphasis in original). As the quotation from *Estate of Gaines* makes clear, the parol evidence rule applies to extrinsic evidence, whether oral or written, from the period *before or contemporaneous* with the signing of the parties' agreement.

Suppose you visit Big Motors to purchase a used vehicle. You claim that the salesperson promised, prior to signing the contract, that the dealership would do an inspection of the car and change the oil for free. When you pick up the car the next day, no inspection was done, and the oil was not changed. The salesperson's alleged oral promise is extrinsic evidence and application of the parol evidence rule determines whether the court will exclude such evidence. The parol evidence rule, however, would not apply to a modification of the parties' agreement because the modification *follows* the signing of the parties' original agreement.

It is important to distinguish between parol evidence rule issues and questions of contract interpretation. The parol evidence rule deals with which terms are included in the parties' agreement. "Application of the parol evidence rule determines only which terms are contained in the parties' final agreement. . . . It does not preclude the admission of extrinsic evidence to interpret those terms." Hessler v. Crystal Lake Chrysler-Plymouth, 788 N.E.2d 405 (Ill. App. Ct. 2003). In other words, a parol evidence rule analysis is about the content of the parties' agreement. Once the court decides what is included in the agreement, it "must still consider the preferred meaning of all of the expressions, i.e., the court must pursue the process of *interpretation.*" JOHN EDWARD MURRAY, JR., MURRAY ON CONTRACTS § 81 (3d ed.) (emphasis in original).

Keep in mind that there are a number of exceptions to the parol evidence rule. As mentioned above, the parol evidence rule does not apply to a modification of the parties' original agreement. The parol evidence rule also does not preclude evidence that the parties' agreement was subject to a condition precedent nor does it "restrict evidence showing that the contract was invalid due to illegality, fraud, duress, mistake or the absence of consideration." 2 Anderson U.C.C. § 2–202:116 (3d ed.).

B. SALES: ARTICLE 2'S PAROL EVIDENCE RULE

Section 2–202 provides, in part, that "a writing intended by the parties as a final expression of their agreement with respect to such terms as are included therein may not be contradicted by evidence of any prior agreement or of a contemporaneous oral agreement." UCC § 2–202. It is beyond peradventure that a party may not introduce extrinsic evidence that contradicts a final expression of its agreement. *See* Taylor v. State Farm Mutual Auto Ins. Co., 854 P.2d 1134 (Ariz. 1993) (stating that "the parol evidence rule prohibits extrinsic evidence to vary or contradict, but not to interpret, the agreement").

But Article 2's parol evidence rule also provides that a writing intended by the parties as their final agreement

> may be explained or supplemented (a) by course of performance, course of dealing, or usage of trade (Section 1–303); and (b) by evidence of consistent additional terms unless the court finds the writing to have been intended also as a complete and exclusive statement of the terms of the agreement.

UCC § 2–202(a), (b). As the structure of § 2–202 makes clear, it is important when analyzing a parol evidence rule problem to distinguish evidence of course of performance, course of dealing, and usage of trade *from* evidence of *other* consistent additional terms. Section 2–202 treats these two categories of evidence differently.

Before discussing in more detail Article 2's parol evidence rule, a brief digression into terminology is in order. In the ensuing discussion, the words "writing" and "contract" are used interchangeably to refer to the document that the parties sign. The word "agreement" is a broader term and includes not only the written contract but also the parties' course of dealing and course of performance, as well as trade usage in the parties' industry.

Notice that the UCC uses the terms "final" and "complete and exclusive." In your first-year Contracts course, you would have learned the terms "partially" and "fully" integrated. The word "final" in § 2–202 corresponds to partially integrated, while "complete and exclusive" means the same thing as fully integrated. If the writing is final (partially integrated), then a party may offer consistent additional terms to supplement that writing. *See* § 2–202(b). But, if the writing is a complete and exclusive statement of the terms of the parties' agreement, i.e., it is fully integrated, then "consistent additional terms" may not be added to that agreement. *See id.*

1. § 2–202(a): WHAT IS COURSE OF PERFORMANCE, COURSE OF DEALING, AND USAGE OF TRADE EVIDENCE?

Course of performance and course of dealing both involve a sequence of conduct between the parties. The difference between them is that the phrase "sequence of conduct" for purposes of course of performance relates to the *current* contract between the parties if that contract involves "repeated occasions for performance by a party." UCC § 1–303(a)(1). Course of dealing, on the other hand, is a "sequence of conduct concerning previous transactions between the parties." UCC § 1–303(b). For example, suppose Road Runner, Inc. (RRI) enters into a contract with Acme to purchase 100 anvils—10 anvils per month for the following 10 months. The contract provides for delivery to RRI's place of business by the first of each calendar month. Acme delivers 10 anvils for the months of March through June, but the deliveries arrive on the 3d through the 5th of each month. RRI accepts the deliveries and makes no complaint to Acme about the anvils arriving late. Acme's delivery and RRI's acceptance of the deliveries constitutes a course of performance. The deliveries after the first of the month are repeated occasions for performance that RRI accepted without objection. *See* § 1–303(a)(2).

Suppose, instead, that in April of 2022, RRI and Acme entered into a contract for the delivery of 100 anvils on June 1, 2022. RRI and Acme had made the same contract for 100 anvils for each of the prior five years (2017–2021), always with delivery on June 1 of the respective calendar year. Each year, however, Acme delivered between June 3 and June 5 with no complaint by RRI. Acme's delivery and RRI's acceptance without objection constitute a course of dealing between the parties that is "fairly to be regarded as establishing a common basis of understanding" that delivery between June 3 and June 5 was and is acceptable.

Usage of trade, unlike course of performance or course of dealing, is not limited to the conduct and interactions of the two parties to the contract. It is "any practice or method of dealing having such regularity of observance in a place, vocation, or trade as to justify an expectation that it will be observed with respect to the transaction in question." UCC

§ 1–303(c). Notice that the definition of trade usage provides for regular observance in a *place, vocation, or trade*. As the Ninth Circuit observed in Nanakuli Paving & Rock Co. v. Shell Oil Co., 664 F.2d 772 (9th Cir, 1981) the drafters' use of the word "or" in the definition of trade usage means that "parties can be bound by a usage common to the place they are in business, even if it is not the usage of their particular vocation or trade." *Id.* at 791. Finally, a usage need not be universal to constitute a usage of trade so long as it is regularly observed. *See* UCC § 1–303, Comment ¶ 6.

2. § 2–202(a): COURSE OF PERFORMANCE, COURSE OF DEALING, AND USAGE OF TRADE EVIDENCE—WHY IT MATTERS

Article 2's parol evidence rule speaks in terms of the parties' *agreement* not *contract*. The UCC distinguishes the word "agreement" from the word "contract." *Compare* UCC § 1–201(b)(3) *with* UCC § 1–203(b)(12). The parties' agreement is their bargain in fact and includes "course of performance, course of dealing, or usage of trade as provided in Section 1–303." UCC § 1–201(b)(3). Unless expressly negated in the terms of the parties' writing, course of performance, course of dealing, and usage of trade are considered part of the parties' agreement. They are *not* extrinsic evidence for purposes of Article 2's parol evidence rule. Instead, they are the backdrop against which the parties contracted. The parties' "writings are to be read on the assumption that the course of prior dealings between the parties and the usages of trade were taken for granted when the document was phrased." UCC § 2–202, Comment ¶ 2.

In Contracts, you likely learned that before admitting evidence to explain the terms of a contract, the court first must decide whether the language at issue is ambiguous. Section 2–202 "definitely rejects . . . [t]he requirement that a condition precedent" to the admission of evidence of course of dealing or performance, or usage of trade, "is an original determination by the court that the language used is ambiguous." UCC § 2–202, Comment ¶ 1(c). Unless carefully negated, such evidence is part of the agreement and may be considered when interpreting the language of the parties' written contract.

As for "supplementing" the agreement with evidence of course of dealing, course of performance, or usage of trade, keep in mind that such evidence already is part of the parties' agreement. In other words, it really is not supplementary extrinsic evidence. Moreover, a course of performance is "[a] sequence of conduct *after* or *under* the agreement." UCC § 1–303, Comment ¶ 2. It *follows* the parties' signing of the written contract. As a noted commentator explains, it is "quite unremarkable" that the UCC allows a party to introduce course of performance evidence because the "UCC follows the usual view that subsequent modifications are not affected by the parol evidence rule." JOHN EDWARD MURRAY, JR., MURRAY ON CONTRACTS § 89F.1 (3d ed.). Thus, unless carefully negated, evidence of course of performance, course of dealing, and usage of trade is admissible, regardless of whether the contract is the final expression *or* the complete and exclusive statement of the parties' agreement.

What does "carefully negated" mean? The Ninth Circuit in *Nanakuli* interpreted the phrase to apply only in narrow circumstances, thereby requiring parties to clearly state that the terms of their written contract override trade usage, course of dealing, or course of performance. *Nanakuli* involved two long-term supply contracts between Nanakuli, an asphaltic paving contractor, and Shell Oil. Nanakuli sued Shell for breach of contract for failing to price protect Nanakuli with respect to 7200 tons of asphalt. (Price protection meant that when Shell raised prices it extended the prior, old price for a certain time period or for a certain tonnage.) The parties' written contract provided that the price for asphalt was "Shell's Posted Price at time of delivery." Shell argued that even if its prior price protection constituted a course of performance and price protection was a usage of trade, price protection could not be read consistently with the express terms of the parties' written contract. The Ninth Circuit disagreed. It concluded that a usage of trade (or course of performance or dealing) "should be allowed to modify the apparent agreement, as seen in the written terms, as long as it does not totally negate it." *Nanakuli,* 664 F.2d at 780. The court explained that the trade usage of price protection was "an exception to, rather than a total negation of, the express price term of 'Shell's Posted Price at time of delivery.' " *Id.* Therefore, the trade usage was part of the parties' agreement.

3. § 2–202(b): CONSISTENT ADDITIONAL TERMS

What happens if a party to the agreement wants to offer evidence that is *not* evidence of course of performance, course of dealing, or usage of trade? In such a case, the court may consider "evidence of consistent additional terms" unless the parties intended their writing to be the "complete and exclusive statement of the terms of the agreement." UCC § 2–202(b). The analysis under § 2–202(b) is really about supplementary evidence. If the court determines that a term or phrase in the parties' writing is ambiguous, then normally evidence explaining terms or phrases in the agreement is admissible in order to interpret the parties' meaning, even if their agreement is complete and exclusive or fully integrated. *See* CLAYTON P. GILLETTE AND STEVEN D. WALT, SALES LAW: DOMESTIC AND INTERNATIONAL 174 (2d ed.) (stating that "[i]n general evidence bearing on the interpretation of the terms of a writing is admissible too, even if the writing is considered the complete expression of the parties' agreement"). This distinction between supplementary and explanatory evidence makes sense. Complete and exclusive means that nothing can be added because there is nothing beyond the agreement that embodies the parties' intent. Thus, if the parties' agreement is complete and exclusive, i.e., fully integrated, then supplementary evidence is excluded. But if the writing is final, i.e., partially integrated, then it may be " '*supplemented* by consistent, additional terms.' " Adams v. Delk

Industries, 2021 WL 354096 (M.D. Tenn. 2021) (emphasis in original).

The court decides whether the parties' writing is partially or fully integrated. This determination is a question of law. *See* Budnick Converting, Inc. v. Nebula Glass International, Inc. 866 F. Supp.2d 976 (S.D. Ill. 2012); Randle v. Glendale Nissan, Inc., 2005 WL 281229 (N.D. Ill. 2005). The presence of a merger clause in the parties' writing is an important, but not necessarily dispositive, factor in a court's analysis of integration. A typical merger or integration clause provides as follows:

> *Entire Agreement.* This Contract constitutes the entire agreement between the parties relating to the subject matter contained in it and supersedes all prior and contemporaneous representations, agreements, or understandings between the parties.

The question, on which opinion is divided, is whether a court ends its integration inquiry upon finding a merger clause in the parties' written agreement. Some courts answer this question in the affirmative. *See* US Salt, Inc. v. Broken Arrow, Inc., 2008 WL 398818 (D. Minn. 2008) (stating that merger clause in parties' agreement was a "clear indicator that the parties intended the Salt Contract to be a complete and final statement of the terms of their agreement"). Others take the merger clause into account, but it is not the sole factor in their integration analysis; other extrinsic evidence as to the parties' intent is also considered. *See* Kominsky v. Dave Smith Chevrolet Oldsmobile Pontiac

Cadillac, Inc., 2010 WL 4920903 (D. Mont. 2010) (stating that the court should consider not only the writing's language but also " 'all extrinsic evidence relevant to the issue of whether the parties intended the written agreement to be a complete integration' "). Bear in mind that a court may be less likely to give dispositive effect to a merger clause in boilerplate language in a standard form contract. In such a case, one party drafted the form contract that the other party did nothing more than sign. Negotiation over terms did not occur and, thus, the merger clause provides little evidence that *both* parties intended the written agreement to be complete and exclusive.

Does the absence of a merger clause automatically mean that the written agreement is *not* complete and exclusive? Not necessarily. The Official Comment to § 2–202 provides the test to determine whether additional terms may be added to the parties' agreement.

> If the additional terms are such that, if agreed upon, they would certainly have been included in the document in the view of the court, then evidence of their alleged making must be kept from the trier of fact.

UCC § 2–202, Comment ¶ 3. For example, in Steel Strip Wheels, Ltd. v. General Rigging, LLC, 2009 WL 3190415 (E.D. Mich. 2009), the court concluded that because a time-for-performance clause certainly would have been included in the parties' contract had they agreed to it, such a clause was *not* part of the parties' agreement, even though the agreement contained no merger clause. *Steel Strip Wheels* involved a contract for the sale of industrial presses. The parties' contract, memorialized after several hours of negotiation in an invoice drafted by the owner of General Rigging, detailed the number and type of presses, the price, payment terms, delivery date, and the responsibility of Steel Strip Wheels to supply General Rigging with open top containers for packing and shipping the presses. A dispute arose as to the time for performance of Steel Strip Wheels' obligation to provide open top shipping containers. General Rigging argued that it discounted the price of the presses because Steel Strip Wheels had promised during negotiations to obtain open top shipping containers within a week of signing the invoice. The invoice, however, contained no deadline for providing the containers. The court explained that the invoice was "very specific with respect to time for payments and ultimate performance" and that the "parties [had] made handwritten changes and amendments" to the invoice. *Id.* at *23. The court noted that General Rigging could have inserted a time-for-performance provision into the agreement. "[S]uch a provision—allegedly so integral to General Rigging—would certainly have been included in the written agreement." *Id.* at *21. Its absence, according to the court, meant that Steel Strip Wheels was not obligated to obtain open top shipping containers by a set date.

C. LEASES: ARTICLE 2A'S PAROL EVIDENCE RULE

The language of § 2A–202 is virtually identical to that of § 2–202. Thus, the Official Comment for § 2–202 also applies to § 2A–202. *See* UCC § 2A–101, Comment: Relationship of Article 2A to Other Articles. Section 2A–202 contains no additional substantive commentary. Moreover, the case law interpreting Article 2's parol evidence rule is relevant to any analysis of § 2A–202. Thus, when analyzing a parol evidence issue for a lease transaction, refer back to the discussion above in Part B of Article 2's parol evidence rule. *See In re* Double G Trucking of the Arklatex, Inc., 432 B.R. 789 (Bankr. W.D. Ark. 2010) (before deciding whether transaction was sale or lease, holding that parol evidence rule precluded consideration of extrinsic evidence of option to purchase, after noting that parol evidence rule of Articles 2 and 2A are "nearly identical").

D. SUMMARY

The parol evidence rule precludes the admission of statements, oral or written, made before or contemporaneous with the signing of a writing if those statements contradict the terms of the writing. Thus, the parol evidence rule bars evidence that contradicts the terms of the parties' written contract.

Unless carefully negated, course of dealing, course of performance, and usage of trade are considered part of the parties' agreement. Such evidence may be offered to explain or to "supplement" the terms of the parties' written contract. As for explanatory evidence, the court need not make a preliminary determination that the language of the writing is ambiguous to consider evidence of course of dealing, course of performance, or usage of trade. Course of performance, course of dealing and usage of trade also may "supplement" the parties' written contract, regardless of whether that agreement is partially or fully integrated, because such evidence is considered part of the agreement already.

For evidence other than course of dealing, course of performance, or usage of trade, it is important to distinguish between explanatory and supplementary evidence. Whether the parties' writing is final or complete and exclusive, explanatory evidence may be used to interpret the written contract so long as the court makes an initial determination that the language at issue is ambiguous. If a party wants to supplement the writing, however, it makes a difference whether the contract is final versus complete and exclusive. If final, then neither § 2–202 nor § 2A–202 bars admission of supplementary evidence that is consistent with, i.e., does not contradict, the parties' written contract. Such evidence is not allowed, however, if the writing is complete and exclusive. A merger clause in a contract negotiated by the parties is some evidence that they intended the contract to be complete and exclusive. While some courts consider a merger clause dispositive on the integration question, many do not. Finally, the Official Comment to § 2–202, which applies both to contracts for sales of goods and to leases, states that if consistent additional terms certainly would have been included in the writing, then the parol evidence rule bars admission of those terms.

CHAPTER 5

ASSIGNMENT AND DELEGATION

A. INTRODUCTION

Before delving into the UCC's provisions on assignment and delegation, a brief discussion of terminology is in order. An assignment involves a transfer of *rights*. With a delegation, a party obligated to perform delegates that *duty* to perform to another person.

There are three parties involved in both an assignment and a delegation. Suppose Carl owes $500 to Anna. Anna assigns her right to payment to Ben. Anna is the assignor while Ben is the assignee. Carl, the obligor or party obligated to pay Anna, now pays Ben instead. Anna no longer has a right to payment from Carl.

Suppose Anna and Carl enter into a contract in which Carl is to deliver goods to Anna. Carl delegates that duty to Ben. Anna is the obligee—the party to whom performance is due. Carl is the delegator and Ben is the delegate. Thus, Ben must deliver the goods to Anna. Carl, however, is not off the hook. The delegation does not discharge Carl's ultimate obligation to perform; if Ben fails to perform, Carl is still obligated to deliver the goods to Anna. *See* UCC § 2–210(1) (stating that delegation does not relieve the delegating party from its duty to perform).

B. SALES: § 2–210

When analyzing an assignment or delegation issue, bear in mind that § 2–210 "recognizes both delegation of performance and assignability as normal and permissible incidents of a contract for the sale of goods." UCC § 2–210, Comment ¶ 1. Section 2–210(1) provides the basic rule on delegation of duties while § 2–210(2) sets forth the test for assignment of rights. A pure assignment involves only a transfer of the assignor's rights under the contract. But an agreement labeled as an assignment *may* involve both an assignment of rights and a delegation of duties.

> An assignment of "the contract" or of "all of my rights under the contract" or an assignment in similar general terms is an assignment of rights and unless the language or the circumstances (as in an assignment for security) indicate the contrary, it is a delegation of performance of the duties of the assignor and its acceptance by the assignee constitutes a promise by him to perform those duties. This promise is enforceable by either the assignor or the other party to the original contract.

UCC § 2–210(5). Therefore, it is important to determine what the parties' agreement accomplishes. *See* RESTATEMENT (SECOND) OF CONTRACTS § 328, Comment ¶ a (stating that "[t]he parties to an assignment, however, may not distinguish between assignment of rights and delegation of duties").

Suppose Widget Company sells widgets on account to various firms, including Pinnacle Corporation. Widget assigns its accounts receivable to Secured Party and satisfies the notice requirements of § 9–406. Pinnacle is an account debtor and must pay Secured Party what it owes to Widget Company. UCC § 9–406(a); *see* UCC § 9–102(a)(3) (definition of account debtor). Section 2–210's rules on assignment are subject to § 9–406, "which makes rights to payment for goods sold ('accounts'), whether or not earned, freely alienable notwithstanding a contrary agreement or rule of law." UCC § 2–210, Comment ¶ 3. Notice that Widget did not delegate its duty of performance to Secured Party.

Suppose Pinnacle Corporation enters into a contract to buy 10,000 widgets from Widget Company. The agreement provides for delivery of the widgets on March 1, with payment due within 30 days of delivery. Widget timely delivers 10,000 widgets to Pinnacle and assigns its right to payment for the widgets to Supplier; Widget owes Supplier for delivery of various raw materials. Is the assignment effective? Yes, the assignment is effective even if the Pinnacle/Widget contract prohibits assignment. "[A] right arising out of the assignor's due performance of his entire obligation can be assigned despite agreement otherwise." UCC § 2–210(2). Widget performed its "entire obligation"—delivering the widgets on time to Pinnacle—and, thus, its right to payment under the contract no longer is executory. "[R]ights which are no longer executory . . . may be assigned although the agreement prohibits assignment." UCC § 2–210, Comment ¶ 3; *see*

RESTATEMENT (SECOND) OF CONTRACTS § 317 (stating that if the obligor's [Pinnacle] only duty is to pay money, then "a change in the person to whom the payment is to be made is not ordinarily material").

What if the right assigned is something other than the right to payment of money? Suppose Pinnacle enters into a requirements contract with Widget in which Pinnacle agrees to purchase all of its widget requirements for the next year from Widget. *See* UCC § 2–306(1). Assume that the parties' agreement contains no anti-assignment language. Pinnacle subsequently assigns the requirements contract to Nadir, Inc. Nadir now has the right to delivery of widgets from Widget and must pay Widget for those deliveries.

Section 2–210's test asks whether the assignment materially changes the duties, burdens, or risks of the non-assigning party (the obligor).

> Except as otherwise provided in Section 9–406, unless otherwise agreed all rights of either seller or buyer can be assigned except where the assignment would materially change the duty of the other party, or increase materially the burden or risk imposed on him by his contract, or impair materially his chance of obtaining return performance.

UCC § 2–210(2). The assignment described above does not involve § 9–406, and there is no prohibition against assignment in the Widget/Pinnacle contract. The issue, then, is whether the assignment materially alters Widget's duties, risks, and burdens under the contract. You could argue that Widget now faces uncertainty because it contracted with Pinnacle for Pinnacle's requirements, not with Nadir for Nadir's requirements. Bear in mind, however, that § 2–306 "removes from the construction of the original contract most of the 'personal discretion' element by substituting the reasonably objective standard of good faith operation of the plant or business to be supplied." UCC § 2–210, Comment ¶ 4. Section 2–306 provides that the buyer cannot demand a quantity "unreasonably disproportionate to any stated estimate." UCC § 2–306(1). Thus, if the Widget/Pinnacle contract contains a stated estimate, that estimate applies to Nadir, the assignee. If the contract has no stated estimate, then Nadir cannot demand a quantity unreasonably disproportionate "to any normal or otherwise comparable" prior requirements. *Id.* As the authors of a noted treatise explain, "the assignee will be taking a contract measured, at baseline, by *assignor's* requirements, and not necessarily by *assignee's* requirements." JAMES J. WHITE, ROBERT S. SUMMERS, DANIEL D. BARNHIZER, WAYNE BARNES, & FRANKLIN G. SNYDER, PRINCIPLES OF SALES LAW 222 (2d ed.) (emphasis in original).

Moreover, Widget may avail itself of § 2–609 on adequate assurance of performance.

> The other party may treat any assignment which delegates performance as creating reasonable grounds for insecurity and may without prejudice to his rights against the

assignor demand assurances from the assignee (Section 2–609).

UCC § 2–210(6). The drafters of § 2–210 explained that "the word 'performance' [in subsection (6)] includes the giving of orders under a requirements contract." UCC § 2–210, Comment ¶ 4. Thus, Widget may allay its concerns about supplying Nadir's requirements by demanding adequate assurance from Nadir as to its performance—that the quantity Nadir orders under the requirements contract is not unreasonably disproportionate to the quantity agreed to or contemplated under the original agreement with Pinnacle.

Recall that if a party to the contract assigns the contract or all of its rights under the contract, then there is both an assignment of rights and a delegation of duties. UCC § 2–210(5). Performance through a delegate is allowed under § 2–210 unless the parties agree otherwise or the non-delegating party "has a substantial interest in having his original promisor perform or control the acts required by the contract." UCC § 2–210(1). Delegation does not relieve the delegating party from "any duty to perform or any liability for breach." *Id.* For example, suppose Pinnacle enters into a contract to buy widgets from Widget Company. Widget delegates its performance to Prime Widget Corporation, which contracts with Widget to assume Widget's duty to deliver widgets to Pinnacle. Prime fails to deliver the widgets. While Prime is liable to Pinnacle, Widget Company's duty to perform is not discharged. *See*

RESTATEMENT (SECOND) OF CONTRACTS § 318, Illustration 10.

What constitutes a substantial interest such that a party to a contract may not delegate its duty of performance? The Seventh Circuit addressed the issue in Sally Beauty Company v. Nexxus Products Company, 801 F.2d 1001 (7th Cir. 1986). In *Sally Beauty,* Nexxus and Best Barber & Beauty Supply Company (Best) made an agreement in which Best would be the exclusive distributor of Nexxus hair care products to hair salons and barbershops in much of Texas. Sally Beauty subsequently acquired Best, which was merged into Sally Beauty. Nexxus then canceled its agreement with Best, claiming that Sally Beauty was a wholly owned subsidiary of Alberto-Culver, a Nexxus competitor. Nexxus argued that its agreement with Best could not be assigned, at least not assigned to Sally Beauty, a competitor. Sally Beauty argued that Nexxus breached by canceling its contract with Best.

The assignment of the Best contract was both an assignment of rights and a delegation of duties. *See* UCC § 2–210(5). Best assigned its rights under the exclusive dealing contract to Sally Beauty, the assignee. Nexxus was the obligor; it owed Best, under the original contract, an obligation to use best efforts to supply the hair care products. *See* UCC § 2–306(2). Best also delegated its performance under the exclusive distributor agreement to Sally Beauty, the delegate. Nexxus was the obligee; Best, under the original agreement, was obligated to use best efforts to promote the sale of Nexxus hair care products. *See id.*

DIAGRAM #3: *SALLY BEAUTY* CASE

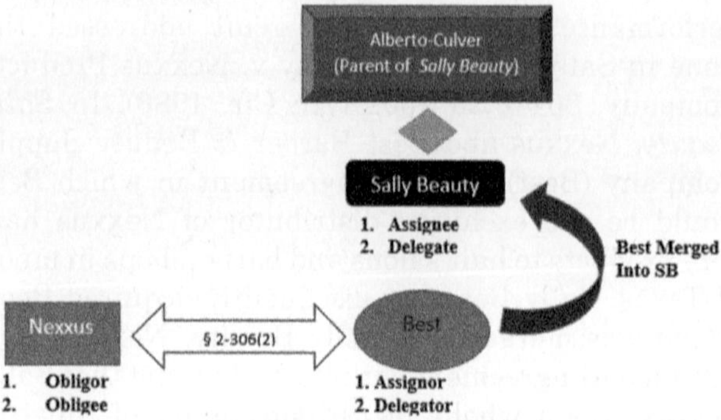

The Seventh Circuit held that Best could not delegate its duties under the exclusive distributorship to Sally Beauty, because Sally Beauty was a wholly owned subsidiary of a Nexxus competitor.

> We hold merely that the duty of performance under an exclusive distributorship may not be delegated to a competitor in the marketplace—or the wholly-owned subsidiary of a competitor—without the obligee's consent. We believe that such a rule is consonant with the policies behind section 2–210, which is concerned with preserving the bargain the obligee has struck. Nexxus should not be required to accept the "best efforts" of Sally Beauty when those efforts are subject to the

> control of Alberto-Culver. It is entirely reasonable that Nexxus should conclude that this performance would be a different thing than what it had bargained for. . . . Sally Beauty may be totally sincere in its belief that it can operate "impartially" as a distributor, but who can guarantee the outcome when there is a clear choice between the demands of the parent-manufacturer, Alberto-Culver, and the competing needs of Nexxus? The risk of an unfavorable outcome is not one which the law can force Nexxus to take. Nexxus has a substantial interest in not seeing this contract performed by Sally Beauty, which is sufficient to bar the delegation under section 2–210.

Sally Beauty, 801 F.2d at 1007–1008. Thus, the majority affirmed the district court's order granting summary judgment to Nexxus.

Judge Posner dissented. He argued that the case should be remanded for trial on the question of whether the merger between Best and Sally Beauty changed the "conditions of performance" to such an extent that Nexxus was justified in canceling the contract. Judge Posner dismissed as "unlikely" the possibility that Sally Beauty's acquisition of Best would adversely harm Nexxus. Posner noted that Sally Beauty distributed products of other Alberto-Culver competitors. He explained that if Alberto-Culver directed Sally Beauty to "go slow in pushing Nexxus" products, there was no guarantee that consumers then would gravitate to Alberto-Culver products. Also, such a move likely would damage

Sally Beauty's ability to sell products from other competing hair care lines. Competitors might be disinclined to sell through Sally Beauty if they learned that Sally Beauty favored Alberto-Culver products. Finally, Judge Posner noted that if Nexxus had reasonable grounds for insecurity about Sally Beauty's performance, it could have demanded adequate assurance of performance. *See* UCC § 2–210(6). It failed to do so. Thus, Judge Posner concluded that the trial court's order for summary judgment should be reversed, and the case remanded for trial.

C. LEASES: § 2A–303

Suppose Nadir, Inc. enters into an agreement to lease equipment for six months from Acme Company with rent due on the first of each month of the rental term. Acme has no obligation under the lease to service, maintain, or upgrade the equipment, but the implied warranty of merchantability is not disclaimed. The lease agreement prohibits assignment. Acme delivers the equipment to Nadir and assigns its right to the monthly rental payments to Pinnacle Corporation. Nadir objects to the assignment and wants to sue Acme for damages for breaching the lease agreement's anti-assignment provision. Does Nadir have a right to recover damages from Acme?

The short answer is "no." A lease provision that prohibits transfer "of a right to payment arising out of the transferor's due performance of the transferor's entire obligation . . . is not enforceable." UCC § 2A–

303(3). Acme, the transferor, performed its entire obligation by delivering the equipment to Nadir. Thus, its right to rent payments "is already due or will become due without further performance" by Acme. UCC § 2A–303, Comment ¶ 3.

How do you determine whether further performance is due by the assignor?

> The basic distinction is between a mere potential duty to respond which is not remaining performance, and an affirmative duty to render stipulated performance. Although the distinction may be difficult to draw in some cases, it is instructive to focus on the difference between "operating" and "non-operating" leases as generally understood in the marketplace.

Id. The Acme/Nadir agreement is a non-operating lease. Acme has no obligation to service, maintain, or upgrade the equipment. Yet the lease agreement does not disclaim the implied warranty of merchantability and Acme may have to respond to any claim by Nadir that the equipment is not fit for its ordinary purpose. Is that further performance? No, it is a "mere potential duty to respond" rather than "an affirmative duty to render stipulated performance." *Id.*

> [T]he fact that the lessor has potential liability under a "non-operating" lease contract for breaches of warranty does not mean that there is remaining performance. In contrast, the lessor would have remaining performance under a lease contract requiring the lessor to regularly

maintain and service the goods or to provide "upgrades" of the equipment on a periodic basis in order to avoid obsolescence.

Id.

Moreover, Nadir has no claim for damages against Acme based on the anti-assignment clause in the parties' lease agreement. Section 2A–303 provides that the party *not* making the transfer—Nadir, in our example—has the "rights and remedies" provided by § 2A–501(2) for breach of a lease provision making a transfer an event of default, and in certain other cases has the right to damages resulting from the transfer. UCC § 2A–303(4). The problem for Nadir, however, is that subsection (4) does *not* apply to the assignment of a right to payment arising out of the transferor's due performance of an entire obligation. "Thus, a lessor can transfer the right to future payments under the lease contract . . . and the transfer will not give rise to the rights and remedies stated in subsection (4) if the lessor has no remaining performance under the lease contract." UCC § 2A–303, Comment ¶ 3; *see* UCC § 2A–303(3) (stating that such a transfer is not a transfer "within the purview of subsection (4)").

As with contracts for the sale of goods, a transfer of "the lease" or of all of a party's rights under the lease constitutes both an assignment of that party's rights and a delegation of that party's duties under the lease. UCC § 2A–303(5). Delegation of performance, however, "does not relieve the transferor as against the other party of any duty to perform or any liability for default." UCC § 2A–

303(6). Thus, the duty of the delegator to perform is not extinguished by the delegation.

Suppose Nadir agrees to lease computer equipment from Acme for two years, with rent due on the first of each month. The agreement requires Acme to perform quarterly maintenance and service on the equipment, and to upgrade the equipment at the end of the first year of the lease. It also prohibits assignment of the lease contract and makes such a transfer an event of default. Before the contract delivery date, Acme assigns the contract to Pinnacle Corporation. Acme has both assigned its rights and delegated its duties under the lease to Pinnacle. Is the transfer of the lease by Acme to Pinnacle effective?

A lease provision that makes a transfer of an interest under the lease contract "an event of default, gives rise to the rights and remedies provided in subsection (4), but a transfer that is prohibited or is an event of default under the lease agreement is otherwise effective." UCC § 2A–303(2). Thus, subject to Nadir's rights and remedies under § 2A–303(4), the transfer from Acme to Pinnacle is "otherwise effective." *Id.* In a case in which the lease agreement makes a transfer, such as Acme's transfer to Pinnacle, an event of default, the party not making the transfer, i.e., Nadir, "has the rights and remedies described in Section 2A–501(2)." UCC § 2A–303(4)(a). Thus, Nadir may avail itself of the rights and remedies provided by Article 2A and the lease agreement. *See* UCC § 2A–501(2) (stating that if the lessor defaults, the lessee has the "rights and remedies as provided in [Article 2A] and, except as limited by [Article 2A], as provided in the lease agreement"); *see also infra* Chapter 11, § E.

What if the Acme/Nadir lease agreement prohibited assignment of the contract but did not make violating the prohibition on transfer an event of default? *See* UCC § 2A–303, Comment ¶ 6 (describing such a scenario as an "unlikely circumstance"). Nadir would have the right to recover "damages caused by the transfer to the extent that the damages could not reasonably [have been] prevented" by Nadir. UCC § 2A–303(4)(b). A court also could "grant other appropriate relief, including cancellation of the lease contract or an injunction against the transfer." *Id.* Thus, subject to Nadir's rights under § 2A–303(4)(b), the transfer of Acme's rights under the lease to Pinnacle is otherwise effective.

If the lease agreement contained neither a prohibition on transfer of the lease nor a provision making such a transfer an event of default, then Nadir has the right to damages and relief described in the preceding paragraph if the transfer "materially impairs the prospect of return performance by, materially chang[ing] the duty of, or materially increase[ing] the burden or risk imposed on" Nadir. UCC § 2A–303(4)(b). What is material? "There is 'materiality' where the contract obligations involve personal services or the exercise of personal skill or discretion." 3 Hawkland UCC Series § 2A–303:3; *cf.* RESTATEMENT (SECOND) OF CONTRACTS § 318 (stating that principal exceptions to permissibility of delegation "relate to contracts for personal services and to contracts for the exercise of personal skill or discretion").

When discussing a question involving an assignment of the contract and the rights and remedies of the non-assigning party—Nadir, in our examples—do not forget Article 2A's rules on adequate assurance of performance. *See* UCC § 2A–401. Nadir may have reasonable grounds for insecurity about Pinnacle's ability to service and upgrade the equipment; thus, Nadir may demand adequate assurance of performance. *Id*; *see* UCC § 2A–303, Comment ¶ 7 (stating that the transferee may propose "adequate cure or compensation for past defaults and adequate assurance of future due performance under the lease contract"); *see also infra* Chapter 10 on the adequate assurance doctrine.

The prior examples involve commercial parties. What happens in the case of a consumer lease? Any lease provision either prohibiting transfer of a lease interest or making such a transfer an event of default "must be specific, by a writing, and conspicuous." UCC § 2A–303(7). The purpose of this requirement is to "protect[ ] a consumer lessee against surprise assertions of default." UCC § 2A–303, Comment ¶ 8. Otherwise, the provisions of § 2A–303 regarding effectiveness of transfers, rights and remedies of the non-transferring party, and the effect of a transfer of all rights under the lease agreement are the same for consumer leases as for commercial leases.

CHAPTER 6
WARRANTIES

A. SALES: INTRODUCTION

This section of the Nutshell covers Article 2's warranty provisions at § 2–312 through § 2–318. It also provides a very brief introduction to the Magnuson-Moss Warranty Act. *See infra* § A.4.c of this Chapter.

Unless modified or excluded, the sale of a good carries with it a warranty of title. UCC § 2–312. Section 2–313 explains how a seller may create an express warranty. Article 2 has two implied warranties: (a) merchantability (§ 2–314); and (b) fitness for a particular purpose (§ 2–315). Section 2–316 addresses warranty disclaimers while § 2–317 provides rules on how to resolve conflicts among warranties. Finally, § 2–318 sets forth three alternatives for states to adopt with regard to third-party beneficiaries of seller warranties.

1. WARRANTY OF TITLE

Section 2–312 has three subsections. Subsection (1) provides the warranty of title. Subsection (2) enumerates the three ways in which the title warranty may be modified or excluded. Finally, § 2–312(3) provides the warranty against infringement.

The title warranty in subsection (1) applies to merchants and non-merchants alike. Unless excluded or modified, the seller in any contract for sale warrants that "the title conveyed shall be good, and its transfer rightful." UCC § 2–312(1)(a). In addition, the seller warrants that "the goods shall be delivered free from any security interest or other lien or encumbrance of which the buyer at the time of contracting has no knowledge." UCC § 2–312(1)(b). For example, in Deere & Co. v. Cabelka, 2014 WL 4744769 (W.D. Okla. 2014), the court held that GTF LLC, the seller of a combine, breached the warranty of title because it conveyed the combine to buyer (i) knowing that Deere had a valid security interest in the combine and (ii) without informing buyer of that security interest. *See* UCC § 2–312(1)(b). The reference to knowledge in § 2–312(1)(b) means actual knowledge, not mere notice. UCC § 2–312, Comment ¶ 1. (You should read this material on the warranty of title in conjunction with the Nutshell's discussion of good faith purchasers and entrustment. *See infra* Chapter 8.)

Unlike the implied warranty of merchantability and implied warranty of fitness for a particular purpose, the warranty of title "is not designated as an 'implied' warranty." UCC § 2–312, Comment ¶ 6. Therefore, § 2–316(3)'s methods for disclaiming implied warranties do not apply to the warranty of title. Instead, the warranty of title may be modified or excluded in only one of three ways: (1) by specific language; (2) by circumstances giving the buyer reason to know that the seller "does not claim title in himself"; or (3) by circumstances giving the buyer reason to know that the seller is selling "only such right or title as he or a third person may have". UCC § 2–312(2). For example, if you purchase goods from the trunk of a car parked in an alley, you have reason to know that the seller "does not claim title in himself." Sheriff sales or sales by executors also may be "so out of the ordinary commercial course" as to alert the buyer that the seller does not warrant title to the goods. *See* UCC § 2–312, Comment ¶ 5.

Finally, § 2–312(3) provides a warranty against infringement which applies only to certain merchant sellers. Unless the parties otherwise agree, a merchant seller regularly dealing in goods of the kind warrants that there is "no claim of infringement of a patent or trademark by a third party that will mar the buyer's title" to the goods sold. UCC § 2–312, Comment ¶ 3. But if the buyer provides the seller with specifications regarding the product, then the buyer "must hold the seller harmless against any such claim [of infringement] which arises out of compliance with the specifications." UCC § 2–312(3). Thus, in order to establish breach of the warranty against infringement, the buyer must establish that the (1) seller was a merchant dealing regularly in the goods sold; (2) "goods were subject to a rightful infringement claim"; (3) buyer did not furnish specifications to the seller; and (4) buyer entered into no agreement with seller to waive or modify the warranty. Innovation Ventures, LLC v. Ultimate One Distribution Corp., 2016 U.S. Dist. LEXIS 44496 (E.D. N.Y. 2016).

In *Innovation Ventures*, FDI, a Florida corporation that sold grocery items and other consumer goods, claimed that Baja Exporting and Dan-Dee Company had sold it counterfeit 5-hour ENERGY, thereby subjecting FDI to suit for trademark infringement by

Living Essentials, the owner of 5-hour ENERGY. The district court granted FDI's motion for summary judgment on its claim of breach of the warranty against infringement. Baja and Dan-Dee both were merchants regularly dealing in 5-hour ENERGY products. By selling counterfeit products to FDI, both companies subjected FDI to a rightful infringement claim by Living Essentials. FDI had neither provided specifications to Baja and Dan-Dee nor entered into any agreement modifying or excluding the warranty against infringement. Therefore, FDI established the elements necessary to prove breach of the warranty against infringement.

2. EXPRESS WARRANTIES

A seller may create an express warranty with regard to the goods it sells in any of the following ways:

- Making an affirmation of fact relating to the goods that becomes part of the basis of the bargain;
- Making a promise relating to the goods that becomes part of the basis of the bargain;
- Giving a description of the goods that is made part of the basis of the bargain;
- Providing a sample of the goods that is made part of the basis of the bargain; or
- Providing a model of the goods that is made part of the basis of the bargain.

UCC § 2–313(1)(a)–(c). The seller may create an express warranty even if she does not use the words "warrant" or "guarantee", and even if she does not have "a specific intention to make a warranty." UCC § 2–313(2). But a statement by the seller of her opinion about the goods or her recommendation to purchase the Goods does not create an express warranty. *Id.* Do not confuse creation of an express warranty with the implied warranty of merchantability. A non-merchant can create an express warranty.

Determining whether the seller created an express warranty is a fact-intensive inquiry. Ask yourself questions about the nature of the statement at issue and the context in which it is made. Is the statement general or specific? Is it capable of objective measurement? Does the seller use "hedging" language? Is the statement the seller's opinion? What is the relative knowledge and skill of buyer and seller? *See* UCC revised Article 2, § 2–313, Comment ¶ 10 (listing eight factors to consider). While no jurisdiction has adopted revised Article 2, the factors mentioned nonetheless are relevant to determining whether a seller creates an express warranty.

Suppose you visit *Wesley's Reliable Cars* (WREC) to buy a used car. You find two cars—one blue and one silver—that you like and ask the salesperson: "In your opinion, which car gets better gas mileage?" The salesperson points to the blue car and says: "I would buy the blue car. I think it probably gets better gas mileage on average than the silver one." You buy the car and discover that the car gets 20 miles to the gallon on the highway. Can you recover against WREC for breach of an express warranty? It is unlikely. First, the statement "better gas mileage" is general, not specific. Second, is "better gas mileage" capable of objective measurement? What does "better" mean in this context? If the silver car got 18 miles to the gallon on the highway, then the blue car actually does have better gas mileage. The salesperson did not say that the blue car would average 25 or even 30 miles to the gallon; she simply told you which car had better gas mileage. Third, you asked for the salesperson's opinion, and she responded with a recommendation as to which car she would purchase. *See* UCC § 2–313(2) (providing that a "statement purporting to be merely the seller's opinion or commendation of the goods does not create a warranty"). Finally, the salesperson hedges. She says the blue car *probably* gets better gas mileage *on average*. This statement is far from a specific, clear factual assertion susceptible to objective measurement.

Affirmations of fact or promises by the seller, however, are not the only ways to create an express warranty. For example, suppose Betty, the buyer for Beta Company, visits Acme's plant. Beta wants to purchase several hundred units of Product X. Betty asks Arnie, the sales representative for Acme, about the dimensions and appearance of Product X. Arnie pulls a sample from a box on the production line and tells Betty: "This is Product X." The sample likely creates an express warranty that the goods that Beta orders will look like the sample. "If the sample has been drawn from an existing bulk, it must be regarded as describing values of the goods contracted for unless it is accompanied by an unmistakable denial of such responsibility." UCC § 2–313, Comment ¶ 6. Arnie drew the sample from goods on the production line in response to Betty's question and stated it *was* Product X. Arnie did not use equivocal language in pointing to the sample and gave no indication that the goods ordered would deviate in any way from the sample.

To sue for breach, the buyer must show that the seller made an express warranty that became part of the basis of the bargain. The UCC does not define the phrase "basis of the bargain," but for many courts the focus is the buyer's reliance on the seller's representations. *See* Berge Helene, Ltd. v. GE Oil & Gas, Inc., 896 F. Supp.2d 582 (S.D. Tex. 2012) (stating in a footnote that "[a]lthough some cases list 'basis of bargain' and 'reliance' as separate elements, other courts blend them together because of their conceptual overlap"). The basis-of-the-bargain analysis is a fact-intensive one.

The courts have adopted three basic approaches to the basis-of-the-bargain analysis.

> U.C.C. § 2–313's [sic] requires that a seller's promise must "become[ ] the basis of the bargain" to form an express warranty. The fifty states use at least three distinct approaches to this "reliance element." First, some states hold that reliance is not an element of an express warranty claim. Second, other states require specific reliance on a seller's statements as a condition of recovery. Finally, a few states hold

that promises relating to goods create a rebuttable presumption of reliance in favor of the buyer.

Chapman v. Tristar Products, Inc., 2017 WL 1433259 (N.D. Ohio 2017); *see* Porcell v. Lincoln Wood Products, 713 F. Supp.2d 1305 (D. N.M. 2010) (in litigation seeking certification of a class of buyers of insulated glass windows, discussion of nine states' requirements as to reliance in a claim for breach of express warranty); *see also* 2 Hawkland UCC Series § 2–313:4 (stating that "courts have used three main approaches to whether the buyer's reliance on the representation is required in order to demonstrate that it is part of the basis of the bargain").

In Koch v. Kaz USA, Inc., 2011 WL 2610198 (D. Colo. 2011), the court held that proof of reliance was not required to make out a claim for breach of express warranty. Shirley Koch sued, in part, for breach of express warranties after suffering burns from the release of hot oil from an oil filled convection radiator heater (HZ-690 heater). Hot oil was released after a fracture occurred at a weld spot on the heater. Koch based her express warranty claims on various statements, e.g., "Machine welded for leak-free operation", appearing on the box in which the heater was sold. The defendant sellers argued that Mrs. Koch could not recover for breach of express warranty because she had not relied on the representations on the box. Her husband bought the heater; therefore, Mrs. Koch did not see those representations prior to the heater's purchase. The district court rejected the defendant sellers' argument. After quoting from

Comment ¶ 3 to § 2–313, the court held that defendant sellers were "not entitled to judgment as a matter of law on Mrs. Koch's claim for breach of express warranty on the basis that she cannot demonstrate reliance on the representations on the box of the HZ-690 heater." *Koch,* 2011 WL 2610198, at *8; *see also* Haynes Mechanical Systems, Inc. v. Bluon Energy, LLC, 2021 WL 3128652 (D. Colo. 2021) (stating that "regardless of what conduct formed the basis of the bargain, reliance is not required to succeed on a breach of express warranty claim").

In some states, however, the buyer must demonstrate that it relied on the seller's representations in order to prevail on a claim for breach of express warranty. *See, e.g.,* MagnetNotes, Ltd. v. Trexan Chemicals, Inc., 2011 WL 3022062 (N.D. Ohio 2011) (stating that "reliance upon the representations is necessary in order for them to become part of the basis for the bargain"); Yocham v. Novartis Pharmaceuticals Corporation, 736 F. Supp. 2d 875 (D. N.J. 2010) (granting summary judgment for defendant seller on buyer's express warranty claim because Texas law "requires some evidence that the claimant relied on the representations in deciding to purchase and use the product" and buyer had "not adduced evidence of reliance"). But, requiring the buyer to show reliance appears at odds with the drafters' intent, as expressed in the Official Comment to § 2–313.

> [Section 2–313] deals with affirmations of fact by the seller, descriptions of the goods or

> exhibitions of samples, exactly as any other part of a negotiation which ends in a contract is dealt with. No specific intention to make a warranty is necessary if any of these factors is made part of the basis of the bargain. In actual practice affirmations of fact made by the seller about the goods during a bargain are regarded as part of the description of those goods; hence no particular reliance on such statements need be shown in order to weave them into the fabric of the agreement. Rather, any fact which is to take such affirmation, once made, out of the agreement requires clear affirmative proof.

UCC § 2–313, Comment ¶ 3. It is difficult to square the language of Comment ¶ 3 with the requirement imposed by some courts that the buyer demonstrate its reliance in order to make out a claim for breach of express warranty.

As the *Chapman* court explained, some courts use a third approach when analyzing § 2–313's "basis-of-the-bargain" language. These courts have adopted a rebuttable presumption that representations by the seller of which the buyer was aware during the bargaining process are presumed to be part of the basis of the bargain. The seller, of course, may overcome the presumption that its statements became part of the basis of the bargain.

> For instance, "the buyer's actual knowledge of the true condition of the goods prior to the making of the contract may make it plain that the seller's statement was not relied upon as one of the inducements for the purchase." . . .

> Additionally, a seller's statement will not be presumed to be part of the basis of the bargain when the buyer knew the statement to be false or was not influenced by it, or when the statement was not made until after the sale of the product.

Kelleher v. Marvin Lumber & Cedar Co., 891 A.2d 477 (N.H. 2005). The "rebuttable presumption" approach is consistent with the language of § 2–313's Official Comment. No "particular reliance" is required to weave the seller's statements into the fabric of the parties' agreement. *See* UCC § 2–313, Comment ¶ 3. Instead, the seller must provide "clear affirmative proof" that the statements were not part of the basis of the bargain. *Id.; see* UCC § 2–313, Comment ¶ 8 (stating that all of the seller's representations become part of the basis of the bargain "unless good reason is shown to the contrary").

Before moving on to the UCC's implied warranties, it is important to recognize the interplay of the parol evidence rule and proof of breach of an express warranty. Suppose Seller makes an express warranty prior to the parties signing a contract; that contract does not include the express warranty. The parol evidence rule may bar the buyer from offering evidence of the existence of the warranty in buyer's breach of warranty lawsuit. *See supra* Chapter 4, § B.3.

3. IMPLIED WARRANTIES

Article 2 has two warranties it designates as implied warranties: (1) the implied warranty of merchantability found at § 2–314; and (2) the implied warranty of fitness for a particular purpose at § 2–315. As you will see below, it is difficult, at times, to distinguish between the implied warranties of merchantability and of fitness.

a. Merchantability

The merchantability warranty is implied in any *sale of goods* by a *merchant seller* that sells goods of that kind. The following sections of this Chapter discuss the merchant requirement, the scope of the merchantability warranty, and breach of that warranty.

1) Merchant

Section 2–104 defines a merchant as follows.

> "Merchant" means a person who deals in goods of the kind or otherwise by his occupation holds himself out as having knowledge or skill peculiar to the practices or goods involved in the transaction or to whom such knowledge or skill may be attributed by his employment of an agent or broker or other intermediary who by his occupation holds himself out as having such knowledge or skill.

UCC § 2–104(1). The word "merchant" as used in § 2–314 refers to the first clause in § 2–104's definition: a person who deals in goods of the kind. Thus, for purposes of § 2–314, the word "merchant" applies to "a much smaller group than everyone who is engaged in business and requires a professional status as to particular kinds of goods." UCC § 2–314, Comment ¶ 2. For example, a used car lot owner is a merchant with regard to cars. But, if the owner sells an old computer used in the business, the implied warranty of merchantability does not apply to that sale. The owner is not a merchant with respect to computers.

Because the merchantability warranty applies to persons with specialized knowledge of the goods, "[a] person making an isolated sale of goods is not a 'merchant'" for purposes of § 2–314. UCC § 2–314, Comment ¶ 3. For example, suppose you place an ad in the local paper to sell a 2018 Honda Accord. Neighbor purchases the car. Neighbor cannot sue you for breach of the implied warranty of merchantability because you are not a merchant.

Finally, it is the status of the *seller,* not the *age* of the goods that determines whether the implied warranty of merchantability applies to the sale. The warranty applies to merchant sellers of both new and used goods. For example, suppose you buy a used car from *Used Car Lot. Used Car Lot* is a merchant seller of cars and, therefore, the implied warranty of merchantability applies to the sale. *See* UCC § 2–314, Comment ¶ 3 (noting that sale of "second-hand goods" carries with it "only such obligation as is appropriate to such goods").

2) Scope of the Warranty

In order to sue for breach of the implied warranty of merchantability, you must prove that the goods are not merchantable. What does merchantable mean?

> Goods to be merchantable must be at least such as
>
> (a) pass without objection in the trade under the contract description; and
>
> (b) in the case of fungible goods, are of fair average quality within the description; and
>
> (c) are fit for the ordinary purpose for which such goods are used; and
>
> (d) run, within the variations permitted by the agreement, of even kind, quality and quantity within each unit and among all units involved; and
>
> (e) are adequately contained, packaged, and labeled as the agreement may require; and
>
> (f) conform to the promise or affirmations of fact made on the container or label if any.

UCC § 2–314(2). The list above is not exhaustive; the drafters of § 2–314 intended to "leave open other possible attributes of merchantability." UCC § 2–314, Comment ¶ 6.

Nonetheless, "[f]itness for the ordinary purposes for which goods of the type are used is a fundamental concept" of § 2–314. UCC § 2–314, Comment ¶ 8; *see* Oddo v. Arcoaire Air Conditioning & Heating, 2017

WL 11631376 (C.D. Cal. 2017) (stating that " 'a core test of merchantability is fitness for the ordinary purpose for which such goods are used' "). For example, floor tiles that do not adhere to the floor and "pop up" and "cup" are not fit for the ordinary purpose of floor tiles, i.e., walking on the tiled floor. *See* Courey International v. Designer Floors of Texas, Inc., 2010 WL 143420 (Tex. Ct. App. 2010). A car that overheats and loses engine power is not merchantable because it fails to provide the owner with "safe and reliable transportation." Matanky v. GM, LLC, 370 F. Supp. 3d 772 (E.D. Mich. 2019). But even though the paint used on a Mercedes had a latent defect that caused blistering and peeling, the seller did not breach the implied warranty of merchantability because the car owner failed to prove that the peeling paint rendered the vehicle unfit for its ordinary purpose of driving. *See* Pinon v. Daimler AG, 2019 WL 11648560 (N.D. Ga. 2019).

It is important to distinguish the ordinary purpose for which goods are to be used from fitness of the goods for a particular purpose under § 2–315. For example, Doe v. Miles, 2000 Mo. App. LEXIS 770 (Mo. Ct. App. 2000), involved an appeal of a trial court verdict against Miles, Inc., which sold Factor VIII concentrate for use by hemophiliacs. Doe sued the firm on behalf of her deceased son, who was a hemophiliac, and claimed, in part, that Miles had breached the implied warranty of fitness for a particular purpose with regard to its sale of Factor VIII. The Missouri Court of Appeals reversed the trial court's verdict for Doe on her claim for breach of the fitness warranty because the company's "Factor

VIII concentrate was purchased and used for its ordinary purpose, and for no particular use other than its ordinary use." *Id.* at *29.

While a lawsuit based on failure of a consumer product likely will include both contract and tort claims, make sure you understand the difference between recovering in contract for breach of the implied warranty of merchantability and recovering in tort for an unreasonably dangerous product. In the context of a claim for breach of the implied warranty of merchantability, a defective good is one unfit for its ordinary purpose. By comparison, for a claim sounding in strict products liability, a defective good is one that is "unreasonably dangerous." For example, a toaster that does not toast bread is not fit for its ordinary purpose even though the failure to toast bread does not make the toaster unreasonably dangerous. Thus, a consumer may recover for breach of the implied warranty of merchantability, even if the good is not unreasonably dangerous, so long as the good is unfit for its ordinary purpose. *See* 3 Anderson U.C.C. § 2–314:615 (3d ed.); *cf.* Herbst v. Deere & Co., 2021 WL 5567379 (S.D. Tex. 2021) (stating that a product may be unreasonably dangerous in the "strict-liability context" yet may be fit for its ordinary purpose).

3) Breach of the Warranty

To prevail on a claim for breach of the implied warranty of merchantability, you must prove not only breach of the warranty but also that the breach "was the proximate cause of the loss sustained." UCC § 2–

314, Comment ¶ 13. Evidence by the seller that it "exercised care in the manufacture, processing or selection of the goods is relevant to the issue of whether the warranty was in fact broken." *Id.* Be careful with this language from the Official Comment. It does *not* mean that the merchant seller is *not* liable for breach of the implied warranty of merchantability if the seller provides evidence of due care in the manufacture, processing, and selection of its goods. It means that evidence of due care is useful to the trier of fact in determining *when* the product was not merchantable. If a product is not merchantable *at the time* it leaves the hands of the merchant seller, then the seller breached the implied warranty of merchantability *regardless of how careful* the seller was in manufacturing, processing, and selecting its goods. In other words, the cause of action for breach of the implied warranty of merchantability, while sounding in contract, is akin to strict liability, not negligence, in tort.

What, then, is the purpose of introducing evidence of due care? It is not easy to determine the time when a product is not merchantable. If the seller exercised due care in producing and selling its products, then a court may determine that the product was merchantable *at the time* it left the seller's hands. In other words, the evidence tends to show that the product became not merchantable in the hands of the *buyer*. In such a case, there is no breach of the implied warranty of merchantability, because it was the *buyer's, not the seller's,* actions that rendered the product not merchantable.

b. Fitness for a Particular Purpose

The implied warranty of fitness for a particular purpose arises in a sale of goods if at the time of contracting the "seller has reason to know any particular purpose for which the goods are required and that the buyer is relying on the seller's skill or judgment to select or furnish suitable goods." UCC § 2–315. In order to prove a breach of the warranty, the buyer must prove that: (1) it had a particular purpose for the goods; (2) the seller had reason to know of that particular purpose; (3) the seller had reason to know that buyer was relying on the seller's skill or judgment in selecting the goods; and (4) the goods were not fit for the particular purpose. Determining whether the warranty arises in any particular sale is a "question of fact." UCC § 2–315, Comment ¶ 1.

The implied warranty of fitness for a particular purpose differs from the implied warranty of merchantability in several ways. First, the fitness warranty applies to a sale by both merchants and non-merchants alike. The implied warranty of merchantability arises only in a sale by a merchant of goods of the kind sold.

Second, as discussed earlier, the goods must be fit for the buyer's *particular* purpose as opposed to the *ordinary* purpose of the goods.

> A "particular purpose" differs from the ordinary purpose for which the goods are used in that it envisages a specific use by the buyer which is peculiar to the nature of his business

> whereas the ordinary purpose for which the goods are used are those envisaged in the concept of merchantability and go to uses which are customarily made of the goods in question.

UCC § 2–315, Comment ¶ 2. The drafters of Article 2 provided an example of the difference between the two warranties. "[S]hoes are generally used for the purpose of walking upon ordinary ground, but a seller may know that a particular pair was selected to be used for climbing mountains." *Id.*

Most courts require that the buyer's particular purpose differ from the ordinary purpose for which the goods are used. For example, in Keffer v. Wyeth, 791 F. Supp.2d 539 (S.D. W.Va. 2011), the plaintiff claimed that she took defendants' hormone replacement therapy drugs for the particular purpose of treating her menopausal symptoms. The court held that plaintiff's claim for breach of the implied warranty of fitness for a particular purpose failed because "the record reveal[ed] that the treatment of menopausal symptoms was the ordinary, rather than the particular, purpose for which the drugs were used." *Id.* at 547. Thus, in a case involving a claim for breach of the implied warranty of fitness for a particular purpose, the court's focus is the buyer's particular or peculiar needs rather than the purpose for which the good ordinarily is used. *See* Parker v. Alexander Marine Co., 2015 WL 12712083 (C.D. Cal. 2015) (holding that plaintiff's argument that he "expected to use the yacht to sail on the open ocean" did not establish "a 'peculiar' intent . . . different from the ordinary purposes for which [such] yachts were used").

Finally, "[r]eliance is not an element of the warranty of merchantability . . . [but] is an element of the warranty of fitness for a particular purpose." Hinderer v. Ryan, 499 P.2d 252 (Wash. Ct. App. 1972). Not only must the seller have reason to know that the buyer is relying on seller's skill or judgment, but the buyer must also actually rely on the seller's skill or judgment. UCC § 2–315, Comment ¶ 1. For example, suppose you own a small business and need to buy a piece of equipment for the office. Friend is very knowledgeable about the type of equipment you wish to purchase, so she accompanies you to the retail outlet where you plan to buy the equipment. If you and Friend examine the equipment and purchase that equipment based on Friend's recommendation, not that of seller's agent, then no implied warranty of fitness for a particular purpose arises.

4. WARRANTY DISCLAIMERS

If the seller makes no warranties, then there is nothing to disclaim. But the implied warranty of merchantability is easy to create; it arises in the sale of goods by a merchant who deals in goods of that kind. Thus, a seller may wish to modify or exclude certain warranties. Section 2–316 provides the rules for warranty disclaimers.

Section 2–316(1) explains the disclaimer rules applicable to express warranties. Specific requirements for disclaiming the implied warranties of merchantability and fitness for a particular purpose are found at § 2–316(2) while § 2–316(3) provides general rules for disclaiming implied warranties. Remember that the warranty of title is "not designated as an 'implied' warranty, and hence is not subject to Section 2–316(3)." UCC § 2–312, Comment ¶ 6. Even if warranties are not disclaimed, the parties' agreement may limit or liquidate damages. UCC § 2–316(4); *see* §§ 2–718, 2–719; *see also infra* Chapter 11, §§ F.1, G.1.

a. Express Warranties

When dealing with disclaimers of express warranties, make sure you distinguish two fact scenarios: (1) the parties signing a contract that contains both an express warranty and a disclaimer of all express warranties, and (2) the seller making an express warranty followed by the parties signing a contract containing a disclaimer of all express warranties.

Scenario #1: Suppose Slate Rock & Gravel Company buys an excavator from Flintrock Machinery. The parties sign a contract that contains an express warranty about the excavator's performance but also states the following: "Seller disclaims all warranties, express and implied." (*See infra* for effect of this language on the implied warranties.) This language is ineffective to disclaim the express warranty about the excavator's performance. Section 2–316 directs that language negating an express warranty "shall be construed wherever reasonable as consistent" with language creating the warranty but that a disclaimer is "inoperative to the extent that such construction is unreasonable." UCC § 2–316(1). It is not possible to read the express warranty and the disclaimer consistently. Therefore, in such a case, the language of disclaimer is denied effect in order to protect buyers from "unexpected and unbargained language of disclaimer by denying effect to such language when inconsistent with language of express warranty." UCC § 2–316, Comment ¶ 1.

Scenario #2: Suppose Barney Rubble buys a used car from Flintrock Motors. The salesman tells Barney that the car gets 30 miles to the gallon in highway driving. The parties then sign a contract that makes no reference to the car's gas mileage and that contains a disclaimer of all express warranties not provided for in the written agreement. After driving the car for a month, Barney discovers that it gets no better than 20 miles to the gallon in highway driving. Barney wants to sue Flintrock Motors and claims that the salesman, an agent of Flintrock, made an express warranty about the vehicle's gas mileage. Barney has a parol evidence rule problem. The court must try to construe the express warranty and the disclaimer as consistent, if possible, "but subject to the provisions of [Article 2] on parol or extrinsic evidence (Section 2–202)." UCC § 2–316(1). The oral warranty is parol evidence—a statement made prior to the parties' final agreement. Flintrock will argue that the warranty contradicts the parties' writing and, therefore, is not admissible. Barney will claim that the writing is final, but not complete and exclusive, and that he is merely trying to supplement the writing with the express warranty on gas mileage. If the contract is complete and exclusive (fully integrated), Barney may argue that he was fraudulently induced into signing the agreement based on the salesman's statement about gas mileage. *See* Poeppel v. Lester, 827 N.W.2d 580 (S.D. 2013) (stating that a "substantial majority of jurisdictions follow the traditional, majority view that the parol evidence rule is inapplicable in cases of fraudulent inducement" and noting that such evidence is admissible even if the parties' contract is fully integrated).

b. Implied Warranties of Merchantability and Fitness for a Particular Purpose

Section 2–316(2) contains very specific requirements for disclaiming the implied warranty of merchantability and the implied warranty of fitness for a particular purpose. These requirements, however, are subject to the disclaimer methods provided by § 2–316(3). Thus, if the seller does not satisfy the disclaimer requirements of § 2–316(2), the seller still may disclaim either implied warranty by complying with the requirements of § 2–316(3).

1) Section 2–316(2)

Section 2–316(2) provides that in order for the seller to disclaim the implied warranty of merchantability, the word "merchantability" must be used. The disclaimer need not be written, but if in writing the disclaimer must be conspicuous. The statement above in *Scenario #1* that "Seller disclaims all warranties, express and implied" does not disclaim the implied warranty of merchantability, because it fails to mention the word "merchantability."

By comparison, no "magic" words must be used to disclaim the implied warranty of fitness for a particular purpose, but the disclaimer must be in writing and conspicuous. Section 2–316(2) provides that the fitness disclaimer suffices if it states: "There are no warranties which extend beyond the description on the face hereof." UCC § 2–316(2).

The UCC defines the word "conspicuous" to mean that the disclaimer is "written, displayed, or presented" such that a reasonable person would notice it. UCC § 1–201(b)(10). The disclaimer is conspicuous if it is in larger type, a different font, or different color from that of the surrounding text. *See* UCC § 1–201(b)(10)(B). A seller also may make text conspicuous by setting it off from surrounding text of the same size with "symbols or other marks that call attention to the language." *Id.*

2) Section 2–316(3)

If the seller's disclaimer does not satisfy § 2–316(2), it still may suffice to disclaim the implied warranties of merchantability and fitness for a particular purpose. Language making "plain that there is no implied warranty," such as "as is" or "with all faults," operates to disclaim all implied warranties. UCC § 2–316(3)(a). Therefore, even though § 2–316(2) requires the seller to mention the word "merchantability" when disclaiming the implied warranty of merchantability, the seller may disclaim that warranty by stating that the buyer is purchasing the goods "as is."

These two implied warranties also may be excluded if the buyer refuses to examine the goods and later tries to rely on a defect that such examination would have revealed. UCC § 2–316(3)(b). Examination, however, is "not synonymous with inspection." UCC § 2–316, Comment ¶ 8. Article 2 provides that the buyer has the right to inspect the goods before accepting them. *See* UCC § 2–513. The mere fact that the buyer has the right to inspect the goods and fails to notice a defect during that inspection does not mean that the implied warranties of merchantability and fitness are disclaimed.

> In order to bring the transaction within the scope of "refused to examine" in paragraph (b), it is not sufficient that the goods are available for inspection. There must in addition be a demand by the seller that the buyer examine the goods fully. The seller by the demand puts the buyer on notice that he is assuming the risk of defects which the examination ought to reveal. The language "refused to examine" . . . is intended to make clear the necessity for such a demand.

UCC § 2–316, Comment ¶ 8. What the buyer *should* discover during such an examination depends on the "buyer's skill and the normal method of examining goods in the circumstances." *Id.* Thus, a professional buyer is held to a higher standard than a consumer or layman. Moreover, the nature of the defect is important. Is the defect obvious or latent? Is it something only discoverable by testing that the circumstances do not permit? For example, implied warranties are not excluded for a latent defect in paint that is discoverable only by chemical testing, not by mere observation or examination. *See* Canadian Pacific Railway Co. v. Williams-Hayward Protective Coatings, Inc., 2005 U.S. Dist. LEXIS 28988 (N.D. Ill. 2005). The analysis boils down to which party bears the risk of the defect. A buyer will bear the risk for obvious defects that an examination would have revealed. The seller bears responsibility, i.e., the warranty is not excluded, for defects that are latent or only discoverable by testing not contemplated under the circumstances.

Finally, the implied warranties of merchantability and fitness for a particular purpose may be excluded by the parties' course of dealing or course of performance, or the usage of trade in which both parties are engaged. UCC § 2–316(3)(c). The key is that the buyer is on notice based on the course of dealing, course of performance, or trade usage. For example, in Frantz v. Cantrell, 711 N.E.2d 856 (Ind. Ct. App. 1999), roofer Frantz argued that its contract to install asphalt shingles on homeowner Cantrell's house excluded the implied warranty of merchantability based on trade usage in the roofing industry. Frantz's expert witness testified that roofers did not provide warranties on the shingles used in their roofing jobs. Cantrell, however, was not a member of the roofing trade and, thus, was unaware of the trade usage. The court concluded that in order to exclude the implied warranty of merchantability from the contract, *both* parties had to be engaged in the relevant trade, or the trade usage was one of which *both* parties were aware or should have been aware.

c. The Magnuson-Moss Warranty Act

The Magnuson-Moss Warranty Act (MMWA) is a federal statute that provides buyers of consumer products with certain warranty-related protections. 15 U.S.C. § 2301 *et seq*. The discussion is this section is limited to MMWA's restriction on the seller's ability to disclaim implied warranties. Please consult another resource for a comprehensive analysis of MMWA.

If the seller makes a written warranty to the buyer, then under the MMWA the seller cannot completely disclaim the implied warranties of merchantability and fitness for a particular purpose. *See* 15 U.S.C. § 2308(a)(1). The seller only may disclaim these implied warranties after the expiration of the written warranty and only if the disclaimer is "conscionable and is set forth in clear and unmistakable language and prominently displayed on the face of the warranty." 15 U.S.C. § 2308(b).

It is important to recognize that MMWA's definition of warranty is not the same as UCC § 2–313's definition of express warranty. MMWA defines a written warranty as:

(A) any written affirmation of fact or written promise made in connection with the sale of a consumer product by a supplier to a buyer which relates to the nature of the material or workmanship and affirms or promises that such material or workmanship is defect free or will meet a specified level of performance over a specified period of time, or

(B) any undertaking in writing in connection with the sale by a supplier of a consumer product to refund, repair, replace, or take other remedial action with respect to such product in the event that such product fails to meet the specifications set forth in the undertaking, which written affirmation, promise, or undertaking becomes part of the basis of the bargain between a supplier and a buyer for purposes other than resale of such product.

15 U.S.C. § 2301(6). The most obvious difference between MMWA's definition and the UCC's definition of an express warranty is that the warranty must be in writing to qualify for protection under MMWA. For example, suppose the seller, in response to questions by the buyer, pulls a sample of the good to show to the buyer. By doing so, the seller makes an express warranty that the goods delivered will "conform to the sample." UCC § 2–313(1)(c). But the seller has not made a written warranty under MMWA.

Notice also that the affirmation of fact or promise under subsection (A) must be for a "specified period of time" to qualify as a written warranty for purposes of MMWA. For example, suppose you purchase a dryer that has a large yellow label on its front that provides the dryer's energy efficiency rating. That yellow label is an express warranty under § 2–313, because it constitutes an affirmation of fact or promise about the dryer's energy efficiency. The label, while written, however, is *not* a written warranty under MMWA because it does not provide for a "specified level of performance over a *specified period of time.*" 15 U.S.C. § 2301(6)(A) (emphasis added); *see* 16 C.F.R. 700.3(a) (stating that while energy efficiency ratings may be express warranties under the UCC they are not written warranties under MMWA because they do not "relate to a specified period of time").

Another difference between the UCC and MMWA is that the latter applies to consumers and consumer products. *See* 16 C.F.R. 700.3(c) (stating that MMWA "generally applies to written warranties covering consumer products"). Section 2–313 contains no such limitation. A consumer product is one "normally used for personal, family, or household purposes." 15 U.S.C. § 2301(1). Suppose Acme Company sells Coyote, Inc. a machine for use in Coyote's factory. An affirmation of fact or a promise related to the machine that becomes part of the basis of the bargain constitutes an express warranty under § 2–313 but is not a written warranty under MMWA because the machine is not a consumer product.

If a seller creates a written warranty, then MMWA limits the seller's ability to disclaim implied warranties. If the seller makes a full warranty, the seller cannot limit "the duration of any implied warranty on the product."15 U.S.C. § 2304(a)(2).

Most sellers make limited, not full, warranties. The seller that makes a limited warranty may disclaim the implied warranties but *only* for the period *after* expiration of the limited written warranty. *See* 15 U.S.C. § 2308(b). Suppose Beth buys a mixer from *Kitchens 'R Us,* which specializes in sales of small kitchen appliances and other gadgets. *Kitchens 'R Us* makes a limited 90-day written warranty on the mixer. Even if *Kitchens 'R Us* follows the rules at § 2–316 for disclaiming implied warranties, that disclaimer is ineffective under MMWA for the 90 days after Beth's purchase. Therefore, if the mixer fails within a month of Beth's purchase, Beth may sue *Kitchens 'R Us* under MMWA for breach of the implied warranty of merchantability. *See* 15 U.S.C. § 2310(d).

5. THIRD-PARTY BENEFICIARIES OF WARRANTIES

A buyer may recover for breach of express or implied warranties against the retail seller from whom she purchased a good. But what if the buyer purchased the good as a gift for a family member or a friend? Suppose the buyer retains the product but when using it injures her neighbor or her neighbor's property. May the neighbor recover for breach of warranty from the retail seller? These examples raise the issue of horizontal privity. While the family member, friend, or neighbor suing the retailer for breach of warranty is not in privity of contract with the retail seller, are they a third-party beneficiary of the contract between the buyer and the retail seller?

Suppose the buyer wants to sue the manufacturer, not the retail seller, of the good. Whether the buyer can recover against the manufacturer raises a vertical privity problem. Vertical privity is an issue in a suit against a party in the chain of distribution of the good—a party with whom the plaintiff filing suit was not in privity of contract.

As a noted commentator explains, horizontal privity answers the question "who may sue?" Vertical privity tells you "who may be sued." JOHN EDWARD MURRAY, JR., MURRAY ON CONTRACTS § 134 (3d ed.)

a. Horizontal Privity

Section 2–318 provides the States with three alternatives for dealing with the question of who, besides the immediate buyer, may sue the retail seller for breach of warranty.

Alternative A, which most States have adopted, is the most restrictive of the three alternatives in terms of who is a third-party beneficiary of the buyer's contract with the retail seller. Alternative A provides that the seller's express or implied warranties

> extend[ ] to any natural person who is in the family or household of his buyer or who is a guest in his home if it is reasonable to expect that such person may use, consume or be affected by the goods and who is injured in person by breach of the warranty.

UCC § 2–318, Alt. A. For example, in Crews v. W.A. Brown & Son, Inc., 416 S.E.2d 924 (N.C. Ct. App. 1992), Foodcraft Corporation sold a walk-in freezer to

Calvary Baptist Church. Crews, a teenager who worked at the church, suffered extensive frostbite damage to her feet, legs, and buttocks after the door latch inside the freezer malfunctioned, trapping her inside. Crews sued Foodcraft for breach of express and implied warranties. The court explained that "a church does not have a 'family' or a 'household' in the ordinary meanings of those terms, . . . [and] cannot be classified as a 'home' ". *Id.* at 930, 931. Therefore, Crews could not be a member of the buyer's family or household, nor a guest in the buyer's home. Because Crews was not a third-party beneficiary of the contract between Foodcraft and the church, she could not recover against Foodcraft for breach of warranty.

Alternative B, unlike Alternative A, does not limit third-party beneficiary status to those in buyer's family or household, or guests in buyer's home. Instead, the seller's warranty "extends to any natural person who may reasonably be expected to use, consume or be affected by the goods and who is injured in person by breach of the warranty." UCC § 2–318, Alt. B. Suppose Barney borrows a hedge trimmer from his next-door neighbor Fred. (Barney bought the trimmer from *Local Hardware.*) Fred and Barney often borrow each other's lawn and garden tools. The trimmer is not fit for its ordinary purpose, malfunctions, and causes serious lacerations to Barney's forearm. In an Alternative B jurisdiction, Barney need not be a member of Fred's family or household, or a guest in Fred's house in order to be a third-party beneficiary of the contract between Fred and *Local Hardware.* Barney was injured in person so the question is whether it is reasonable to expect that Barney would "use, consume or be affected" by the hedge trimmer. Barney will argue that neighbors often borrow tools from each other and, therefore, it is reasonable to expect that Barney would use the trimmer that Fred purchased from *Local Hardware*.

Before moving on to discuss Alternative C, keep in mind that the "seller may not exclude or limit the operation" of Alternative A or Alternative B. UCC § 2–318, Alt. A, Alt. B. What does this language mean? An example should help to clarify. Suppose Retail Seller sells a bike to Buyer. The parties' agreement provides that Seller disclaims the implied warranty of merchantability but only as to third parties, not as to Buyer. Buyer gives the bike as a birthday gift to Son, who lives at home while attending college. The bike is not fit for its ordinary purpose and Son is injured in person while riding it one day. Son sues Retail Seller for breach of the implied warranty of merchantability. Son is not in privity of contract with Retail Seller but in either an Alternative A or Alternative B jurisdiction, Son is a third-party beneficiary of Buyer's contract with Retail Seller. Retail Seller's attempt to disclaim the implied warranty of merchantability only as to parties other than Buyer is ineffective. The drafters of the Code intended to extend any warranties created in the sale between buyer and seller to any party who qualifies as a third-party beneficiary under the § 2–318 alternative adopted by the jurisdiction.

But what if Retail Seller properly disclaims the implied warranty of merchantability (or any other warranty) as to Buyer? In that case, there is no warranty to extend to any third-party beneficiaries. If the Retail Seller properly disclaims some or all warranties in its sale with Buyer, then neither the Buyer nor any third party may sue for breach of warranty. What the final sentence of Alternative A and Alternative B "forbids is exclusion of liability by the seller to the persons to whom the warranties which he has made to his buyer would extend" under § 2–318. UCC § 2–318, Comment ¶ 1. In other words, if the seller fails to properly disclaim a warranty as to the buyer, the seller may not disclaim that warranty as to a third party who qualifies as a beneficiary of the warranty under § 2–318.

Unlike Alternatives A and B, Alternative C applies to any person, not just natural persons. Therefore, in an Alternative C jurisdiction, artificial entities that qualify as persons under the law may file suit as third-party beneficiaries. *See, e.g.*, City of Perry, Iowa v. Procter & Gamble Company, 188 F. Supp.3d 276 (S.D. N.Y. 2016) (denying defendants' motion to dismiss breach-of-warranty claims and noting that Iowa, which had adopted Alternative C, defined the word "person" to include governmental units). In addition, the third-party beneficiary must "reasonably be expected to use, consume or be affected by the goods." UCC § 2–318, Alt. C. But recovery under Alternative C is not limited to damages for personal injury; it includes recovery for property damage. A seller in an Alternative C jurisdiction may exclude or limit a third-party beneficiary's recovery for property damage but, as in

Alternative A and Alternative B jurisdictions, not for personal injury.

TABLE #2: § 2–318: COMPARISON OF ALTERNATIVES A, B, AND C

	Alternative A	Alternative B	Alternative C
Type of Person	Natural	Natural	Legal (includes artificial entities)
Class of Persons	Family or household of buyer; guest in buyer's home	—	—
Limitation on who may sue	Only person who may reasonably be expected to use, consume or be affected by goods	Only person who may reasonably be expected to use, consume, or be affected by goods	Only person that may reasonably be expected to use, consume, or be affected by goods
Type of injury	Personal injury	Personal injury	Personal injury and property damage
Can seller exclude beneficiaries?	No	No	Yes, but only for property damage

b. Vertical Privity

Vertical privity problems involve lawsuits against parties in the chain of the product's distribution. For example, if Bella purchases a blender from *Home Stuff,* a local retailer of kitchen appliances and home décor, Bella is in privity of contract with *Home Stuff.* But if Hamilton Beech manufactured the blender sold by *Home Stuff,* Bella is not in privity of contract with Hamilton Beech. Can Bella sue Hamilton Beach?

A majority of states have adopted Alternative A, which lists the beneficiaries of a warranty as natural persons in the "family or household or *his* buyer" or who are a "guest in *his* home." UCC § 2–318, Alt. A (emphasis added). In the Hamilton Beech example above, *his* buyer refers to Home Stuff, *not* Hamilton Beech because Bella is Home Stuff's buyer. The language of Alternative A, then, addresses only horizontal privity questions. That does not mean, however, that an Alternative A jurisdiction cannot eliminate the vertical privity bar to bringing suit against the manufacturer of a good or some other entity in the chain of distribution of that good. The Official Comment to § 2–318 provides that Alternative A "is neutral and is not intended to enlarge or restrict the developing case law on whether the seller's warranties, given to his buyer who resells, extend to other persons in the distributive chain." UCC § 2–318, Comment ¶ 3. In other words, using our Hamilton Beech example, a court in an Alternative A jurisdiction may hold that

Bella can sue the manufacturer of the blender even though she is not in privity with the manufacturer.

What about Alternatives B and C? Neither contains the "his buyer" language. The language is broader, and a plaintiff could argue that the warranty of a remote seller, e.g., a manufacturer, extends to any natural person (Alternative B) or any person (Alternative C) who reasonably may be expected to use, consume or be affected by the good. *See, e.g.*, UCC § 2–318, Comment ¶ 3 (stating that Alternative B "is designed for states where the case has already developed further and for those that desire to expand the class of beneficiaries").

In fact, courts in most jurisdictions, regardless of whether an Alternative A, B, or C jurisdiction, have held that the purchaser of a consumer good may sue the manufacturer of that good for personal injury resulting from breach of warranty, even though the consumer is not in privity with the manufacturer. Eliminating the requirement of vertical privity for the consumer purchaser makes sense for both express and implied warranties. After all, consumers generally purchase goods through a retailer, not directly from the manufacturer. The manufacturer's express warranties are directed to the ultimate consumer. For example, a car dealer only cares about gas mileage and the power train warranty as it relates to the dealer's ability to sell vehicles. The dealer does not intend to drive the car. It is the consumer, not the dealer intermediary between the consumer and manufacturer, who is interested in the car's daily and long-term performance—its gas mileage and how long the manufacturer warrants the vehicle's power train. Similarly, it is the consumer who is interested in whether the good is fit for its ordinary purpose. Moreover, many manufactured goods are sold in boxed form; the retailer never opens the boxes to use the goods. Therefore, it is the consumer, not the retailer, who will discover, upon using the good, that it is not merchantable.

c. Vouching in

Suppose Byer purchases a good from Retailer and the good was not fit for its ordinary purpose when it left Retailer's store. The good arrived at Retailer's store in a box, and Retailer did nothing more than unload the delivery from Manufacturer and place the boxes on the store shelf. Recall that the Retailer's due care is only relevant to determining *when* the good was not fit for its ordinary purpose; due care does not relieve Retailer of liability for breach of the implied warranty of merchantability if the good was not merchantable when it left Retailer's store. Thus, Byer may sue and recover from Retailer for breach of the implied warranty of merchantability. But, if the good was not fit for its ordinary purpose when it left the hands of Manufacturer, Retailer will sue Manufacturer to recover for the damages it incurred due to Manufacturer's breach of the warranty.

If Byer sues only Retailer, then Retailer should use § 2–607(5) to vouch in Manufacturer. *Cf.* 2 Hawkland UCC Series § 2–607:6 (stating that § 2–607(5) "remains particularly useful where the vouchee is not subject to personal jurisdiction in the underlying action"). Article 2 provides a mechanism by which Retailer, sued for breach of warranty, may vouch in Manufacturer.

> Where the buyer is sued for breach of a warranty or other obligation for which his seller is answerable over
>
> (a) he may give his seller written notice of the litigation. If the notice states that the seller may come in and defend and that if the seller does not do so he will be bound in any action against him by his buyer by any determination of fact common to the two litigations, then unless the seller after seasonable receipt of the notice does come and defend he is so bound.

UCC § 2–607(5)(a). Suppose Retailer in the example above provides notice to Manufacturer of the litigation. That notice complies with the requirements of § 2–607(5) but Manufacturer declines to come into the litigation and defend. The court in the Byer v. Retailer litigation rules in favor of Byer. Retailer then sues Manufacturer for breach of the implied warranty of merchantability. Manufacturer is bound by any findings of fact common to the Byer v. Retailer and the Retailer v. Manufacturer lawsuits.

For example, in The Hertz Corp. v. Century Products, Inc., 1999 WL 459291 (Del. Sup. Ct. 1999), Hertz sought indemnification and/or contribution from Century, the manufacturer of a child car seat. Hertz rented a car and provided a car seat produced by Century to the Bealers. A metal clip on the seat burned the Bealers' infant daughter. The Bealers sued both Hertz and Century, but Century was dismissed from the litigation for lack of personal jurisdiction. Hertz used § 2–607(5) to vouch in Century but Century declined to participate in the litigation. The jury in the original lawsuit found against Hertz and in favor of the Bealers. Hertz then filed suit against Century and moved for partial summary judgment on the issues of the car seat's defective condition and the damages associated with the defect. The *Hertz* court granted the motion for partial summary judgment. Century argued that Hertz's litigation strategy was inadequate and, thus, Century should not be bound by the prior court's liability determination. The *Hertz* court disagreed, noting that one of § 2–607(5)'s primary purposes is "preserv[ing] judicial resources."

> In fact, the purpose of this Section is to prevent attempts at relitigating issues that *should have* been decided in prior litigation, the exact situation occurring in this case. Century cannot stand idly by while litigation involving its product proceeds, and then claim, after the fact, that Hertz did a poor job. The way to correct this problem was to join in, or take over, the defense of [the prior action]; not to wait until the dust settles and poke holes in Hertz's defense.

Hertz, 1999 WL 459291, at *3 (emphasis in original). The court held that the determinations in the prior litigation as to the dangerous condition of the car seat and the amount of damages were binding on Century, and granted Hertz's motion for summary judgment on those issues.

One caveat is in order. A party vouched in that fails to defend is only bound by the outcome of a "full-dress adversarial proceeding[ ] conducted in good faith." 2 Hawkland UCC Series § 2–607:6. For example, Hertz could not invoke § 2–607(5) if it had settled the original litigation with the parents of the child injured by the defective car seat. *See, e.g.*, Kaiser Aluminum & Chemical Sales, Inc. v. PG Industries, Inc., 42 F.3d 1147 (7th Cir 1994) (stating that "[t]he voucher method may not be invoked, however, when the underlying action was settled instead of fully litigated to judgment").

B. LEASES

1. WARRANTIES

Article 2A's provisions on express and implied warranties are almost identical to those of Article 2's warranty provisions. The differences largely reflect the difference in the underlying transactions: a lease versus a sale.

> All of the express and implied warranties of the Article on Sales (Article 2) are included in [Article 2A], revised to reflect the difference between a sale of goods and a lease of goods. Sections 2A–210 through 2A–216. The lease of goods is sufficiently similar to the sale of goods to justify this decision.

UCC § 2A–210, Comment: Purposes. Thus, the language of § 2A–210 on express warranties largely tracks that of § 2–313, while the language of § 2A–212 and § 2A–213 on implied warranties tracks that of § 2–314 and § 2–315, respectively. Note that Article 2A's implied warranty of merchantability and its implied warranty of fitness for a particular purpose do not apply to finance leases. *See* UCC §§ 2A–212, 2A–213. The reason is that the lessee in a finance lease typically looks to the supplier or manufacturer in the event of a breach of warranty. *See supra* Chapter 1, § B.3.

What *is* different in Article 2A is the absence of a title warranty, as there is in a sale of goods. *See* UCC § 2–312. The reason, of course, is that the lessee does not take title to the goods in a lease transaction; instead, it has a limited interest in the goods for the lease term. Thus, § 2A–211, while modeled on § 2–312, was modified to "reflect the limited interest transferred by a lease contract [compared to] the total interest transferred by a sale." UCC § 2–211, Comment: Changes.

Section 2A–211, Article 2A's counterpart to § 2–312, provides warranties against interference and infringement. In all lease transactions, the lessor warrants that "no person holds a claim to or interest in the goods that arose from an act or omission of the lessor, other than a claim for infringement or the like, which will interfere with the lessee's enjoyment of its leasehold interest." UCC § 2A–211(1). This is the warranty of quiet possession, which Article 2 abolished for sales of goods. *See* UCC § 2A–211,

Comment: Changes (stating that "Section 2A–211(1) reinstates the warranty of quiet possession with respect to leases," which "was abolished with respect to sales of goods").

The warranty against infringement, unlike the warranty against interference in subsection (1), applies only if the lessor is a merchant that regularly deals in goods of the kind that are the subject of the lease. In such a case, the lessor warrants that "the goods are delivered free of the rightful claim of any person by way of infringement or the like." UCC § 2A–211(2). This warranty against infringement does not apply to a finance lease. *See id.* Again, the lessee under a finance lease must look to the supplier or manufacturer for warranties. *See* UCC § 2A–211, Comment: Purposes. But, if the lessee provides specifications to a lessor or supplier, then the lessee "shall hold the lessor and the supplier harmless against any claim by way of infringement or the like that arises out of compliance with the specifications." UCC § 2A–211(3).

2. WARRANTY DISCLAIMERS

The rule for disclaiming an express warranty in a lease transaction is the same as the rule for disclaiming an express warranty in a contract for the sale of goods. *Compare* UCC § 2A–214(1) *with* UCC § 2–316(1).

A disclaimer of the implied warranty of merchantability in a lease agreement must use the word "merchantability." *See* UCC § 2A–214(2). The rule is the same for a contract for the sale of goods.

See UCC § 2–316(2). But, for a lease agreement, unlike a contract for the sale of goods, the disclaimer must be in writing and conspicuous. *Compare* UCC § 2A–214(2) *with* UCC § 2–316(2).

A disclaimer of the implied warranty of fitness for a particular purpose also must be in writing and conspicuous, which also is the rule for disclaiming the warranty in a contract for the sale of goods. *Compare* UCC § 2A–214(2) *with* UCC § 2–316(2). Section 2A–214(2) provides the following example of a valid disclaimer of the fitness warranty: "There is no warranty that the goods will be fit for a particular purpose." UCC § 2A–214(2). This example is more specific than the example of a fitness warranty disclaimer found at § 2–316(2), which provides that "[t]here are no warranties which extend beyond the description on the face hereof." UCC § 2–316(2).

The lessor may disclaim all implied warranties by using terms or phrases such as "as is" or "with all faults." UCC § 2A–214(3)(a); *see* UCC § 2–316(3)(a). Implied warranties also may be disclaimed by course of dealing, course of performance, or usage of trade. *See* UCC § 2A–214(3)(c); *see also* UCC § 2–316(3)(c). The lessee's full examination or refusal to examine the goods also may result in a disclaimer of an implied warranty "with regard to defects that an examination ought in the circumstances to have revealed." UCC § 2A–214(3)(b). As to what constitutes an examination, *see supra* § A.4.b.2 of this Chapter.

The warranty against interference or against infringement may be excluded or modified by course of dealing, course of performance, or usage of trade. UCC § 2A–214(4). Other circumstances that give the lessee "reason to know that the goods are being leased subject to a claim or interest of any person" also may result in an exclusion or modification of the warranty. *Id.* Otherwise, a disclaimer of the warranty against interference or against infringement must be in writing, use specific language, and be conspicuous. *Id.*

3. BENEFICIARIES OF WARRANTIES

Suppose Leonard leases equipment from Big Box Store for a home improvement project. Leonora, Leonard's daughter, is helping him with the project. While working, Leonora is injured when a piece of equipment malfunctions. Assuming that the equipment is not fit for its ordinary purpose, can Leonora, who is not a party to the contract between Big Box Store and her father, recover for her injuries? Section 2A–216 provides the rules for determining which third parties are beneficiaries of the lease agreement. *See supra* § A.5 of this Chapter on privity of contract; *cf.* UCC § 2–318.

In addition to § 2A–216, § 2A–209 states the rules regarding the lessee's beneficiary status under a finance lease. The lessee is not a party to the supplier's and lessor's agreement, but § 2A–209 provides that the lessee is a beneficiary of the promises and warranties made in the supply contract. Article 2 has no counterpart to § 2A–209.

a. Third Party Beneficiaries

Article 2A's three alternatives for states to adopt with regard to third-party beneficiary status are much the same as those of Article 2. The drafters advised legislators to consider choosing the alternative that is "parallel to the choice it made with respect to Section 2–318, as interpreted by the courts." UCC § 2A–216, Comment: Purposes.

Alternative A is the "least favorable to the injured person as the doctrine of privity imposed by other law is abrogated to only a limited extent." UCC § 2A–216, Comment: Purposes. Alternative A extends only to a natural person in the "family or household of the lessee or who is a guest in the lessee's home." UCC § 2A–216, Alt. A. It must be reasonable to expect that the family, household member, or guest may "use, consume or be affected by the goods" and that person must be "injured in person by breach of the warranty." *Id.*

Alternatives B and C are "more favorable to the injured person." UCC § 2A–216, Comment: Purposes. Alternative B applies to "any natural person" while Alternative C is more expansive and applies to "any person." UCC § 2A–216, Alt. B, Alt. C. The person claiming third-party beneficiary status must "reasonably be expected to use, consume or be affected by the goods." *Id.* Alternative B applies to personal injuries. *See* UCC § 2A–216, Alt. B. Alternative C, again, is more expansive and applies to a person "injured by breach of the warranty". UCC § 2A–216, Alt. C. Therefore, a person may recover in an Alternative C jurisdiction for personal injury and property damage.

The lessor is free to disclaim any and all warranties. Such a disclaimer also is enforceable against third-party beneficiaries. What the lessor cannot do is selectively discriminate against a party that otherwise satisfies the requirements of a third-party beneficiary under § 2A–216. *See* UCC § 2A–216, Comment: Purposes (stating that the last sentence of each alternative "forbids selective discrimination against the beneficiaries under this section"). The one exception is in an Alternative C jurisdiction. The lessor may exclude property damage as recoverable by a third-party beneficiary; however, the lessor that provides a warranty to the lessee may not exclude recovery for personal injuries by a third-party beneficiary. UCC § 2A–216, Alt. C. Thus, with the limited exception for property damage exclusions in an Alternative C jurisdiction, if a warranty is not disclaimed as to the lessee, then it is not disclaimed as to eligible third-party beneficiaries. If the lessor validly disclaims a warranty, then that disclaimer operates not only against the lessee but also against any party that otherwise would qualify as a third-party beneficiary under § 2A–216.

b. Lessee Under a Finance Lease

Recall that neither the warranty of merchantability nor the warranty of fitness for a particular purpose is implied in a finance lease. *See* UCC § 2A–212, § 2A–213; *see also supra* § B.1 of this Chapter. The reason is that the lessor in a finance lease plays an "extremely limited" role. UCC § 2A–209, Comment ¶ 1. Instead, the lessee in a finance lease looks to the supplier for warranties. *See id.* In other words, the lessee is a beneficiary of the warranties in the contract between the supplier and the finance lessor.

> The benefit of a supplier's promises to the lessor under the supply contract and all warranties, whether express or implied, including those of any third party provided in connection with or as part of the supply contract, extends to the lessee to the extent of the lessee's leasehold interest under a finance lease related to the supply contract, but is subject to the terms of the warranty and of the supply contract and all defenses or claims arising therefrom.

UCC § 2A–209(1).

The "extension of the benefit of the supplier's promises and warranties to the lessee" does not change the supplier's and lessor's rights and obligations under the supply contract. UCC § 2A–209(2); *see* UCC § 2A–209, Comment ¶ 4 (stating that § 2A–209(2) preserves the "supplier's and lessor's rights and obligations"). It also does not impose on the lessee any "duty or liability under the supply contract." UCC § 2A–209(2); *see also* UCC § 2A–209, Comment ¶ 4 (stating that § 2A–209(2) "absolves the lessee of any duties with respect to the supply contract that might have been inferred from the extension of the benefits thereof").

But the extension of beneficiary status to the lessee comes with a cost to the lessee. Once the lessee under a non-consumer finance lease accepts the goods, the lessee's promises to the lessor under their lease agreement become "irrevocable and independent." UCC § 2A–407(1); *see* UCC § 2A–209, Comment ¶ 3 (stating that "the benefit extended by [§ 2A–209] is not without a price"); *see also infra* Chapter 9, § B.6 on irrevocable promises.

While the lessee is the beneficiary of the supplier's promises and warranties, it also is bound by the supplier's exclusion of warranties. If the supplier properly disclaims the implied warranty of merchantability or of fitness for a particular purpose in its agreement with the lessor, then that disclaimer is effective against the lessee, as well. *See* United States Achievement Academy, LLC v. Pitney Bowes, Inc., 458 F. Supp. 2d 389 (E.D. Ky. 2006) (concluding that conspicuous disclaimer in software supply contract of all warranties, express or implied, except for a 90-day repair-or-replace warranty, was effective against lessee in a finance lease transaction). What the supplier cannot do is "selective[ly] discriminate" by excluding "liability to the lessee with respect to warranties made to the lessor." UCC § 2A–209, Comment ¶ 1. The supplier also may limit remedies or provide for liquidated damages; these provisions in the supply contract are binding on the lessee under a finance lease. *See id.*

What happens if the warranties in the supply contract are modified? For example, suppose the duration of an express warranty in the supply contract is changed from four years to one year. *See* UCC § 2A–209, Comment ¶ 5. Is the modification effective as between the supplier and the lessee? It depends.

> Any modification or rescission of the supply contract by the supplier and the lessor is effective between the supplier and the lessee unless, before the modification or rescission, the supplier has received notice that the lessee has entered into a finance lease related to the supply contract.

UCC § 2A–209(3). If the requisite notice was provided before the express warranty was modified, then the change in duration of the warranty is not effective between the supplier and the lessee. *See* UCC § 2A–209, Comment ¶ 5 (stating that a modification or rescission "is not effective between the supplier and the lessee if, before the modification or rescission occurs, the supplier received notice that the lessee has entered into the finance lease").

What if the supplier did not receive notice before the supplier and lessor changed the duration of the express warranty in the supply contract? In that case, the change is effective between the supplier and the lessee. But the lessor assumes the "promises of the supplier to the lessor and warranties that were so modified or rescinded as they existed and were available to the lessee before modification or rescission." UCC § 2A–209(3). In our warranty-duration example, suppose that after one year but before four years have passed, there is a breach of that express warranty as to the leased good. As between the supplier and the lessee, the express warranty is good for only one year; the modification is effective between them. But the lessor is liable to the lessee, because it assumed, upon the modification, an obligation to honor the express warranty as it existed prior to the modification. *See* UCC § 2A–209, Comment ¶ 5.

CHAPTER 7

UNCONSCIONABILITY

A. SALES: § 2–302

Section 2–302 provides a court with three avenues for redressing contractual unconscionability, either of the contract as a whole or of any particular contractual clause. The court may (i) "refuse to enforce the contract;" (ii) enforce the contract without the unconscionable clause; or (iii) "limit the application of any unconscionable clause as to avoid any unconscionable result." UCC § 2–302(1); *see also* UCC § 2–302, Comment ¶ 2. The court rules on unconscionability "as a matter of law" and the determination is made based on whether the contract or any contractual clause was unconscionable at the time that the contract was made, not at the time of litigation. UCC § 2–302(1).

The UCC does not define the term "unconscionable." But the Official Comment provides some guidance.

> The basic test is whether in the light of the general commercial background and the commercial needs of the particular trade or case, the clauses involved are so one-sided as to be unconscionable under the circumstances existing at the time of the making of the contract. . . . The principle is one of the prevention of oppression and unfair surprise.

UCC § 2–302, Comment ¶ 1. Because the commercial context matters, the parties must be given a reasonable opportunity to present evidence on the contract's "commercial setting, purpose, and effect" to assist the court in determining whether the contract (or contractual clause) is unconscionable. UCC § 2–302(2).

Most courts require that the party claiming unconscionability demonstrate both procedural and substantive unconscionability. *See, e.g.,* Haft v. Haier US Appliance Solutions, Inc., 578 F. Supp. 3d 436 (S.D. N.Y. 2022); Horizon Ventures of West Virginia v. American Bituminous Power Partners, LP, 857 S.E.2d 33 (W.Va. 2021). "Courts generally have applied a sliding-scale approach to determine overall unconscionability, considering the relative levels of both procedural and substantive unconscionability." Delta Funding Corporation v. Harris, 912 A.2d 104 (N.J. 2006). Nonetheless, a high degree of procedural unconscionability does not negate the need for the party claiming unconscionability to demonstrate that the contract or a contractual provision is substantively unconscionable. *See, e.g., Horizon,* 857 S.E.2d at 40 (stating that notwithstanding application of a sliding scale, both procedural and substantive unconscionability must be present); *cf.* Whirlpool Corporation v. Grigoleit Company, 713 F.3d 316 (6th Cir. 2013) (interpreting Michigan law and concluding that substantive unconscionability alone does not suffice to find an agreement unconscionable); *but see* Fiser v. Dell Computer Corporation, 188 P.3d 1215 (N.M. 2008) (holding that class action ban in consumer contract was "contrary to fundamental New Mexico public policy" and unconscionable on basis of substantive unconscionability alone).

Procedural unconscionability relates to the formation of the contract. A court may look at a number of factors, including the relative bargaining power of the contracting parties, the relative sophistication, e.g., education and experience of the contracting parties, whether terms were hidden or unduly complex, and whether the contract was one of adhesion. As these factors suggest, e.g., sophistication and bargaining power, the unconscionability doctrine is applied more often in consumer cases than in commercial dealings between business firms. *See* Braun v. E.I. du Pont de Nemours & Company, 2006 WL 290552 (D. S.D. 2006) (stating that courts are more inclined to find unconconscionability in a consumer as opposed to a commercial case).

For example, in *Delta Funding*, Alberta Harris, a "78-year-old woman with a sixth-grade education and little financial sophistication, whose sole source of income was social security payments", entered into a mortgage loan agreement with Delta Funding. Although the case does not involve the sale of goods, the court's discussion of unconscionability is instructive for analyzing claims of unconscionability under § 2–302. The loan contract included an arbitration agreement by which either party could elect binding arbitration to resolve certain issues. Harris argued that the arbitration agreement was unconscionable. The case came before the New Jersey Supreme Court on a question of law certified and submitted by the Third Circuit as to whether an arbitration clause in a consumer loan contract was unconscionable under New Jersey law. The New Jersey Supreme Court held that the arbitration agreement was ambiguous and required interpretation by the arbitrator, but that several parts of the agreement might be unenforceable based on unconscionability, depending on the arbitrator's interpretation. Without deciding that the arbitration agreement was unconscionable, the court noted that Harris had alleged facts "suggest[ing] a high level of procedural unconscionability." *Delta Funding,* 912 A.2d at 111. The contract was one of adhesion with Delta, which not only had "superior bargaining power" but also was "the more sophisticated party in the transaction." *Id.*

In Boston Helicopter Charter, Inc. v. Agusta Aviation Corporation, 767 F. Supp. 363 (D. Mass. 1991), the court concluded that a durational limitation on a repair-or-replace warranty was not unconscionable. In its discussion of procedural unconscionability, the court noted that the "commercial, as opposed to consumer, setting [was] significant." *Id.* at 375. In addition, an attorney represented Boston Helicopter in its acquisition of the helicopter. Moreover, Boston Helicopter negotiated for transfer of the warranty from the helicopter's prior owner, which suggested to the court that Boston Helicopter was not "the uninformed buyer that section 2–302 seeks to protect against unfair surprise." *Id.; see also Horizon,* 857 S.E.2d at 42 (concluding there was no procedural unconscionability because the parties were "two sophisticated businesses" and there was "no evidence of uneven bargaining power; any adhesion; or hidden or unduly complex contract terms"); *In re* Caterpillar, Inc., 2015 WL 4591236 (D. N.J. 2015) (stating that plaintiffs, who were mostly "corporate entities", had failed to allege facts showing a "disparity in sophistication or buying power" and that they were unable to buy comparable vehicles from another seller).

The substantive unconscionability inquiry focuses on the substance of the contractual provisions at issue. Are they so one-sided or unreasonably favorable to one party that the terms are oppressive to the party alleging unconscionability? For example, in *Fiser*, the consumer purchased a computer using Dell's website. The terms and conditions on the website required buyers to arbitrate claims individually and precluded them from bringing class action suits. Fiser's alleged damages did not exceed $20. The New Mexico Supreme Court first explained that the state's policy required that "consumers with small claims have a mechanism for dispute resolution via the class action." *Fiser,* 188 P.3d at 1220. But consumers with small claims could not afford to invoke the state's consumer protection laws when the cost of litigation far exceeds any damages they might recover. As a result, Dell's class action ban effectively exempted the company from operation of the state's consumer protection statutes. "Because it violates public policy by depriving small claims consumers of a meaningful remedy and exculpating [Dell] from potential wrongdoing, the class action ban meets the test for substantive unconscionability." *Id.*

at 1221. The court found that the class action ban was not severable from the arbitration provision and, therefore, it held that the arbitration provision was unenforceable. Interestingly enough, the court's decision rested solely on substantive unconscionability. While it briefly discussed procedural unconscionability, the court did not rule on that basis, instead invalidating the arbitration agreement on the basis of "an overwhelming showing of substantive unconscionability." *Id.*

B. LEASES: § 2A–108

Section 2A–108 is the UCC's provision on unconscionability for leases. Like § 2–302, § 2A–108 provides three avenues by which a court may provide redress to a party that demonstrates that a lease or a lease provision is unconscionable. UCC § 2A–108(1); *see supra* § A of this Chapter. The court rules as a matter of law and the determination of unconscionability is based on the lease contract at the time it was made. UCC § 2A–108(1); *see* UCC § 2A–108, Comment: Changes (stating that "[s]ubsection (1) is taken almost verbatim from the provisions of Section 2–302(1)). Thus, the unconscionability analysis used by courts in evaluating contracts for the sale of goods also applies to lease contracts. *See* § A of this Chapter. Courts look at both procedural and substantive unconscionability when evaluating whether a lease contract or lease clause is unconscionable. *See, e.g.*, United States Achievement Academy, LLC v. Pitney Bowes, Inc., 458 F. Supp.2d 389 (E.D. Ky. 2006) (finance lease).

But § 2A–108 differs from § 2–302 in several respects. First, § 2A–108 provides that a court may grant "appropriate relief" in a case involving a consumer lease if the court determines that the lease was "induced by unconscionable conduct" or "unconscionable conduct has occurred in the collection of a claim" arising from the lease contract. UCC § 2A–108(2). Notice that subsection (2) covers *both* unconscionable conduct at the formation of the lease *and* post-lease conduct in connection with collecting a claim. The focus is on procedural unconscionability. In other words, the consumer lessee need not prove that the lease contract itself or any particular clause is substantively unconscionable if the lessor's unconscionable conduct induced the consumer to enter into the lease contract or the lessor engaged in unconscionable conduct in collecting on a lease-related claim. *See* UCC § 2A–108, Comment: Purposes (stating that subsection (2) applies to a situation in which a "consumer lease may not itself be unconscionable but that the agreement would never have been entered into if unconscionable means had not been employed to induce the consumer to agree"). The Official Comment to § 2A–108 provides an example. "To make a statement to induce the consumer to lease the goods, in the expectation of invoking an integration clause in the lease to exclude the statement's admissibility in a subsequent dispute, may be unconscionable." *Id.* Section 2–302 has no comparable provision.

Oden v. Vanguard Car Rental USA, Inc., 2008 WL 901325 (E.D. Tex. 2008) is one of the few cases examining § 2A–108(2). In *Oden,* the district court dismissed a consumer's claim under § 2A–108(2). In a footnote, the court explained that the disputed refueling service charge was disclosed in the contract, the consumer had received a copy of the lease contract, and she had initialed the part of the agreement related to the disputed charge. The court noted that the consumer had not alleged fraud and that the complaint "[fell] short of alleging that the circumstances surrounding the execution of the agreement were 'grossly unfair,' as required to state a claim for procedural unconscionability." *Oden,* 2008 WL at *10, n.1.

The discussion in *Oden* is brief and there is otherwise scant case law on § 2A–108(2). But the Notes accompanying a 1996 draft of revisions to Article 2 contain two examples that provide some insight as to the meaning of the phrase "induced by unconscionable conduct." In this draft, the phrase "induced by unconscionable conduct" was added to § 2–302, which was renumbered § 2–106. (No state has adopted amendments to Article 2, and the "induced" language is not part of current § 2–302.)

> What is "unconscionable conduct" that induces a contract that is otherwise conscionable? Possible examples include cases where excessive pressure is place [sic] upon senior citizens (a used car dealer takes the keys to the car of prospective buyers and won't let them leave for food or medication until they buy the used car) or the contract is presented in a manner so that the purchaser cannot see that an important term has been changed. In short, the

conduct approaches but does not clearly reach defenses such as duress or fraud.

The Emerged and Emerging New Uniform Commercial Code Volume II, National Conference of Commissioners on Uniform State Laws Draft, November 1, 1996, § 2–106, Notes ¶ 1 (ALI-ABA Study Materials). While the comment above was included in a draft of proposed revisions to Article 2's unconscionability provision, "[t]he phrase 'induced by unconscionable conduct' [was] taken from § 2A–108(2)." *Id.* Therefore, the explanation of the phrase's meaning is relevant to interpreting the same language in § 2A–108(2).

A second difference between § 2A–108 and § 2–302 lies in the language of subsection (3) of the Article 2A provision. Both § 2A–108 and § 2–302 give the parties a reasonable opportunity to present evidence if the court is to decide whether a contract or contractual clause is unconscionable. Section 2–302(2) provides for evidence as to "the commercial setting, purpose and effect" while § 2A–108(3) omits the modifier "commercial" and provides for evidence as to "the setting, purpose and effect." The reason for omitting the word "commercial" is that § 2A–108(3) is "concerned with all leases and the relevant standard of conduct is determined by the context." UCC § 2A–108, Comment: Purposes.

Another difference between § 2–302(2) and § 2A–108(3) is that the latter covers unconscionable conduct; subsection (2) of § 2–302 only applies to unconscionable contracts and unconscionable contractual clauses. *See* UCC § 2A–108, Comment:

Changes (stating that "Subsection (3), taken from the provisions of Section 2–302(2), has been expanded to cover unconscionable conduct"). Thus, before the court determines that a lease contract or lease provision is unconscionable, or that a consumer lease contract or clause was induced by unconscionable conduct or unconscionable conduct occurred in collecting a claim arising from a consumer lease, the parties should have a reasonable opportunity to present evidence of the setting, purpose and effect of the contract, clause, or conduct. UCC § 2A–108(3). Unlike unconscionable conduct that induced the consumer lessee to enter into the lease agreement, post-lease unconscionability may be ongoing. Thus, the court may "enjoin[ ] the lessor from repeating the unconscionable acts, not only with respect to the lessee but with respect to other leases." 4C Anderson U.C.C. § 2A–108:38 (3d ed.). In addition, the court may "require the lessor to give the lessee credit for money improperly collected under the authority of the outlawed provision." *Id.*

A final difference between § 2–302 and § 2A–108 is that the latter provides for the recovery of attorney's fees in the case of consumer leases. If the court decides that the consumer lease contract or one of its provisions is unconscionable or was induced by unconscionable conduct, or that the lessor engaged in unconscionable conduct in collecting on a lease-related claim, it shall award the lessee reasonable attorney's fees. UCC § 2A–108(4)(a). The amount that the consumer lessee recovers under § 2A–108(1) or (2) does not control the amount of attorney's fees that the court may award. UCC § 2A–108(4)(c). If the court does not find unconscionability and also determines that the consumer lessee brought or maintained a claim that she knew was groundless, then the court shall award reasonable attorney's fees to the party against whom that claim was brought. UCC § 2A–108(4)(b).

CHAPTER 8

GOOD FAITH PURCHASERS, SUBSEQUENT LESSEES, AND SUBLESSEES

A. SALES

Part 4 of Article 2 includes only three sections. This Nutshell covers only two of those three sections. The first, § 2–401, provides the rules on passing of title. The second, § 2–403, covers good faith purchasers and entrustment.

1. PASSING OF TITLE: § 2–401

Article 2's provisions on the "rights, obligations, and remedies of the seller, the buyer, purchasers or other third parties appl[y] irrespective of title to the goods except where the provision refers to such title." UCC § 2–401. In general, the legal consequences of contracting flow "directly from the contract and action taken under it" *not* from which party has title to the goods or when title to the goods passed. UCC § 2–101, Comment. In other words, Article 2 "deals with the issues between seller and buyer in terms of step by step performance or non-performance under the contract for sale and *not in terms of whether or not 'title' to the goods has passed.*" UCC § 2–401, Comment ¶ 1 (emphasis added). Thus, with the exception of a provision that specifically refers to title, Article 2's provisions apply to a transaction in goods regardless of which party has title to the goods.

Why, then, is § 2–401, which, in part, is entitled "Passing of Title", necessary? There are cases not covered by Article 2's provisions in which title to the goods does matter. Which party has title to the goods is important for other purposes, such as determining liability for sales and use taxes, resolving issues in bankruptcy, or deciding whether an insurance policy covers the goods. *See* 2 Hawkland UCC Series § 2–401:1 (stating that title may be relevant for determining tax liability, insurance coverage, and "the application of other principles of law found in bankruptcy, products liability law, regulation of products, regulation of unfair trade practices, or other areas of state or federal law").

For example, in Media Graphics, Inc. v. Director, Division of Taxation, 7 N.J. Tax 23 (N.J. Tax Ct. 1984), Media Graphics argued that it was not liable under the New Jersey Sales and Use Tax Act for printed materials sold to out-of-state customers. Media Graphics claimed that because the goods were delivered out of state, those sales took place out of state and, therefore, were not subject to taxation under New Jersey law. The Tax Court of New Jersey disagreed. After explaining that the New Jersey Sales and Use Tax Act defined a sale as the transfer of title or possession, the court looked to § 2–401's rules on passage of title.

> The present contracts were for the sale of nonexistent and yet to be identified printed matter, *i.e.* future goods. The goods became identified to the contract when they were made. Title to the printed material could therefore pass

> at any subsequent time. Under N.J.S.A. 12A:2–401(2), title passed to plaintiff's customers at the time and place at which plaintiff completed its performance with reference to the physical delivery of the goods, meaning on delivery at a post office in New Jersey. Title to the printed matter therefore passed in New Jersey, performance was completed in this State and the sale of the printed matter was properly taxable by this State.

Media Graphics, 7 N.J. Tax at 29–30.

Section § 2–401's rules on passage of title also may be relevant in a bankruptcy case to determine whether goods are part of the debtor's bankruptcy estate. For example, in Riddle Farm Equipment v. Boles (*In re* Boles), 2004 Bankr. LEXIS 2384 (Bankr. M.D. N.C. 2004), Wesley and Cindy Boles, the married debtors, purchased a new Kubota tractor from Riddle Farm Equipment in April of 2003 prior to filing for relief under the Bankruptcy Code. As part of an adversary proceeding seeking to declare certain debts nondischargeable, Riddle Farm moved to recover possession of the Kubota tractor claiming that title to the tractor never passed from Riddle Farm to the debtors. Citing to the language of § 2–401(2), the bankruptcy court noted that it was "undisputed" that Riddle Farm had "completed its performance with reference to the delivery of the new Kubota tractor in April of 2003." *Riddle Farm,* 2004 Bankr. LEXIS 2384, at *5. The court explained that the parties had made no agreement that title did not pass until the debtors had obtained financing for the tractor and even had the parties had such an agreement, at most it would amount to a reservation of a security interest by Riddle Farm, pursuant to § 2–401(1). Thus, the bankruptcy court concluded that title to the tractor passed to the debtors in April of 2003 and Riddle Farm did "not have a valid and enforceable claim for turnover of the tractor." *Id.* at *7.

Section 2–401's rules also are relevant in the insurance context. The court in Gross v. Powell, 181 N.W.2d 113 (Minn. 1970), applied the rule at § 2–401(2) to hold that Proctor Motor, the seller of a vehicle, was not the owner of that vehicle for purposes of the Minnesota Safety Responsibility Act (MSRA). The case began with the purchase by Hendricksen of a 1962 Oldsmobile from Proctor Motor. After buying the car, Hendricksen arranged to have Powell drive the 1962 Olds back to Hendricksen's hometown. En route, Powell was in an accident that resulted in the death of Michael Culbert. When Gross filed a wrongful death action on behalf of Culbert's heirs, Powell filed a third-party complaint against Travelers, Proctor Motor's insurance carrier. Powell claimed that because Hendricksen's check to pay for the Olds was later dishonored, title did not pass to Hendricksen but remained with Proctor Motor and, thus, Travelers was obligated to defend Powell in the litigation. The Minnesota Supreme Court rejected Powell's argument. The court explained that for purposes of the MSRA, the owner of the vehicle is the person holding legal title to it and that pursuant to § 2–401, "title passes to the buyer at the time and place at which the seller completes his performance with reference to physical delivery of the goods." UCC § 2–401(2). The court determined that title had passed to Hendricksen "no later than at the time when unrestricted possession was delivered" to him. *Gross*, 181 N.W.2d at 118. Therefore, at the time the accident occurred, Hendricksen had title to and was the owner of the car, which meant that Travelers, as insurer for Proctor Motor, had no obligation to defend Powell.

Of course, the parties to the contract may expressly agree on the manner of and on any conditions to passage of title from seller to buyer. UCC § 2–401(1). But, in the absence of such agreement, § 2–401 provides default rules for passage of title. *See* UCC § 2–401(2), (3) (introductory language stating "[u]nless otherwise explicitly agreed").

First, title to goods cannot pass before the goods are identified to the contract. UCC § 2–401(1); *see* UCC § 2–501 (identification). If the seller retains or reserves title when it ships or delivers the goods, that retention or reservation is limited to reservation of a security interest. UCC § 2–401(1).

The bankruptcy court in Ivey v. Wilson (*In re* Payne), 2006 Bankr. LEXIS 4199 (M.D. N.C. 2006) addressed the issue of a seller's attempt to retain or reserve title in the context of the sale of a car. *Ivey* involved an adversary proceeding brought by the Chapter 7 trustee against the debtor Payne. Prior to bankruptcy, the Wilsons, parents of Payne, purchased a car for Payne. Mrs. Wilson and Payne were listed on the certificate of title for the vehicle, which was paid in full by the Wilsons. Subsequently, and before Payne filed for bankruptcy, Payne and Mrs. Wilson entered into what they termed an installment sales agreement with Payne agreeing to buy the car from Mrs. Wilson and to make monthly payments over 68 months. Payne signed a promissory note and a security agreement granting her mother a security interest in the car. Mrs. Wilson, however, never perfected that security interest. Payne subsequently filed for relief under Chapter 7 of the Bankruptcy Code. Agreeing with the Chapter 7 trustee, not the Wilsons, the bankruptcy court concluded that the UCC, not the North Carolina Motor Vehicle Act, applied to the case because the transaction at issue involved the sale and financing of a car, not "tort law and liability insurance coverage." The court explained that the documents in the case, e.g., promissory note, security agreement, bankruptcy schedules, showed that Mrs. Wilson had sold the car to Payne and had reserved a security interest in the vehicle. Under § 2–401, title passed to Payne upon the sale. "Any attempted reservation of title by Mrs. Wilson in the Vehicle [was] limited to a reservation of a security interest." *Ivey,* 2006 Bankr. LEXIS 4199, at *22. The bankruptcy court explained that it was "irrelevant" that Mrs. Wilson's name still appeared on the certificate of title. Moreover, because Mrs. Wilson failed to perfect her security interest, she was an unsecured creditor in Payne's Chapter 7 bankruptcy case.

Second, if the parties' agreement does not provide for how and when title passes, title passes to the buyer "at the time and place at which the seller completes his performance with reference to the physical delivery of the goods." UCC § 2–401(2). In the case of a shipment contract, title passes to the buyer "at the time and place of shipment." UCC § 2–401(2)(a). For a destination contract, title passes to the buyer when the goods are tendered at their destination. UCC § 2–401(2)(b).

Third, for contracts in which goods are to be delivered without moving them, e.g., bailments, the default title-passage rules depend on whether title documents are involved. If the seller is supposed to deliver a document of title, then title passes "at the time when and the place where [seller] delivers such documents." UCC § 2–401(3)(a). If no such documents are to be delivered and the goods are identified at the time of contracting, then "title passes at the time and place of contracting." UCC § 2–401(3)(b).

Finally, subsection (4) to § 2–401 provides the rule for cases in which the buyer rejects the goods or revokes its acceptance. If the buyer rejects the goods, even if the rejection is wrongful, title revests in the seller. If the buyer justifiably revokes its acceptance of the goods, title also revests in the seller. UCC § 2–401(4). "Such revesting occurs by operation of law and is not a 'sale.' " *Id.*

In conclusion, title is not an obsolete concept. Nonetheless, which party has title to the goods is largely irrelevant in determining the parties' rights under various provisions of Article 2. Which party has *good title* to the goods is important, however, when a conflict exists between two parties claiming to own those goods. Section 2–403, discussed in the next section, provides the rules for deciding those conflicts.

2. GOOD FAITH PURCHASERS AND ENTRUSTMENT: § 2–403

Suppose Mother purchases from Seller an antique broach as a gift for Daughter. If Seller is a non-merchant who later attempts to retrieve the broach from Daughter, then the nature of Seller's, Mother's, and Daughter's title to the broach is relevant. *See* UCC § 2–403(1). But suppose Mother entrusted the broach to Seller, a jewelry merchant, who sold the broach to Bella. If Mother attempts to retrieve the broach from Bella, then the entrustment subsections of § 2–403 apply. *See* UCC § 2–403(2), (3).

a. Good Title, Voidable Title, and Void Title: § 2–403(1)

If Mother purchased the broach from a non-merchant seller, then the rules at § 2–403(1) apply. Understanding the meaning of several terms—good title, voidable title, and void title—is critical to reaching the correct result in the action by Seller against Daughter. Good title is self-explanatory. A party with good title defeats one with voidable *or* void title. Void title is at the opposite end of the spectrum from good title. A party with void title has *no title*. Between these two extremes lies voidable title. A party with voidable title loses to a party with good title, but a party with voidable title may transfer good title to a good faith purchaser for value.

The starting point for the analysis is with the three sentences in § 2–403(1). The first sentence states: "A purchaser of goods acquires all title which his transferor had or had power to transfer except that a purchaser of a limited interest acquires rights only to the extent of the interest purchased." It is important to look up terms and not assume that Article 2 uses those terms in the way in which people use them in daily life. A purchaser is a "person that takes by purchase," and a purchase is defined broadly to mean "taking by sale, lease, discount, negotiation, mortgage, pledge, lien, security interest, issue or reissue, gift, or any voluntary transaction creating an interest in property." UCC § 1–201(b)(29), (30).

In our example, then, Daughter, is a purchaser because she took by gift. If Mother had good title to the broach, then so did Daughter. Under the first sentence of § 2–403(1), Daughter, as a purchaser, takes whatever title her transferor Mother had; it does not matter that Daughter did not pay value. The requirement of a "good faith purchaser for value" appears in the *second, not the first, sentence* of § 2–403(1).

The second sentence of § 2–403(1) provides that a person with voidable title may transfer good title to a good faith purchaser for value. The third sentence then states four situations in which the purchaser has voidable title.

> When goods have been delivered under a transaction of purchase the purchaser has such power [to transfer good title] even though
>
> (a) the transferor was deceived as to the identity of the purchaser, or
>
> (b) the delivery was in exchange for a check which is later dishonored, or
>
> (c) it was agreed that the transaction was to be a "cash sale", or
>
> (d) the delivery was procured through fraud punishable as larcenous under the criminal law.

UCC § 2–403(1).

Suppose that Mother paid for the broach with a check that her bank later dishonored. In such a situation, Mother has voidable title. *See* UCC § 2–403(1)(b). Under the first sentence of § 2–403(1), Daughter takes whatever title Mother had; therefore, Daughter also has voidable title. While Daughter qualifies as a purchaser, she is not a purchaser for value because the broach was a gift and Daughter gave no value for it. *See* UCC § 1–204. If Seller has good title, the Seller can reclaim the broach from Daughter who has only voidable title.

Suppose that before Seller took any action to reclaim the broach from Daughter, Daughter sold the broach to Friend for its market value. Friend is not in the business of selling or buying jewelry; she simply enjoys wearing antique jewelry. Moreover, Friend knew nothing about Mother's bounced check.

See UCC § 1–201(b)(20) (definition of good faith). When Seller contacts Daughter about the broach, Daughter tells Seller that she has sold the broach to Friend. Seller cannot reclaim the broach from Friend, who has good title. Daughter had voidable title and transferred good title to Friend, who was a good faith purchaser for value. While this result may seem unfair, there are two innocent parties here: Seller, who was cheated by Mother, and Friend, who knew nothing about Mother's actions and paid value for the broach. Seller's recourse is against Mother, not against Friend.

Suppose that Seller, unbeknownst to Mother, was a thief who had stolen the broach from Owner. Mother paid Seller in cash for the broach and gave the broach to Daughter as a gift. Both Mother and Daughter have void title, because a thief breaks the chain of title. Owner can reclaim the broach from Daughter. Even if Daughter sold the broach to Friend, who paid value and acted in good faith, Owner could still reclaim the broach from Friend. Friend, like Mother and Daughter, did not have title to the broach due to Seller's theft.

b. Entrustment: § 2–403(2) & (3)

Suppose Mother owned an antique broach that had been given to her by her grandmother. Mother planned to give Daughter the broach as a graduation gift, but the broach had a broken clasp. Mother took the broach to Merchant, a dealer in antique jewelry. Mother left the broach with Merchant for repair. Merchant repaired the broach and then put it out for sale in his store's display cabinet. Bella saw the broach in the cabinet and purchased it during Merchant's normal business hours and without knowledge that the broach belonged to Mother.

This fact scenario involves the rules on entrustment under § 2–403(2) and (3). First, Mother entrusted the broach to Merchant.

> "Entrusting" includes any delivery and any acquiescence in retention of possession regardless of any condition expressed between the parties to the delivery or acquiescence and regardless of whether the procurement of the entrusting or the possessor's disposition of the goods have been such as to be larcenous under the criminal law.

UCC § 2–403(3). Mother left the broach with Merchant for repair. She is the entruster and Merchant is the entrustee. Mother acquiesced in Merchant's retention of possession even though it was solely for the purpose of repair and not for sale of the broach. Merchant's sale to Bella, even if larcenous under the jurisdiction's criminal law, does not alter the fact that Mother's leaving the broach constituted entrustment.

Second, entrusting goods to a merchant who deals in goods of that kind gives that merchant the "power to transfer all rights of the entruster to a buyer in ordinary course of business." UCC § 2–403(2). Mother entrusted the broach to Merchant, who deals in antique jewelry. Therefore, Merchant had the power to transfer all of Mother's rights to Bella, if Bella was a buyer in the ordinary course of business.

Notice that § 2–403(2) does not use the term "good faith purchaser for value" from § 2–403(1). Instead, the buyer under § 2–403(2) must be a "buyer in the ordinary course." To qualify as a buyer in the ordinary course, the buyer must satisfy the following three requirements. First, the buyer must buy in good faith. Second, the buyer cannot have "knowledge that the sale violates the rights of another person in the goods." Finally, the buyer must purchase the goods "in the ordinary course from a person, other than a pawnbroker, in the business of selling goods of that kind." UCC § 1–201(b)(9).

Taking these elements in reverse order, Bella purchased the broach in the ordinary course of business from Merchant, who sells goods of the kind. Bella bought the broach at Merchant's store during normal business hours. The broach was displayed in the sale cabinet and there are no facts to indicate that Bella knew that she was buying a broach that Merchant had no right to sell. In fact, Bella did not know that the broach belonged to Mother. Finally, Bella acted in good faith. There is no evidence that she was not honest in fact, or that "reasonable commercial standards of fair dealing" were not observed. UCC § 1–201(b)(20).

While it may seem unfair that Mother loses the broach to Bella, remember that there are two innocent parties involved: Mother and Bella. Article 2 provides a rule for deciding which of these two innocent parties has the right to the broach. Mother may sue Merchant for conversion. Thus, she is not without recourse, even though her recourse is against Merchant, not Bella.

c. Summary

If you have a problem involving a conflict between parties as to who owns the goods, start by asking whether the seller is a merchant in goods of that kind and whether the original owner seeking to reclaim those goods from the purchaser entrusted them to the merchant seller. If so, then determine whether the purchaser of the goods was a buyer in the ordinary course. If the purchaser bought the goods from the merchant in the ordinary course, then the purchaser prevails over the original owner who entrusted the goods to the merchant. The original owner entruster's recourse is limited to claims against the merchant entrustee. But, if the purchaser does not qualify as a buyer in the ordinary course, then the original owner entruster can reclaim the goods from the purchaser.

If the fact scenario does not involve a merchant entrustee, then the rules of § 2–403(1) apply. First, determine the nature of the seller's title. If the seller was a thief, then the buyer (and any subsequent purchaser in the chain) has void title. That means that the owner from whom the thief stole the goods may reclaim them from the person with current possession of those goods. If the seller had good title, then the buyer has good title *even if* the buyer was not a good faith purchaser for value. Why? The first sentence of § 2–401(1) provides that a purchaser acquires whatever title her transferor had. There is no requirement that the purchaser be a good faith purchaser for value. That requirement is in the *second, not the first, sentence* of § 2–403(1). Therefore, a seller with good title transfers good title. Remember that a purchase involves more than a sale; it also includes gifts.

The second and third sentences of § 2–403(1) come into play when the seller has voidable title. A seller with voidable title may transfer good title to a good faith purchaser for value. Thus, a buyer who purchases for value (not a gift) and in good faith may have good title even if the buyer purchased the goods from a seller with voidable title.

B. LEASES

1. SUBSEQUENT LESSEES: § 2A–304

Section 2A–304 on subsequent lessees, while modeled on § 2–403, was "significantly revised to reflect leasing practices and to integrate [Article 2A] with certificate of title statutes." UCC § 2A–304, Comment: Changes. Nonetheless, the drafters intended § 2A–304 to be "read in conjunction with Section 2–403." UCC § 2A–304, Comment ¶ 2. Both sections use the phrase "transaction of purchase", which includes taking by sale or by lease. *See* UCC § 1–201(b)(29) and UCC § 2A–103(1)(v) (definitions of purchase).

Section 2A–304 contains three subsections. The first states the rights of a lessee that leases goods already covered by an existing lease. UCC § 2A–

304(1). Subsection (2) sets forth the rule on entrustment to a merchant lessor that deals in goods of the kind. UCC § 2–304(2). Finally, subsection (3) covers the rights of a subsequent lessee in a transaction to which a jurisdiction's certificate of title law applies. UCC § 2A–304(3).

Subsection (1) states as follows:

> Subject to Section 2A–303, a subsequent lessee from a lessor of goods under an existing lease contract obtains, to the extent of the leasehold interest transferred, the leasehold interest in the goods that the lessor had or had power to transfer, and except as provided in subsection (2) and Section 2A–527(4), takes subject to the existing lease contract. A lessor with voidable title has power to transfer a good leasehold interest to a good faith subsequent lessee for value, but only to the extent set forth in the preceding sentence. If goods have been delivered under a transaction of purchase, the lessor has that power even though:
>
> (a) the lessor's transferor was deceived as to the identity of the lessor;
>
> (b) the delivery was in exchange for a check which is later dishonored;
>
> (c) it was agreed that the transaction was to be a "cash sale"; or
>
> (d) the delivery was procured through fraud punishable as larcenous under the criminal law.

UCC § 2A–304(1).

The first sentence of § 2A–304(1) describes the rights of a lessee that leases goods subject to another existing lease agreement. The last two sentences of § 2A–304(1) address the problem of the lessor with voidable title. The second sentence explicitly uses that phrase while the third sentence provides four examples of transactions in which the lessor has such voidable title. *Cf.* UCC § 2–403.

Consider the following example. Office Supplies Company (OSC) sells and leases office equipment. Suppose that on February 1, 2022, OSC signs an agreement to lease various pieces of office equipment for one year to New Firm (New). The lease begins on March 1, 2022, and ends the following year on February 28, 2023. On December 1, 2022, OSC signs an agreement to lease the same equipment, starting January 1, 2023, to Small Biz (Small). The two leases overlap for two months—January and February of 2023. What rights do New and Small have?

There is no entrustment by New to OSC; therefore, subsection (2) of § 2–304 does not apply. *See infra* for entrustment discussion. Section § 2A–527(4) also is inapplicable. While Small is the subsequent lessee, its transaction with OSC is not a re-lease of the goods after a default by New. *See* 3 Hawkland UCC Series § 2A–527:4 (stating that purpose of § 2A–527(4) is "to maximize the release rent by giving third parties the assurance that the goods will not be reclaimed from them when they have acquired them in good faith").

At the time that it leased to Small, OSC had an existing lease agreement with New that covered the equipment for the remaining months of January and

February. Unfortunately, then, for Small, it takes subject to the lease that OSC has with New, including New's rights under that lease. *See* UCC § 2A–304(1); § 2A–304, Comment ¶ 4. In other words, for the months of January and February, New's right to possession of the equipment is superior to that of Small's.

What happens if New, after signing the lease with OSC, entrusts the equipment to OSC for a limited time period but during that time OSC leases it to another firm? Suppose that on February 20, OSC signs a one-year lease with New for equipment. The lease term begins March 1. New pays the first month's rent and the agreement provides for delivery of the equipment on March 1. As its name indicates, New is a new enterprise and while it had planned to open its doors on March 5, problems arose. New contacts OSC to hold the equipment and deliver it on March 15, not March 1. OSC agrees to the new delivery date. On March 10, OSC signs an agreement to lease to Small the equipment already leased to New. *See* 3 Hawkland UCC Series § 2A–304:7 (example modified here). Assume that Small acts in good faith, is unaware of the New lease, and leases in the ordinary course of OSC's business. Small is a subsequent lessee in the ordinary course of business. *See* UCC § 2A–103(1)(*o*). What are New's and Small's rights?

Small, once again, is the subsequent lessee but the result differs from the result in the earlier OSC/New example because the current scenario involves entrustment. Subsection (2) of § 2A–304 provides the rule on entrustment.

> A subsequent lessee in the ordinary course of business from a lessor who is a merchant dealing in goods of that kind to whom the goods were entrusted by the existing lessee of that lessor before the interest of the subsequent lessee became enforceable against that lessor obtains, to the extent of the leasehold interest transferred, all of that lessor's and the existing lessee's rights to the goods, and takes free of the existing lease contract.

UCC § 2A–304(2). OSC is a merchant dealing in goods of the kind—the equipment. New entrusted the equipment to OSC by acquiescing in OSC's retention of possession of the equipment until March 15. Section 2–403(3)'s definition of entrustment applies to § 2A–304. *See* UCC § 2A–304, Comment ¶ 6; *see also* UCC § 2A–103(3). New entrusted the equipment before Small's interest as a subsequent lessee became enforceable against OSC. As a result, Small "takes free of the existing lease contract" between OSC and New. UCC § 2A–304(2).

The final subsection of § 2A–304 provides the rule for leases of goods covered by a jurisdiction's certificate of title statute. This subsection deals with leases of motor vehicles. The rule is that a subsequent lessee in such a case "takes no greater rights than those provided both by [§ 2A–304] and by the certificate of title statute." UCC § 2A–304(3). The drafters intended to incorporate into § 2A–304 the construction by the jurisdiction's courts of the relationship between § 2–403 and the jurisdiction's certificate of title statute. UCC § 2A–304, Comment ¶ 7. If the certificate of title statute does not address the issue of transfer, then § 2A–304's rules control. *See id.*

2. SUBLESSEES: § 2A–305

Like § 2A–304, § 2A–305 is modeled on § 2–403, albeit with significant revisions to reflect leasing practice and to integrate Article 2A with statutes dealing with certificates of title. *See* UCC § 2A–305, Comment: Changes. Section 2A–305 is divided into three subsections, which track the structure and language of § 2A–304. Section 2A–305(1) states the rights of a buyer or sublessee that purchased or sublet goods from the lessee of goods under an existing lease contract. Subsection (2) sets forth the rule on entrustment to a merchant that deals in goods of the kind. UCC § 2–305(2). Finally, § 2A–305(3) covers the rights of a buyer or sublessee in a transaction to which a jurisdiction's certificate of title law applies.

Subsection (1) states as follows:

> Subject to the provisions of Section 2A–303, a buyer or sublessee from the lessee of such goods under an existing lease contract obtains, to the extent of the interest transferred, the leasehold interest in the goods that the lessee had or had power to transfer, and except as provided in subsection (2) and Section 2A–511(4), takes subject to the existing lease contract. A lessee with a voidable leasehold interest has power to

> transfer a good leasehold interest to a good faith buyer for value or a good faith sublessee for value, but only to the extent set forth in the preceding sentence. If goods have been delivered under a transaction of purchase, the lessee has that power even though:
>
> (a) the lessor's transferor was deceived as to the identity of the lessee;
>
> (b) the delivery was in exchange for a check which is later dishonored; or
>
> (c) the delivery was procured through fraud punishable as larcenous under the criminal law.

UCC § 2A–305(1).

Suppose that on February 1, Equipment Company (EC), which manufactures farm equipment, leases six combines to Fannie Farmer Company (Fannie) for a one-year term—February 1 through January 31 of the following year. Under the parties' lease, EC agreed to defer until April 1 Fannie's rent payment for the lease's first two months. On March 1, Fannie, after realizing that it needed only four of the six combines, subleased two of the six combines to Small Field, Inc. (Small) for a one-year term—from March 1 through February 28 of the following year. *See* UCC § 2A–301, Comment ¶ 3 (hypothetical modified here). What are Small's and EC's rights?

Small takes subject to the lease agreement between EC and Fannie. UCC § 2A–305(1). Fannie's right to possession under its lease with EC ends on

January 31. Because Fannie has no right to possession of the combines past January 31, neither does Small. In other words, EC has the right to return of all six combines, including the two sublet to Small, by the end of the day on January 31. The exceptions to operation of this rule under § 2A–305(2) and § 2A–511(4) do not apply. There is no entrustment, because Fannie is not a merchant in farm equipment. *See* § 2A–305(2) (entrustment). Also, Small did not buy or sublet the equipment after Fannie had rightfully rejected it. *See* § 2A–511(4) (rights of purchaser from lessee upon rightful rejection).

But § 2A–305(1) is subject to the provisions of § 2A–303. Suppose that the lease between EC and Fannie prohibited Fannie from subletting the combines or made subletting the combines an event of default. The transfer to Small still would be effective. *See* UCC § 2A–303(2). But EC would have the rights and remedies provided by § 2A–303(4). *See* UCC § 2A–301, Comment ¶ 3(d); *see also supra* Chapter 5, § C.

What if Fannie is unable to pay the deferred rent on April 1? Remember, Small takes subject to the lease agreement between Fannie and EC. *See* UCC § 2A–305(1). Fannie's default means that EC may recover the combines, including the two combines held by Small. *See* UCC § 2A–523; *see also* UCC § 2A–301, Comment ¶ 3(h). But Small can sue Fannie for damages. *See* UCC §§ 2A–211(1), 2A–508; *see also* Section UCC § 2A–301, Comment ¶ 3(h).

Let's move on from the first to the second and third sentences of § 2A–305(1). The last two sentences of § 2A–305(1) address the problem of the lessee with a "voidable leasehold interest." The second sentence explicitly uses that phrase while the third sentence provides three examples of transactions in which the lessor has such a voidable leasehold interest. Notice that the "cash sale" provision of § 2A–304(1)(c) is not included in § 2A–305(1). The reason is that the transaction at issue in § 2A–305(1) is the original lease. Because that transaction is a lease, it makes no sense to talk about a "cash sale."

Suppose Cards, Inc. (Cards) enters into a one-year lease of computer equipment from Computer World (CW). Cards is a small greeting card business that struggles financially. The parties' lease provides that Cards must make the first rental payment upon delivery of the equipment. Cards pays CW with a check that is later dishonored. Before CW learns that the check bounced, Cards decides that it cannot afford the equipment. In order to recoup the cost of the lease payments and also make some extra cash, Cards signs a two-year lease for the equipment with Biz. Assume that Biz acted in good faith in its dealings with Cards. Cards has a voidable leasehold interest because it paid with a dishonored check. *See* UCC § 2A–305(1)(b). Biz is a good faith sublessee for value. Thus, Cards transferred a good leasehold interest to Biz. Nonetheless, Biz's leasehold interest is subject to the lease between Cards and CW, which is only a year long. *See* UCC § 2–305(1). At the end of that year, CW may reclaim the computer equipment from Biz.

Subsection (2) of § 2A–305 provides the rule on entrustment.

> A buyer in the ordinary course of business or a sublessee in the ordinary course of business from a lessee who is a merchant dealing in goods of that kind to whom the goods were entrusted by the lessor obtains, to the extent of the interest transferred, all of the lessor's and lessee's rights to the goods, and takes free of the existing lease contract.

UCC § 2A–305(2).

The final subsection of § 2A–305 provides the rule for leases of goods covered by a jurisdiction's certificate of title statute. This subsection deals with leases of motor vehicles. The rule is that a "buyer or sublessee from the lessee of goods that are subject to an existing lease contract and are covered by a certificate of title . . . takes no greater rights than those provided both by [§ 2A–305] and by the certificate of title statute." UCC § 2A–305(3).

For example, in CIT Group/Equipment Financing, Inc. v. M&S Grading, Inc. (*In re* M&S Grading, Inc.), 457 F.3d 898 (B.A.P. 8th Cir. 2006), CIT leased equipment, subject to Nebraska's Certificate of Title Act, to Fehrs Nebraska Tractor & Equipment Company. Fehrs subsequently sold the equipment to M&S Grading, the debtor. Fehrs did not deliver a certificate of title to the debtor, because CIT held it. When the debtor filed for bankruptcy, CIT learned that the equipment it had leased to Fehrs was now in the debtor's possession. Debtor claimed the equipment as part of its bankruptcy estate. Under Nebraska's certificate of title statute, the buyer of a vehicle does not obtain title unless it has physical possession of and a certificate of title on the vehicle. The bankruptcy court held that while debtor was a buyer in the ordinary course of business from Fehrs, a merchant dealing in goods of the same kind, debtor had not received a certificate of title. Therefore, CIT held a superior interest in the equipment. The Bankruptcy Appellate Panel (BAP) affirmed the bankruptcy court decision and rejected the debtor's argument that the bankruptcy court had misapplied § 2A–305.

The BAP also rejected the debtor's argument that the Nebraska Supreme Court's decision in Dugdale of Nebraska v. First State Bank, 420 N.W.2d 273 (Neb. 1988), which analyzed the interplay between § 2–403 and Nebraska's certificate of title statute, also applied to § 2A–305(3). The *CIT* debtor based its argument that *Dugdale* controlled the outcome on Article 2A's Official Comments.

> Where the relationship between the certificate of title statute and Section 2–403, the statutory analogue to this section, has been construed by a court, that construction is incorporated here.

UCC § 2A–304, Comment ¶ 7; *see* UCC § 2A–305, Comment: Purposes (directing the reader to compare the Official Comment to § 2A–304).

The BAP, however, held that *Dugdale* did not apply to its analysis of § 2A–305. The court explained that § 2A–305 incorporated Nebraska's certificate of title statute, unlike § 2–403. Moreover, Nebraska enacted § 2A–305 *after* the Nebraska Supreme Court's decision in *Dugdale*.

> [A] legislature is presumed to have knowledge of judicial precedent relating to the subject matter under inquiry, so § 2A–305's specific incorporation of the certificate of title act cannot be disregarded, even if the comments to the statute suggest a contrary interpretation. The Nebraska legislature might have intended to draft § 2A–305 to incorporate the holding in *Dugdale*, but the statutory language does not reflect that intent. If anything, the specific incorporation of the certificate of title act into § 2A–305 suggests that the Nebraska legislature intended to preclude the application of *Dugdale* to § 2A–305.

CIT Group, 457 F.3d at 901. Therefore, the BAP affirmed the bankruptcy court's decision that CIT's interest in the equipment was superior to debtor's interest.

CHAPTER 9
PERFORMANCE

A. SALES

This portion of the Chapter covers those provisions of Article 2 dealing with performance of the parties' contract for sale. It covers: (1) the perfect tender rule; (2) what constitutes acceptance versus rejection of goods by the buyer; (3) when the seller has the right to cure a nonconforming delivery; (4) when the buyer may revoke acceptance of goods; (5) which party bears the risk of loss for damaged or destroyed goods; and (6) when contract performance is excused.

1. THE PERFECT TENDER RULE: § 2–601

In first-year Contracts, you likely read Jacob & Youngs v. Kent, 230 N.Y. 239 (1921), and studied the doctrine of substantial performance. The substantial performance doctrine does not apply to the sale of goods. Instead, the drafters of Article 2 created what is known as the perfect tender rule.

The UCC's perfect tender rule provides that with the exception of installment contracts, a buyer that receives a shipment of goods that "fail[s] in any respect to conform to the contract" may reject the whole shipment, accept the entire shipment, or "accept any commercial unit or units and reject the rest." UCC § 2–601. For example, suppose Buyer agrees to purchase 500 blue widgets—ten boxes of 50 each. Seller delivers ten boxes to Buyer, who inspects the delivery and discovers that two boxes contain green, not blue, widgets. Buyer may accept the eight boxes of blue widgets and reject the two boxes that do not conform to the contract. UCC § 2–601(c). Buyer may reject the entire shipment. UCC § 2–601(a); *see* § 2–602. If Buyer accepts the entire shipment, Buyer still may sue Seller for breach for making a nonconforming delivery. UCC § 2–601(b); *see* UCC § 2–601, Comment ¶ 1 (stating that "[a] buyer accepting a non-conforming tender is not penalized by the loss of any remedy otherwise open to him").

Bear in mind that § 2–601 speaks in terms of a non-conforming delivery by the seller. If the seller delivers goods that conform to the contract, i.e., a perfect tender, then any rejection of the goods, either in whole or in part, by the buyer is wrongful as against the seller. The buyer, then, is in breach and the seller may avail itself of the remedies provided by Article 2. *See infra* Chapter 11, § B.

a. Installment Contracts: § 2–612

The perfect tender rule does not apply to installment contracts. Article 2 defines an installment contract as a contract that "requires or authorizes the delivery of goods in separate lots to be separately accepted, even though the contract contains a clause 'each delivery is a separate contract' or its equivalent." UCC § 2–612(1); *see, e.g.,* Emanuel Law Outlines, Inc. v. Multi-State Legal Studies, Inc., 899 F. Supp. 1081 (1995) (contract to provide "950 copies of each of two volumes of capsule summaries" each year for three years "require[d] the delivery of goods in separate lots to be separately accepted" and, therefore, was an installment contract). The buyer may reject a non-conforming installment if the "nonconformity substantially impairs the value of the installment and cannot be cured." UCC § 2–612(2). If the non-conformity does not substantially impair the value of the entire contract, the buyer must accept the installment if the "seller gives adequate assurance of its cure." UCC § 2–612(2).

In most jurisdictions, what constitutes a "substantial impairment" is a question of fact. *See, e.g.*, Bill's Coal Co. v. Board of Public Utilities, 887 F.2d 242 (10th Cir. 1989) (stating that the "case law indicates that the question of 'substantial impairment' under the Code presents a question of fact"); *but see* Nutrisoya Foods Inc. v. Sunrich, LLC, 641 F.3d 282 (8th Cir. 2011) (stating that "[u]nder Minnesota law, unlike many other states, while '[t]he determination of substantial impairment necessarily involves factual findings,' the 'ultimate conclusion' is 'legal in character' "). Neither Article 1 nor Article 2 defines the phrase "substantially impairs." The Official Comment to § 2–612 provides that substantial impairment may relate not only to the quality of the goods but also to "factors [such as] time, quantity, assortment, and the like." UCC § 2–612, Comment ¶ 4; *see* Stinnes Interoil, Inc. v. Apex Oil Co., 604 F. Supp. 978 (S.D. N.Y 1985) (stating that "failure to comply with a delivery deadline can constitute substantial impairment" but noting that not every "delay necessarily impairs the value of an installment in all circumstances"). Moreover, substantial impairment "must be judged in terms of the normal or specifically known purposes of the contract." UCC § 2–612, Comment ¶ 4.

Section 2–610 on anticipatory repudiation also uses the term "substantially impairs" and the Official Comment to that section provides a bit more guidance.

> The test chosen to justify an aggrieved party's action under this section is the same as that in the section on breach in installment contract—namely the substantial value of the contract. The more useful test of substantial value is to determine whether material inconvenience or injustice will result if the aggrieved party is forced to wait and receive an ultimate tender minus the part or aspect repudiated.

UCC § 2–610, Comment ¶ 3; *see* 4 Anderson U.C.C. § 2–612:22 (3d ed.) (noting that while the UCC does not define "substantially impairs," the term "is defined to some extent by the Official Code Comments to U.C.C. § 2–610 and U.C.C. § 2–612").

Use of the phrase "substantially impairs" in the UCC's section on anticipatory repudiation demonstrates the link between the concepts of substantial impairment and material breach. In Midwest Mobile Diagnostic Imaging, L.L.C. v. Dynamics Corporation of America, 965 F. Supp. 1003 (W.D. Mich. 1997), the district court explained that "whether nonconformity rises to the level of substantial impairment may be judged by reference to the concept of material breach under traditional contract law." The Eighth Circuit in Barry & Sewall

Industrial Supply Co. v. Metal-Prep of Houston, Inc., 912 F.2d 252 (8th Cir. 1990), noted that substantial impairment and material breach are related concepts, and quoted the observation by White & Summers that " '[t]he common law concept of 'material breach' is at least a first cousin to the concept of 'substantial nonconformity.' " *Id.* at 257 (quoting 1 White & Summers, Uniform Commercial Code § 8–3, p. 403 (3d ed. 1988)); *see also* Johannsen v. Minnesota Valley Ford Tractor Co., 304 N.W.2d 654 (Minn. 1981) (quoting White & Summers for proposition that a determination of substantial impairment is " 'akin to the determination of a material breach' "). Thus, in determining whether a non-conformity substantially impairs the value of an installment, the Restatement's test for material breach provides useful guidance. *See* RESTATEMENT (SECOND) OF CONTRACTS § 241 (listing five "circumstances" relevant to whether a party's failure to perform is material, including the extent to which non-performance deprives the injured party of the contract's benefit and the extent to which the non-performing party's conduct "comports with standards of good faith and fair dealing").

Deciding that a non-conformity substantially impairs the value of an installment does not end the analysis under § 2–612(2), however. The buyer still must accept the installment, notwithstanding substantial impairment, if the "nonconformity is curable and the seller gives adequate assurance of cure." UCC § 2–612, Comment ¶ 5. Cure may consist of a reduction in the price for the goods. *See id.* (stating that cure "in the first instance can usually be afforded by an allowance against the price"). The standard for determining whether the seller provided adequate assurance of cure is the same as the standard under § 2–609 on the right to adequate assurance of performance. *See id.; see also infra* Chapter 10, § A.2 on adequate assurance doctrine.

If the nonconformity does not substantially impair the installment's value, e.g., minor flaw, the buyer cannot reject the installment. Nonetheless, the seller still is liable to the buyer for any damages flowing from that minor nonconformity, because the seller failed to deliver goods that conformed to the contract. Of course, the seller could simply do an offset to the price to avoid any suit for damages and to address the minor nonconformity of the installment.

Even if the buyer's rejection of an installment is proper, the buyer may not be able cancel the entire contract. The test for cancellation is whether the "non-conformity or default with respect to one or more installments substantially impairs the value of the whole contract." UCC § 2–612(3).

> Whether the non-conformity in any given installment justifies cancellation as to the future depends, not on whether such non-conformity indicates an intent or likelihood that the future deliveries will also be defective, but whether the non-conformity substantially impairs the value of the whole contract.

UCC § 2–612, Comment ¶ 6. The court looks at the totality of the circumstances, mindful that "defects in prior installments are cumulative in effect, so that acceptance does not wash out the defect 'waived.' " *Id.* Nonetheless, in certain circumstances, a buyer may cancel after the first installment if the nonconformity substantially impairs the value of the entire contract. For example, in *Midwest Mobile Diagnostic Imaging*, the court held that the buyer's cancellation of the parties' contract after delivery of only one installment was proper. Midwest Mobile Diagnostic Imaging (Midwest) entered into a contract with Ellis & Watts (E&W) to buy from E&W four mobile MRI trailers in separate installments. The first trailer did not conform to the contract, and E&W attempted a cure. E&W, however, failed to correct the problems with the trailer and Midwest rejected the trailer. Midwest also canceled the parties' contract. The court noted that "one of the primary purposes" of the contract was to provide Midwest with the ability to satisfy the "growing demand for its services [and] [t]hus, impairment of one of the four installments would have a substantial negative impact" on Midwest. *Midwest Mobile Diagnostic Imaging,* 965 F. Supp. at 1016. In addition, E&W was aware that early delivery was "of primary importance" to Midwest. The court explained that E&W's failure to effect a cure "substantially delayed completion of the remainder of the contract which delayed [Midwest's] ability to begin use of the 1.5T MRI trailer it had promised to its customers" at an earlier open house. *Id.* Therefore, the court concluded that Midwest had rightfully canceled the contract.

Unlike § 2–612(2), which applies only to the buyer, § 2–612(3) applies to both buyers and sellers. For example, in L&M Enterprises, Inc. v. BEI Sensors &

Systems Company, 231 F.3d 1284 (10th Cir. 2000), the seller BEI canceled the parties' agreement because the buyer L&M had "completely failed to make timely payments." The Tenth Circuit concluded that L&M's failure to pay for shipments constituted substantial impairment of the entire contract.

> We agree with the courts that have held implicitly that an undisputed failure to pay for shipments establishes, as a matter of law, substantial impairment justifying cancellation as to the future undelivered balance of a contract.

L&M, 231 F.3d at 1288. Thus, the Tenth Circuit affirmed the district court's decision that L&M's failure to make timely payments justified BEI's cancellation of the parties' agreement. *Cf.* UCC § 2–612, Comment ¶ 7 (stating that under subsection (3) "a seller may withhold a delivery pending payments for prior ones, at the same time delaying his decision as to cancellation").

2. ACCEPTANCE VERSUS REJECTION OF GOODS: § 2–606 AND § 2–602

Suppose Barney Company (BC) and Slate, Inc. enter into a valid, enforceable contract for the purchase and sale of a machine that BC plans to use in its factory. Slate delivers the machine to BC's plant. If plant personnel conduct a test run of the machine, has BC accepted the machine? No. Unless the parties agreed to the contrary, BC has the right to inspect the machine prior to acceptance. Inspection may occur after the goods arrive at the buyer's location, if the parties' agreement requires or authorizes the seller to send the goods to the buyer. UCC § 2–513(1). Conducting a test run is a perfectly reasonable way to inspect a machine intended for factory use.

When does acceptance occur, then? Article 2 provides three basic ways in which a buyer accepts the goods. Let's walk through our example above to see when acceptance occurs.

First, if BC inspects the machine and contacts Slate to say that it accepts it, then acceptance has occurred. What if an inspection reveals a minor defect with the machine but BC contacts Slate and says that it will keep the machine? Acceptance occurs if the buyer "after a reasonable opportunity to inspect the goods signifies to the seller that the goods are conforming or that he will take or retain them in spite of their nonconformity." UCC § 2–606(1)(a). In other words, a buyer may accept non-conforming goods. Acceptance precludes the buyer from rejecting the goods. UCC § 2–607(2). Moreover, if the buyer accepts with knowledge of the non-conformity, as BC does in our example, then the buyer cannot revoke acceptance unless the buyer accepted on the reasonable assumption that the seller would cure the nonconformity. *Id.*; *see* UCC § 2–607, Comment ¶ 2; *see also infra* § A.4 of this Chapter. But remember, the buyer does not lose the right to sue the seller for damages resulting from the nonconformity simply because the buyer accepts nonconforming goods. *See* § 2–601, Comment ¶ 1.

Second, BC may end up accepting the goods by simply holding onto the goods. The buyer accepts goods by "fail[ing] to make an effective rejection (subsection (1) of Section 2–602), but such acceptance does not occur until the buyer has had a reasonable opportunity to inspect them." UCC § 2–602(1)(b). What if Slate delivers the machine but BC fails to inspect it and does not operate the machine for several weeks? Slate demands the contract price but BC claims that it does not owe the price until it has accepted and that it does not accept until it inspects the machine. Is BC correct? No. Section 2–606 speaks in terms of a "reasonable opportunity to inspect." If the rule were the one articulated by BC, then buyers could simply hold onto goods indefinitely by delaying their inspection. *See* UCC § 2–602, Comment ¶ 1 (stating that "[a] tender of delivery of goods made pursuant to a contract for sale, even though wholly non-conforming, requires affirmative action by the buyer to avoid acceptance"). If BC has had a reasonable opportunity to inspect the machine, then BC has accepted the machine simply by failing to reject it in a timely fashion.

Third, subsection (c) states that the buyer accepts by doing "any act inconsistent with the seller's ownership; but if such act is wrongful as against the seller it is an acceptance only if ratified by him." UCC § 2–606(1)(c). For example, if plant personnel at BC modify the height of the machine by sawing an inch off the bottom of the legs and affixing a wide foot to the end, then BC has done an act inconsistent with Slate's ownership and by doing so has accepted the machine, regardless of whether BC has inspected or had an opportunity to inspect the machine.

The example above deals only with the first clause of § 2–606(1)(c). What does the second clause mean? It applies to situations in which the buyer, after initially rejecting the goods, takes an action inconsistent with the seller's ownership. For example, suppose BC inspects the machine, finds it nonconforming, and contacts Slate to reject the delivery. Slate provides BC with instructions for return of the rejected goods. Any action taken in good faith by BC in complying with Slate's instructions does not constitute acceptance. UCC § 2–603(3). But instead of following Slate's return instructions, BC begins using the machine. While nonconforming, the machine still operates. BC's post-rejection use of the machine is an "exercise of ownership" and is "wrongful as against the seller". UCC § 2–602(2)(a). "The second clause of paragraph (c) . . . makes it clear that 'acceptance' in law based on the wrongful act of the acceptor is acceptance only as against the wrongdoer and then only at the option of the party wronged." UCC § 2–606, Comment ¶ 4. In other words, Slate may treat BC's post-rejection use as acceptance, but it is Slate, not BC, which makes that determination.

But, what if BC, after rejecting the machine, calls Slate back and says it has changed its mind and wants to accept the machine? If Slate has held open the tender, then BC may withdraw its rejection. *See* UCC § 2–601, Comment ¶ 2 (stating that buyer may withdraw its "original refusal to accept" if the seller is holding open the tender); UCC § 2–606, Comment ¶ 4 (stating that once the buyer rejects, § 2–606(1)(a) does not operate in the buyer's favor unless, for example, the seller has held open the tender).

Suppose that in the interim between BC's call rejecting the machine and its subsequent call attempting to accept and withdraw that rejection, Slate arranges to sell the machine to another buyer. In this case, BC is liable to Slate for any damage resulting from BC first rejecting and later attempting to accept the machine. *See* UCC § 2–601, Comment ¶ 1 (stating that if buyer attempts to accept after first rejecting goods, it "must answer for any ensuing damage" resulting from the seller making other arrangements for the goods). Moreover, even if Slate treats BC's "action as acceptance rather than conversion," BC still is liable for any damages Slate incurs, because "the damage flows from the misleading notice." UCC § 2–601, Comment ¶ 2.

Thus, the buyer may accept by affirmatively telling the seller that it accepts, by failing to reject after having had a reasonable opportunity to inspect the goods, or by taking any action inconsistent with the seller's ownership of the goods. If the buyer rejects the goods and later attempts to withdraw that rejection and accept, it is an acceptance only at the seller's option.

3. CURE: § 2–508

Article 2's rules on cure mitigate the harshness of its perfect tender rule. The seller may cure an imperfect tender or delivery in two circumstances.

The first is when the buyer rejects nonconforming goods and the "time for performance has not yet expired." UCC § 2–508(1). The second extends the right to cure beyond the time for contract performance when the buyer rejects nonconforming goods that the seller "had reasonable grounds to believe would be acceptable with or without money allowance." UCC § 2–508(2). In both cases, of course, the seller must notify the buyer of its intention to cure.

a. Before Contract Performance Date

Suppose Acme Company enters into a valid, enforceable contract to sell 500 anvils to Road Runner, Inc. (RRI) with delivery to occur on May 7. Acme delivers the anvils to RRI on May 1. RRI inspects the shipment and rejects it, after finding non-conforming goods. Acme has the right to cure.

> Where any tender or delivery by the seller is rejected because non-conforming and the time for performance has not yet expired, the seller may seasonably notify the buyer of his intention to cure and may then within the contract time make a conforming delivery.

UCC § 2–508(1). In order to invoke the right to cure, Acme must seasonably notify RRI of its intention to cure. Seasonable means that Acme provides notice of its intent to cure "within a reasonable time." UCC § 1–205(b). The analysis is fact intensive. If Acme notified RRI of its intent to cure when RRI contacted Acme to reject the anvils, such notice is timely. "The closer, however, it is to the contract date, the greater is the necessity for extreme promptness on the seller's part in notifying of his intention to cure if such notification is to be 'seasonable' " for purposes of § 2–508(1). UCC § 2–508, Comment ¶ 1. If the seller decides to cure, it must "within the contract time make a conforming delivery." UCC § 2–508(1). If Acme tells RRI that it intends to cure, then Acme must deliver conforming goods to RRI by May 7, the original contract performance date.

Keep in mind that the seller is not required to cure. But, if the buyer rejects the goods prior to the contract performance date and the seller does not cure, then the seller is liable for damages for breach of contract. *See infra* Chapter 11, § C. If Acme invokes its right to cure and adheres to the requirements of § 2–508(1), can RRI refuse Acme's offer to cure? No, it cannot. If RRI does so, then it is in breach of contract and Acme can sue for damages. *See infra* Chapter 11, § B.

b. Reasonable Grounds

Even if the time for performance under the contract has passed, the seller may have a right to cure a non-conforming delivery.

> Where the buyer rejects a non-conforming tender which the seller had reasonable grounds to believe would be acceptable with or without money allowance the seller may if he seasonably notifies the buyer have a further reasonable time to substitute a conforming tender.

UCC § 2–508(2). For example, in Bartus v. Riccardi, 55 Misc.2d 3 (Utica City Ct. 1967), the buyer, in January, signed a contract to purchase a Model A-660 hearing aid from Seller, a franchise representative of Acousticon, a hearing-aid manufacturer. In February, however, Seller fitted Buyer with Model A-665, a "modified and improved" model of the A-660. Buyer wore the hearing aid for about 15 hours in total but returned it stating it gave him a headache and was not the model he had ordered. Seller offered to replace the A-665 or to order an A-660 for Buyer, but Buyer refused. The court held that Seller had reasonable grounds to believe that tender of the A-660 would be acceptable to Buyer because it was the "newer and improved version of the model" that Buyer had ordered. Because Buyer refused Seller's offer of a cure, the court awarded damages to Seller for Buyer's breach of contract.

The *Bartus* case is a reminder that § 2–508 uses the word "non-conforming." Non-conforming does *not* mean defective. It simply means that the goods delivered are not what the buyer ordered. The parties' course of dealing, course of performance, or the usage of trade also may provide the seller with reasonable grounds to believe that its tender of the goods would prove acceptable to the buyer. UCC § 2–508, Comment ¶ 2; *see* Western Sky Industries, LLC v. Colttech, LLC, 2009 WL 2168914 (D. Kan. 2009) (denying buyer's motion for summary judgment and holding that based on the parties' "prior course of dealing, a disputed issue of material fact exists as to whether [seller] had reasonable grounds to believe the circuit boards it delivered to [buyer] would be acceptable").

As discussed earlier, the seller must seasonably notify the buyer of its intent to cure. How much time does the seller have to cure? Subsection (2) states that the buyer has a "further reasonable time to substitute a conforming tender." UCC § 2–508(2). What constitutes a "further reasonable time" is a question of fact and "depends upon the attending circumstances." UCC § 2–508(2), Comment ¶ 3. But the drafters made clear that the "words 'a further reasonable time to substitute a conforming tender' are intended as words of limitation to protect the buyer." *Id.* For example, in B&F Machine Co., Inc. v. Electro-Methods, Inc., 2010 WL 2593269 (Conn. Super. Ct. 2010), B&F agreed to manufacture and ship mechanical parts to Electro-Methods. The parties' agreement provided that time was of the essence. B&F delivered the parts, but Electro-Methods rejected them as non-conforming. When Electro-Methods rejected, B&F timely invoked its right to cure under § 2–508(2). B&F then shipped conforming parts but five months after Electro-Methods had returned the original shipment of non-conforming goods.

The court held that B&F "failed to substitute the 'conforming tender' within a 'further reasonable time.'" *B&F,* 2010 WL 2593269, at *3. The court noted that not only did the parties' contract provide that time was of the essence but also that Electro-Methods originally had wanted delivery of the parts within one month of the contract's effective date.

Thus, timely delivery of conforming goods was important to Electro-Methods. Yet, B&F took five months to cure. The court concluded that B&F's "five-month delay in correcting its breach [was] not 'substitution in a further reasonable time.' " *Id.* at *4. Therefore, it held that B&F had breached the parties' contract and ruled in favor of Electro-Methods.

4. REVOCATION OF ACCEPTANCE: § 2–608

A buyer can no longer reject goods after having accepted them. "Acceptance of goods by the buyer precludes rejection of the goods accepted." UCC § 2–607(2). In certain circumstances, however, the buyer may revoke its acceptance of the goods.

> The buyer may revoke his acceptance of a lot or commercial unit whose non-conformity substantially impairs its value to him if he has accepted it
>
> (a) on the reasonable assumption that its non-conformity would be cured and it has not been seasonably cured; or
>
> (b) without discovery of such non-conformity if his acceptance was reasonably induced either by the difficulty of discovery before acceptance or by the seller's assurances.

UCC § 2–608(1). The buyer must revoke its acceptance within a reasonable time after the buyer discovers or should have discovered the basis for revocation. UCC § 2–608(2). A buyer cannot revoke its acceptance if "any substantial change in condition of the goods . . . not caused by their own defects" has occurred. *Id.* Finally, revocation is "not effective until the buyer notifies the seller" of the revocation. *Id.*

Thus, in order to revoke acceptance, the buyer must satisfy all of the following requirements.

1. The nonconformity must ***substantially impair*** the value of the good to the buyer;

2. The buyer must have accepted the good under ***one of three*** conditions:

   a. the buyer reasonably assumed the seller would cure the nonconformity, but the nonconformity has not been seasonably cured; *or*

   b. the buyer did not discover the nonconformity prior to acceptance due to the difficulty of discovery, e.g., a latent defect; *or*

   c. the buyer did not discover the nonconformity prior to acceptance because the seller's assurances induced the buyer to delay in discovering the nonconformity;

3. The buyer must ***revoke within a reasonable time*** of discovering the nonconformity or within a reasonable time of when it *should* have discovered the nonconformity;

4. The buyer must ***revoke before there has been a substantial change*** in the good, but the buyer may revoke if a substantial

change has occurred due to defects in the good itself; *and*

5. The buyer must ***notify the seller*** that it is revoking acceptance of the good.

a. Substantial Impairment

With one important exception, the analysis of substantial impairment under § 2–608 is similar to that for installment contracts under § 2–612. *See* § A.1.a of this Chapter. Unlike § 2–612, however, § 2–608 provides that the non-conformity must substantially impair the value of the good *to the buyer*. This language suggests a subjective test. *See, e.g.,* Barry & Sewall Industrial Supply Co. v. Metal-Prep of Houston, Inc., 912 F.2d 252 (8th Cir. 1990) (comparing revocation with breach of warranty and noting that for revocation "the U.C.C. engages a more subjective standard: revocation may be sought for goods whose nonconformity substantially impairs the value to the buyer"); Herring v. Home Depot, Inc., 565 S.E.2d 773 (S.C. Ct. App. 2002) (stating that substantial impairment test for revocation is subjective).

A majority of courts, however, use a combined subjective-objective test. 4 Anderson U.C.C. § 2–608:140 (3d ed.) (stating that the " 'subjective-objective' test [ ] is the prevailing rule"). Courts articulate this test in different ways. For example, in Tibbets v. Riverside Motorcars, LLC, 2007 WL 2938315 (Conn. Super. Ct. 2007), the court explained that " '[t]he test for substantial impairment is both subjective and objective.' " *Id.* at *25. The subjective portion of the test focuses " 'on the needs and circumstances of the particular buyer' " while the objective piece considers whether " 'the value of the goods to the buyer has in fact been impaired.' " *Id.* In Hardy v. Winnebago Industries, 706 A.2d 1086 (Md. Ct. Spec. App. 1996), the court explained that substantial impairment "necessarily involves consideration of subjective factors, i.e., the particular needs and circumstances of the individual buyer." *Id.* at 1092. Nonetheless, more is required "than the buyer's subjective assertion that the value of the product to him was impaired." *Id.* What more? The buyer must present "evidence from which the trier of fact, applying objective standards, can infer that the needs of the buyer were not met because of the nonconformity." *Id.*

What the *Tibbetts* and *Hardy* courts describe does not make sense. A subjective test, as provided for by § 2–608, would look at the buyer's needs and circumstances and decide whether the nonconformity in the good substantially impairs its value to the buyer, considering the buyer's needs and circumstances. How exactly does a court determine substantial impairment on an *objective* basis if its initial focus is on the needs and circumstances of the particular buyer? Is the court saying that the analysis moves from the particular buyer to buyers in general? If that is the case, then, the court is *not* taking into consideration the needs and circumstances of the particular buyer but rather is deciding substantial impairment on the basis of a reasonable buyer's needs and circumstances. Interestingly enough, the *Tibbets* court, while stating that the test contains both subjective and objective elements, nonetheless made its substantial impairment determination on the basis of the buyer's credible testimony and his reason for entering into the transaction—in other words, a subjective analysis.

After articulating the subjective-objective test, the court in Leshine Carton Co. v. Matik of North America, 2008 WL 5252908 (Conn. Super. Ct. 2008), explained that White & Summers consider the test to be "goofy."

> "The cases seem to require both subjective and objective elements. The buyer must provide objective evidence that the value of the goods was substantially impaired, but this value is to be viewed through the unique needs and circumstances of that particular buyer and not those of the average buyer. However, we dress it, this concept looks goofy. How can something be objective, and, at the same time, subjective? Perhaps the courts are asking us to listen to *this* buyer's complaint—but not too closely."

Id. at *37 (quoting 1 White & Summers, Uniform Commercial Code § 8–4, p. 367 (5th ed.) (emphasis in original). The *Leshine* court noted that this observation by White & Summers is "disheartening" for the jury or judge that must render a decision on substantial impairment.

b. Acceptance and Discovery of the Non-Conformity

A buyer may revoke acceptance of goods even if the buyer knew of the non-conformity at the time of acceptance if the buyer reasonably assumed that the seller would cure but has failed to do so. UCC § 2–608(1)(a). For example, in Vemex Trading Corp. v. Technology Ventures, Inc., 2011 WL 3270841 (S.D. Tex. 2011), Vemex, the buyer, purchased equipment that it discovered during the installation process was missing parts and did not function properly. Vemex notified Technology Ventures (TV), the seller, of the defects with the equipment. Even though TV assured Vemex that it would cure the defects during installation, TV failed to cure. The court held that while Vemex had accepted the equipment, it had done so "on the reasonable assumption that the non-conformity would be seasonably cured." *Id.* at *7. Because Vemex satisfied the other requirements of § 2–608, the court held that Vemex had "effectively and timely revoked its acceptance" of the equipment. *Id.*

The other two bases for revoking acceptance of goods involve situations in which the buyer accepts the goods without discovering that they are nonconforming. The first involves the buyer who accepts the goods without discovering their non-conformity due to the difficulty of discovery. UCC § 2–608(1)(b). Not all defects manifest themselves upon inspection. If goods have a latent defect, the buyer, notwithstanding a thorough inspection, may be unable to discover the non-conformity. In such a situation, if the buyer satisfies the other requirements of § 2–608, she may be able to revoke acceptance of the goods because of the difficulty of discovering the defect prior to acceptance.

Finally, the buyer may accept goods without discovering their defects because acceptance was reasonably induced by the seller's assurances. UCC § 2–608(1)(b). In Steel Bar Service, Inc. v. Connors Steel Co., 1979 WL 208144 (Ohio Ct. App. 1979), Connors entered into a contract to sell to Steel Bar 100 tons of 1.5" round steel with carbon content of "35 and under". Connors delivered the steel, which Steel Bar rejected because it was "tagged '35 carbon and over.' " This initial delivery was returned to Connors, which then sent another shipment of steel to Steel Bar. Steel Bar accepted that shipment. Steel Bar did not test the carbon content of this replacement shipment, apparently relying on the tagging of the steel by Connors. Steel Bar later discovered that much of the replacement delivery had a carbon content above 35. The court explained that Steel Bar had relied on Connors' assurances in the form of the carbon content tags. The court found that such reliance was reasonable because Connors had "accepted the first steel shipment rejection based solely upon the carbon content tags." *Id.* at **3–4. The court concluded that the case "typifie[d] the situation where a buyer delays discovery based on a seller's assurances." *Id.* Because Steel Bar satisfied all of the requirements for revocation of acceptance, the Ohio Court of Appeals reversed the trial court's judgment in favor of Connors.

c. Substantial Change in Condition of the Goods

The buyer must revoke its acceptance of the goods prior to "any substantial change in condition of the goods which is not caused by their own defects." UCC § 2–608(2). A substantial change, however, may affect the value of the goods either positively or negatively. The Official Comment focuses on a negative change in condition. "[T]he buyer may not revoke his acceptance if the goods have materially deteriorated except by reason of their own defects." UCC § 2–608, Comment ¶ 6.

The court in Village Mobile Homes, Inc. v. Porter, 716 S.W.2d 543 (tex. Ct. App. 1986), relying on the Official Comment, interpreted § 2–608's "substantial change" language to mean a negative or detrimental change in the condition of the goods. In *Village Homes,* Terry Porter, the buyer, purchased a mobile home from the seller Village Homes. While living in the mobile home, Porter noticed that the exterior paint was cracking and peeling. To protect the exterior of the home, she painted it. There were several other problems with the mobile home, the most significant being defects in title to the home. Porter subsequently revoked her acceptance of the mobile home based on the title defects. Village Homes argued that Porter could not revoke her acceptance because she had substantially changed the home prior to her revocation by painting its exterior. The Texas Court of Appeals rejected the seller's argument. The court explained that the purpose of the "substantial change" requirement is to "protect the seller from changes which deteriorate or take away from the value of the goods sold." *Id.* at 552. As the trial court jury found, painting the exterior of the mobile home had increased its value by $1,000. Because painting the exterior had improved, rather than damaged, the value of the mobile home, the court rejected Village Homes' argument that Porter was ineligible to revoke acceptance of the home.

The interpretation of § 2–608's "substantial change" language to mean a change to the goods that reduces their value to the seller makes sense. This interpretation is consistent with the intent to do "substantial justice in regard to the condition of the goods restored to the seller." UCC § 2–608, Comment ¶ 6. After all, if a change made by the buyer to a good has no effect on value or increases the good's value, the seller is not harmed.

d. Right to Cure?

Recall that § 2–608(1)(a) applies to situations in which the buyer knows of the non-conformity but accepts the goods based on the reasonable assumption that the seller will cure. What about the case in which the buyer revokes its acceptance of the goods based on a non-conformity discovered after acceptance? UCC § 2–608(1)(b). Does the seller have a right to cure in such a case?

A majority of courts have held that the seller has no right to cure. *See, e.g.,* Car Transportation Brokerage Co. v. Blue Bird Body Co., 322 F. App'x 891 (11th Cir. 2009) (while not deciding the issue, stating that where the buyer accepts goods "as described in UCC § 2–608(1)(b), the majority rule is that he may revoke the acceptance without waiting for a cure, seasonable or otherwise, by the seller"); Economy Folding Box Corp. v. Anchor Frozen Foods, Corp., 2007 WL 844878 (N.D. Ill. 2007) (holding that "Illinois courts would find that a right to cure does not exist when the revocation is based on a subsequently discovered defect"), *aff'd* 515 F.3d 718 (7th Cir. 2008); Johannsen v. Minnesota Valley Ford Tractor Co., 304 N.W.2d 654 (Minn. 1981) (holding that "the seller has no right to cure defects which substantially impair the good's value"). The reason for the majority rule lies in the language of § 2–508, which gives the seller the right to cure when the buyer *rejects* the goods. Section 2–508 fails to mention revocation of acceptance. Thus, based on the "plain text" of § 2–508, the court in CB Aviation, LLC v. Hawker Beechcraft Corp., 2011 U.S. Dist. LEXIS 128988 (E.D. Penn. 2011), concluded that under Kansas law the seller "only has a right to cure when the buyer rejects delivery."

A small minority of courts, however, has concluded that § 2–608(3) provides the seller with the right to cure prior to the buyer's revocation of acceptance of the goods. Section 2–608(3) provides that the buyer "has the same rights and duties with regard to the goods involved as if he had rejected them." UCC § 2–608(3). The contention is that allowing the seller to cure is one such duty of the buyer. Thus, the revoking buyer, like the rejecting buyer, must afford the seller the opportunity to cure in certain circumstances. *See, e.g.*, David Tunick, Inc. v. Kornfeld, 838 F. Supp. 848

(S.D. N.Y. 1993) (explaining that under New York law, "[o]ne duty imposed upon the buyer" under § 2–608(3) is to provide the seller with the chance to cure, but ultimately holding that cure was not possible in the particular case); Fitzner Pontiac-Buick-Cadillac, Inc. v. Smith, 523 So. 2d 324 (Miss. 1988) (stating in a footnote that "[t]he law's policy of minimization of economic waste strongly supports recognition of a reasonable opportunity for cure" in the case of a revoking buyer).

For a flowchart of the buyer's and seller's basic performance obligations in a contract that is *not* an installment contract, *see* Flowchart #4: Performance.

FLOWCHART #4: PERFORMANCE

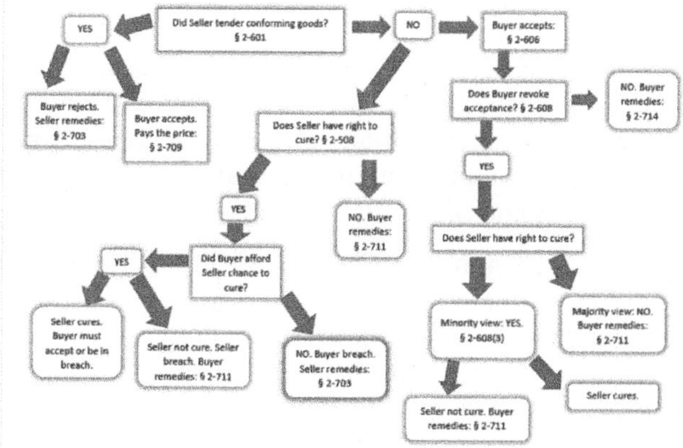

5. RISK OF LOSS: § 2–509 AND § 2–510

Risk of loss rules determine which party—buyer or seller—bears the loss of goods that are damaged, destroyed, or stolen after contract formation but prior to the buyer taking possession of the goods. When analyzing a risk-of-loss problem, make sure that you understand the relationship among risk of loss, breach of contract, and excuse.

The fact that a party has the risk of loss does *not* mean that the party is in breach of contract. In fact, Article 2 has different risk-of-loss rules for cases involving no breach of contract versus cases involving breach by the buyer or seller. *Compare* UCC § 2–509 *with* UCC § 2–510. An example should make clear the distinction. Suppose Acme Company makes a valid, enforceable contract with Road Runner, Inc. (RRI) to sell RRI 100 anvils. The contract provides for delivery to RRI's business via Beep, Inc. (BBI), a third-party carrier neither owned nor operated by Acme. While Acme has the risk of loss the 100 anvils are destroyed. Destruction of the anvils does not put Acme in breach of contract. But, because Acme has the risk of loss, it still must deliver 100 anvils to RRI. If Acme fails to do so, claiming that the goods were destroyed, Acme *then* will be in breach of contract.

The breach analysis changes if the seller makes out a case for excuse of performance. Suppose Newman makes a valid, enforceable contract with Costanza for the purchase and sale of a car previously owned by the actor Jon Voight. While Newman has the risk of loss the car is destroyed through no fault of Newman or Costanza. Because the contract called for the sale of one particular vehicle for which there is no replacement, Newman's performance under the contract is excused and his failure to deliver the Voight car to Costanza is not a breach of contract. *See* UCC § 2–613.

When tackling a risk-of-loss problem, ask yourself the following question: Has either the buyer or the seller breached the contract? If your answer is "no" to this question, then proceed to § 2–509. If the answer is "yes," then use the rules at § 2–510.

a. § 2–509: Risk of Loss in the Absence of Breach

If neither buyer nor seller has breached the contract, then § 2–509 provides default rules for determining which party has the risk of loss. The parties always may allocate the risk of loss as they see fit in their contract. *See* UCC § 2–509(4) (stating that § 2–509's provisions "are subject to contrary agreement of the parties"). If the parties' contract does not allocate the risk of loss, then § 2–509 applies. It covers four situations: (1) a contract that requires or authorizes shipment of the goods by a third-party carrier (§ 2–509(1)); (2) a contract in which the goods held by a bailee are to be delivered without being moved (§ 2–509(2)); (3) any contract not covered by § 2–509(1) or (2); and (4) a sale on approval (§ 2–509(4)).

1) Third-Party Carrier: § 2–509(1)

Before embarking on a discussion of § 2–509(1), a brief digression to explain relevant terms is in order. Notice that the heading of this section of the Nutshell says: "third-party carrier." A third-party carrier is a company *other than the seller* that transports goods, for example by truck. Section 2–509(1) applies when the goods are to be transported by third-party carrier, not by the seller's own vehicles. *See* UCC § 2–206, Comment ¶ 2 (stating that the word "shipment" in § 2–206 is "used in the same sense as in Section 2–504; it does not include the beginning of delivery by the seller's own truck"); 2 Hawkland UCC Series § 2–509:3.

The parties' contract may contain abbreviations such as F.O.B. or F.A.S. The abbreviation "F.O.B." means "free on board." UCC § 2–319(1). The abbreviation "F.A.S." means "free alongside". UCC § 2–319(2). The meaning of other abbreviations, such as C.I.F. or C.F., can be found at § 2–320.

Risk of loss rules involving a contract to ship the goods require you to determine whether the contract is a *shipment* or a *destination* contract. The following example illustrates how to analyze a contract that falls within the language of § 2–509(1). Recall the contract described above between Acme and RRI for the purchase and sale of 100 anvils. Acme's plant is located in Gary, Indiana, while RRI's store is in Grand Rapids, Michigan. The parties' contract provides that the anvils will be sent "F.O.B. Gary." Acme hires Beep, Inc. (BBI), a reputable trucking firm, to deliver the anvils.

The term "F.O.B. Gary" means that this is a shipment contract. To decide whether you have a shipment or a destination contract, look at what follows the abbreviations "F.O.B." or "F.A.S." If what follows is the seller's location, e.g., the seller's business, plant, or city, then it is a shipment contract.

That means that the seller "bear[s] the expense and risk of putting [the anvils] into the possession of the carrier." UCC § 2–319(1)(a). Thus, in a shipment contract, "the risk of loss passes to the buyer when the goods are duly delivered to the carrier." UCC § 2–509(1)(a). Therefore, in our example, if the anvils are destroyed on the way to Grand Rapids, then RRI has the risk of loss. RRI must pay the price for the destroyed anvils even though those anvils never arrived in Grand Rapids. *See* UCC § 2–709(1)(a); *see also infra* Chapter 11, § B.1.d.

Of course, the seller must make a reasonable contract for transportation of the goods. *See* UCC § 2–504(a). Thus, a contract to ship frozen goods across several states in non-refrigerated trucks is not a reasonable contract for carriage. The seller also must provide to the buyer any documents that the buyer needs to take possession of the goods, and the seller must "promptly notify the buyer of the shipment." UCC § 2–504(b), (c). One purpose of notification is to ensure that the buyer has in place insurance coverage for the goods while in transit.

What happens if there is no "F.O.B." or "F.A.S." term, but the contract requires delivery by carrier? The contract is a shipment contract.

> [T]he "shipment" contract is regarded as the normal one and the "destination" contract as the variant type. The seller is not obligated to deliver at a named destination and bear the concurrent risk of loss until arrival, unless he has specifically agreed so to deliver or the

> commercial understanding of the terms used by the parties contemplates such delivery.

UCC § 2–503, Comment ¶ 5. Be careful! The mere fact that the parties' agreement provides for delivery to the buyer's business does *not* make the contract a destination contract. After all, the delivery must go somewhere. What is critical is whether the seller's or the buyer's location, e.g., plant, business, city, follows the term "F.O.B." or "F.A.S."

Now, suppose Acme and RRI make the same contract for delivery of 100 anvils, but the contract provides for delivery "F.O.B. Grand Rapids." The contract now is a destination contract because Grand Rapids is the buyer RRI's city. When the parties' contract requires the seller to deliver to a particular destination and the goods are "there duly tendered while in the possession of the carrier, the risk of loss passes to the buyer when the goods are there duly so tendered as to enable the buyer to take delivery." UCC § 2–509(1)(b); *see* § 2–319(1)(b) (stating that in a destination contract "the seller must at his own expense and risk transport the goods" to the destination and tender delivery of the goods as provided in § 2–503). To tender delivery, the seller must "put and hold conforming goods at the buyer's disposition and give the buyer any notification reasonably necessary to enable him to take delivery." UCC § 2–503(1). In our example, if the anvils are destroyed in transit to Grand Rapids, then Acme has the risk of loss. The risk of loss did not pass to RRI because the goods were not duly tendered to RRI in Grand Rapids. Therefore, even though the goods were destroyed, Acme must tender another delivery of 100 anvils to RRI or be in breach of contract.

Notice that § 2–319(1)(a) and (b) speak in terms of which party bears both the risk of loss and the expense of transporting the goods. Section 2–319(1)(a) provides that in a shipment contract, the seller bears the cost of putting the goods into the carrier's possession. In a destination contract, the seller bears the cost of transporting the goods to the destination. UCC § 2–319(1)(b). While the cost of transport is not relevant to this discussion on risk of loss, it is important for any discussion of damages. *See infra* Chapter 11.

2) *Bailment: § 2–509(2)*

If the parties' agreement provides "for delivery of the goods . . . without removal from the physical possession of a bailee," then § 2–509(2) provides the rules for when risk of loss passes from seller to buyer. UCC § 2–509, Comment ¶ 4. The rules at § 2–509(2) "parallel the seller's tender of delivery obligation stated in Section 2–503(4)." 2 Hawkland UCC Series § 2–509:3.

Courts generally reject arguments by the seller that § 2–509(2) provides the risk-of-loss rules when the seller holds goods for the buyer. *See, e.g.,* Silver v. Wycombe, Meyer & Co., Inc, 124 Misc.2d 717 (N.Y. Civ. Ct. 1984) (concluding that seller's argument that § 2–509(2) controlled risk of loss on furniture that buyer asked seller to hold at its plant was "entirely without merit"); Conway v. Larsen Jewelers, Inc., 104 Misc.2d 872 (N.Y. Civ. Ct. 1980) (finding that

§ 2–509(3), not § 2–509(2), applied to risk of loss of a necklace purchased by buyer on "lay away" and stolen from seller's jewelry store, noting that parties "did not have a true bailor-bailee relationship"). In other words, for purposes of the rules at § 2–509(2), the bailee is not the seller, but a third party, e.g., a warehouseman, with physical possession of the goods who "continue[s] to hold them after consummation of the sale." *Silver,* 124 Misc. 2d at 719.

Section 2–509(2) provides three rules for when the risk of loss passes to the buyer in a case involving a bailee. In a case in which a bailee holds the goods and delivery occurs without moving the goods, the risk of loss passes to the buyer when one of the following events occurs: (1) the buyer receives "a negotiable document of title covering the goods"; (2) the bailee acknowledges "the buyer's right to possession of the goods"; or (3) the buyer receives a "non-negotiable document of title or other written direction" to the bailee to deliver the goods. UCC § 2–509(2); *see* § 2–503(4).

Section 2–509(2)(b) does not make clear whether the bailee's acknowledgment must be to the *buyer*. The text says merely "on acknowledgment by the bailee." But in Jason's Foods, Inc. v. Peter Eckrich & Sons, Inc. 774 F.2d 214 (7th Cir. 1985), the Seventh Circuit held that the bailee's acknowledgment must be to the buyer. Jason's Foods, the seller, made a contract to sell 38,000 pounds of pork ribs to Eckrich & Sons with delivery to occur by a transfer of the ribs from seller's account in an independent warehouse to Eckrich's account in that same warehouse. Jason's

Foods notified Eckrich that the transfer would occur between January 10 and January 14; Jason's notified the warehouse on January 13 to transfer the ribs to Eckrich's account. The warehouse clerk noted the transfer on the warehouse's books but failed to timely make an acknowledgment to Eckrich. Eckrich received the warehouse receipt of the transfer on January 24, but a week earlier, the ribs had been destroyed in a fire. The Seventh Circuit held that the bailee's acknowledgment must be to the buyer, noting that it would be "very strange" to read the word "acknowledgment" in § 2–509(2)(b) as an acknowledgment to *the seller*. While the warehouse clerk sent Eckrich a warehouse receipt, the court explained that the acknowledgment contemplated by § 2–509(2) need not be formal or even a written receipt; it can be a phone call. The court rejected the seller's argument that the risk of loss had passed on January 13, when the transfer occurred on the warehouse books and, thus, affirmed the trial court's ruling that Jason's Foods bore the risk of loss.

3) Residuary Clause: § 2–509(3)

If the parties' contract does not fit within either the carrier or bailment scenarios under § 2–509(1) or § 2–509(2), respectively, then § 2–509(3) provides the rule on risk of loss. The rule differs based on the status of the seller. If the seller is a merchant, then the "risk of loss passes to the buyer on his receipt of the goods." UCC § 2–509(3). Article 2 defines the word "receipt" to mean "taking physical possession" of the goods. UCC § 2–103(1)(c). The Official

Comment explains why the merchant seller retains the risk of loss until the buyer takes possession.

> The underlying theory of this rule is that a merchant who is to make physical delivery at his own place continues meanwhile to control the goods and can be expected to insure his interest in them. The buyer, on the other hand, has no control of the goods and it is extremely unlikely that he will carry insurance on the goods not yet in his possession.

UCC § 2–509, Comment ¶ 3.

If the seller is *not* a merchant, however, the risk of losses "passes to the buyer on tender of delivery." UCC § 2–509(3). Recall that tender of delivery requires the seller to "put and hold conforming goods at the buyer's disposition and give the buyer any notification reasonably necessary to enable him to take delivery." UCC § 2–503(1).

Two examples should illustrate how the risk-of-loss rules of § 2–509(3) operate.

Suppose Stan placed an ad in the local paper to sell his used band saw and several other wood working tools for $1,200. On Thursday, Beulah stopped by to look at the tools and offered to pay $1,000. Stan accepted and wrote out a short contract that both parties signed. Beulah gave Stan $100 towards the $1,000 contract price, and the parties agreed that Beulah would return on Saturday with the rest of the cash and a pick-up truck to take the tools. Beulah did not come by on Saturday, however. She waited until the end of the following week. When she arrived at

Stan's house the next week, she discovered that a thief had stolen equipment from various homes in the neighborhood, including the tools in Stan's outdoor shed. Who has the risk of loss? Beulah. Stan tendered delivery of the tools. He kept the tools "available for the period reasonably necessary to enable the buyer to take possession." UCC § 2–503(1)(a). Two days, which is the time the parties agreed for pickup of the tools, was the "period reasonably necessary" for Beulah to take possession.

Suppose, however, that on Saturday, Beulah went to *Big Box Store* (BBS) to buy a stationery band saw. The model she wanted was not in stock, but BBS placed an order for the saw, and Beulah paid with her credit card. Two days later on Monday, BBS contacted Beulah and told her that the band saw had arrived and that she could pick it up at the store at any time during store hours. Because BBS is a merchant, the risk of loss on the band saw does not pass to Beulah until she takes possession of it.

4) Sale on Approval: § 2–509(4)

What is a sale on approval?

A "sale on approval", sometimes also called a sale "on trial" or "on satisfaction", deals with a contract under which the seller undertakes a risk in order to satisfy its prospective buyer with the appearance or performance of the goods that are sold. The goods are delivered to the proposed purchaser but they remain the property of the seller until the buyer accepts them. The price has already been agreed. The buyer's willingness to receive and test the goods is the consideration for the seller's engagement to deliver and sell.

UCC § 2–326, Comment ¶ 1. Unless the parties otherwise agree, the buyer in a sale on approval may return delivered goods, even if they conform to the contract. UCC § 2–326(1). Under a sale on approval, the risk of loss passes to the buyer upon acceptance of the goods, unless the parties agree to the contrary. UCC § 2–327(1).

Suppose Design Firm (DF), hoping to expand its business, entered into a contract with Savannah Anchor, a local newscaster, to redecorate the living area of Anchor's million-dollar home. The parties' agreement provided that the suite of furniture to be delivered and placed in Anchor's living room was on a trial or "on approval" basis. DF delivered the furniture to Anchor's home. At some point after delivery, a tornado swept through the neighborhood, destroying much of Anchor's home and the entire suite of furniture delivered by DF.

If DF sues Anchor for the price of the furniture, the court must determine whether Anchor had accepted the furniture. The mere use of the furniture by Anchor did not constitute acceptance, because "use of the goods consistent with the purpose of trial is not acceptance." UCC § 2–327(1)(b). But, if Anchor failed to seasonably notify DF that she was electing to return the furniture, then she accepted it. *See id.* If the furniture conformed to the contract, accepting any piece of furniture constituted acceptance of the entire suite of furniture delivered. *See id.* The UCC defines the word "seasonable" to mean that an action is taken "within a reasonable time" if the parties did not agree upon a specific time period. UCC § 1–205(b). If Anchor failed to seasonably notify DF that she did not approve of the furniture, then she bears the risk of loss and must pay DF the contract price. Otherwise, the risk of loss remained with DF. *See* Valley Bank & Trust Co. v. Gerber, 526 P.2d 1121 (Utah 1974) (explaining that a reasonable basis existed for determining that couple had accepted home furnishings provided on an "on approval" basis because more than two months had elapsed since delivery and the couple had not notified seller that they disapproved of the furnishings).

b. § 2–510: Effect of Breach on Risk of Loss

Section 2–510 provides the rules for risk of loss when one party to the contract, whether buyer or seller, breaches. Section 2–510(1) and (2) state the risk-of-loss rules in the case of a seller breach. Section 2–510(3) provides the rule on risk of loss when the buyer breaches the contract before the risk of loss has passed to the buyer.

1) § 2–510(1): Buyer Has Right of Rejection

The rule at § 2–510(1) applies when the seller's "tender or delivery so fails to conform to the contract as to give [the buyer] a right of rejection." In such a case, the risk of loss stays with the seller until either the seller cures or the buyer accepts the goods. UCC § 2–510(1).

Suppose Lovely Lighting, Inc. (LLI) manufactures solar lights for use in gardens and on patios. LLI's plant is located in Toledo, Ohio. The Patio Store (TPS) sells patio furniture, decorations, and a full range of outdoor lighting. TPS is located in Troy, Michigan. LLI and TPS enter into a valid, enforceable contract in which LLI agrees to sell and TPS to buy 5000 boxes of garden lights, 8 lights to a box. (Each light comes with a plastic stake that fits into the bottom of the light shaft and permits the homeowner to push the stake and, thus, the light into the ground or grass.) The parties' agreement provides that the lights would be sent "FOB LLI plant." LLI arranges for shipment with a reliable third-party carrier but when TPS inspects the boxes upon arrival, it discovers that the plastic stakes are missing from the boxes. TPS contacts LLI to say that it is rejecting the shipment. LLI immediately sends a replacement shipment. The entire original shipment is destroyed in an accident on the return trip from TPS to LLI's plant. LLI has the risk of loss on that shipment.

Had the goods conformed to the contract, risk of loss would have passed to TPS when the boxes were loaded onto the carrier because this was a shipment contract. But LLI "cannot shift the risk of loss to the buyer unless his action conforms with all the conditions resting on him under the contract." UCC § 2–510, Comment ¶ 1.

Moreover, the fact that LLI cured by sending a replacement shipment does *not* mean that the risk of loss for the original nonconforming shipment rests with TPS. The drafters intended the word "cure" in § 2–510(1) to have a more limited meaning.

> The "cure" of defective tenders contemplated by subsection (1) applies only to those situations in which the seller makes changes in goods already tendered, such as repair, partial substitution, sorting out from an improper mixture and the like since "cure" by repossession and new tender has no effect on the risk of loss of the goods originally tendered.

UCC § 2–510, Comment ¶ 2. In our example, the cure is repossession and new tender, which has no effect on the risk of loss, which remains on the seller during transit back to LLI's plant after rejection.

It is important to recognize that you measure whether the goods conform to the contract at the point of tender. In a shipment contract, tender occurs at the time that the goods are loaded onto the carrier. If tender occurred when the goods arrived at the buyer's place of business, then any damage to the goods during transit would render the tender imperfect. In other words, all shipment contracts involving non-conforming goods would become destination contracts. Therefore, make sure that you correctly identify the point at which tender of delivery occurs.

2) § 2–510(2): Buyer Revokes Acceptance

What if the buyer accepts the goods and subsequently revokes her acceptance under § 2–608?

If the goods are destroyed, which party bears the risk of loss?

> Where the buyer rightfully revokes acceptance, he may to the extent of any deficiency in his effective insurance coverage treat the risk of loss as having rested on the seller from the beginning.

UCC § 2–510(2). Note that unlike § 2–510(1), which speaks in terms of "a right of rejection", § 2–510(2) states that the buyer has rightfully revoked acceptance. In other words, § 2–510(2) is limited to cases in which the buyer actually revokes acceptance, and that revocation is rightful under § 2–608. In addition, the risk of loss rests on the seller to the extent that the buyer's insurance does not cover the entire loss.

For example, suppose Sampson Company makes a contract to sell a machine to Benson Corporation "FOB Sampson's Factory." Sampson delivers the machine, which has a latent defect that substantially impairs its value to Benson. *See* UCC § 2–608. The machine malfunctions after several weeks. Benson contacts Sampson and revokes its acceptance of the machine. Before Sampson picks up the machine, it is destroyed in a fire at Benson's plant. If Benson has insurance on the machine with a $1,000 deductible, then Sampson must pay the $1,000.

3) § 2–510(3): Buyer Repudiates or Otherwise Is in Breach

Section 2–510(3) provides the rule on risk of loss when the buyer is in breach.

> Where the buyer as to conforming goods already identified to the contract for sale repudiates or is otherwise in breach before risk of their loss has passed to him, the seller may to the extent of any deficiency in his effective insurance coverage treat the risk of loss as resting on the buyer for a commercially reasonable time.

UCC § 2–510(3). Notice that like subsection (2), subsection (3) speaks in terms of a deficiency in insurance coverage. The reason is that § 2–510(3) covers situations in which the seller is in control of the goods; therefore, the seller is likely to have insurance covering those goods.

> In cases where there has been a breach of the contract, if the one in control of the goods is the aggrieved party, whatever loss or damage may prove to be uncovered by his insurance falls upon the contract breaker under subsections (2) and (3) rather than upon him.

UCC § 2–510, Comment ¶ 3. For example, if the parties have a shipment contract and the buyer breaches before the seller loads the goods on the carrier, the risk of loss will not have passed to the buyer. The seller, who is the aggrieve party, will retain and be in control of the goods. If the goods are damaged or destroyed, then the seller's insurance carrier will pay for the loss. But if the seller's insurance does not completely cover the loss, then the buyer will have the risk of loss as to the deficiency for a commercially reasonable time.

The reason for the phrase "commercially reasonable time" is to avoid having the buyer become an indefinite backstop to the seller's insurance coverage. For example, in the example above, suppose the contract provided for delivery of the goods no later than June 2. Seller intended to deliver the goods to the carrier on May 28, but Buyer contacted Seller and breached on May 26. If the goods are destroyed in a fire at Seller's plant on May 29, then Buyer is responsible for any deficiency in Seller's insurance coverage. But what if Seller does not resell the goods and they are destroyed in a fire at Seller's plant in early August? Section 2–510(3)'s language makes clear that Buyer is not indefinitely on the hook for any deficiency in Seller's insurance coverage.

6. EXCUSE: § 2–613 THROUGH § 2–616

A seller or buyer that can establish an excuse for non-performance of its contractual obligations is not in breach of contract. Instead, the contract is avoided. The UCC contains two sections that provide for contract avoidance based on excuse: §§ 2–613 and 2–615. Section 2–613 is similar, although not identical, to the common law doctrine of impossibility that excused contractual performance when unique goods were destroyed. Section 2–615 expands the common law impossibility doctrine to cover cases in which performance has become impracticable.

Section 2–614, sandwiched between §§ 2–613 and § 2–615, does not provide for contract avoidance. Instead, it excuses only contractual obligations considered incidental to the primary obligation to tender and pay for goods. Section 2–614 provides that when the contractually agreed facilities, methods of delivery, or type of carrier fail or become commercially impracticable an available commercially reasonable alternative must be tendered and accepted.

Make sure you distinguish between the UCC's excuse provisions and its risk-of-loss provisions when evaluating a legal problem. Both sets of provisions deal with situations in which goods are damaged, lost, or destroyed. But under § 2–613 or § 2–615, the contract is avoided; therefore, the failure to perform does not constitute a breach of contract. By comparison, a party with the risk of loss must perform or be in breach. For example, suppose Buyer and Seller contract for the purchase and sale of widgets. While Seller has the risk of loss, the widgets are destroyed. If Seller cannot satisfy the requirements of § 2–613 or § 2–615, then Seller must tender conforming widgets to Buyer, notwithstanding the destruction of the original order of widgets. If Seller fails to do so, Buyer may sue Seller for breach of contract.

a. Casualty to the Goods: § 2–613

In order for § 2–613 to apply, the parties' contract must "require[ ] for its performance goods identified when the contract is made, and the goods suffer casualty without fault of either party before the risk of loss passes to the buyer." UCC § 2–613. If the loss of the goods is total, then the "contract is avoided." UCC § 2–613(a). In other words, the failure to perform is excused and there is no breach.

If the loss is partial, the buyer has two options. The buyer may treat the contract as avoided with the same result as if the loss of the goods was total. Or the buyer may accept the goods with an offset to the purchase price but with no "further rights against the seller." UCC § 2–613(b). While § 2–613's language is not limited to the "seller," as is that of § 2–615, nonetheless it typically is the seller that invokes § 2–613 to avoid its performance obligations under the contract.

There are several important points to keep in mind. First, § 2–613 applies regardless of *when* the goods are damaged or destroyed so long as its other requirements are satisfied. For example, if the goods already were destroyed when the parties entered into their contract, § 2–613 applies so long as neither party knew of the goods' destruction. UCC § 2–613, Comment ¶ 2. *Compare* mutual mistake (event at time of contract formation) *with* impracticability (supervening event).

Second, § 2–613 only applies "where the continuing existence of identified goods is a presupposition of the agreement." Colley v. Bi-State, 586 P.2d 908 (Wash. Ct. App. 1978). If the good is unique, e.g., a Matisse painting, then § 2–613 applies. But § 2–613 does not require that the good be unique. *See* 2 Hawkland UCC Series § 2–613:1. Nonetheless, "with respect to fungible goods more than just an identification in a sales contract by kind and amount is necessary to come within the meaning of the section." Valley Forge Flag Co. v. New York Dowel & Moulding Import Co., 395 N.Y.S.2d 138 (N.Y. Civ. Ct. 1977). The reason for requiring more than the "kind and amount" of the good is to prevent the seller from using § 2–613 to excuse its performance in contracts for ordinary goods that the seller could replace on the open market.

For example, in *Valley Forge,* the parties entered into a contract for the purchase and sale of 130,000 Ramin dowels. The dowels were destroyed on board a ship in transit during a heavy storm while the seller still had the risk of loss. Seller failed to deliver. Buyer covered on the open market and then sued Seller for the difference between the contract and the cover price. *See infra* Chapter 11, § C.1.a on cover damages. Seller claimed that it was excused from delivery under § 2–613 because the goods were totally destroyed. The court disagreed. It noted that the dowels were fungible. "A dowel is a round wooden rod or stick and interchangeable. Nor is a particular type of wood required." *Valley Forge*, 395 N.Y.S.2d. at 139. Moreover, the seller admitted that it could have replaced the destroyed shipment by buying more dowels on the open market. Nothing indicated that *only* the destroyed dowels were required for contract performance. Therefore, the court held that § 2–613 did not apply and awarded buyer its damages for cover.

In Clark v. Wallace County Cooperative Equity Exchange, 986 P.2d 391 (Kan. Ct. App. 1999), Clark entered into a contract to sell 4,000 bushels of corn to the Equity Exchange. A fall freeze damaged the corn crop and Clark delivered only 2,207 bushels, claiming that he was excused under § 2–613 from delivering the remaining bushels due to the freeze. The court rejected Clark's argument and concluded that § 2–613 did not apply "because the goods were not identified at the time the contract was made." *Id.* at 393. While "there may have been corn planted somewhere in Kansas" at the time of contract formation, the contract did not require corn from any particular land or grower. The court held that § 2–613 does not excuse a grain seller from performing under a contract "when the grain is not identified by a specific tract of land on which it is to be grown." *Id.*; *see also* Bende and Sons, Inc. v. Crown Recreation, Inc., 548 F. Supp. 1018 (E.D. N.Y. 1982) (seller not excused from delivering combat boots destroyed in train derailment because the particular boots destroyed were not specified in the contract and "any combat boots would have fit the general description outlined in the purchase orders").

Third, "without fault of either party" includes not only willful wrongs, but also negligence. UCC § 2–613, Comment ¶ 1.

Fourth, if the buyer has the risk of loss when the goods are damaged or destroyed, then the damage or destruction of the goods is a matter for the buyer's insurance carrier. Section 2–613 does not apply. *See* UCC § 2–613, Comment ¶ 2 (stating that where risk of loss "has passed to the buyer before the casualty, [§ 2–613] has no application"). For example, suppose the parties enter into a contract for the purchase and sale of widgets. The contract provides for delivery "FOB Seller's Plant." If the goods were conforming and are destroyed in transit, the buyer has the risk of loss. *See* UCC § 2–509(1)(a); *see supra* § A.5.a.1 of this Chapter. The buyer is not excused from performance; buyer must pay the seller the contract price for the goods. *See* § 2–709(1)(a); *see also infra* Chapter 11, § B.1.d. (action for the price).

Finally, bear in mind that there is some overlap between § 2–613 and § 2–615. Therefore, a seller seeking to avoid the contract may argue both § 2–613 and § 2–615 as grounds for excusing its performance under the contract. *See, e.g., Clark, supra* (rejecting seller's claim that his obligation to deliver 4,000 bushels of corn was excused under § 2–613 and § 2–615); *Colley, supra* (rejecting seller's arguments under both § 2–613 and § 2–615 that weather conditions excused his contractual obligations to deliver 20,000 of 25,000 bushels of wheat promised under the parties' contracts).

b. Substituted Performance: § 2–614

Section 2–614 addresses both failure of agreed facilities, carriers, and manner of delivery of goods, *and* failure of an agreed means or manner of payment for goods. Subsection (1) covers three situations: (1)

failure of "agreed berthing, loading, or unloading facilities"; (2) unavailability of "an agreed type of carrier"; and (3) commercial impracticability of "the agreed manner of delivery." UCC § 2–614(1). If any of these three situations arises and a "commercially reasonable substitute is available," then that "substitute performance must be tendered and accepted." Subsection (1)'s rule applies only if neither party is at fault for the failure.

Subsection (2) provides that if domestic or foreign regulation results in the failure of the "agreed means or manner of payment," then the seller may "withhold or stop delivery unless the buyer provides a means or manner of payment which is commercially a substantial equivalent." UCC § 2–614(2). In a case in which the buyer already has taken delivery of the goods, the buyer may pay "by the means or in the manner provided by the regulation unless the regulation is discriminatory, oppressive or predatory." UCC § 2–614(2). Section 2–614(2) "deals with instances in international trade where a buyer cannot make payment in seller's currency as a result of some governmental regulation." R.C. Craig, Ltd. v. Ships of the Sea, Ltd., 401 F. Supp. 1051 (S.D. Ga. 1975). For example, if the parties' contract required "payment in gold specie and the government subsequently forb[ade] payment in gold," then § 2–614(2) would apply. Eastern Air Lines, Inc. v. Gulf Oil Corp., 415 F. Supp. 429 (S.D. Fla. 1975) (example drawn from case). The payment failure must result from operation of a government regulation. *See* Allied Plywood Corp. v. Western Pulp, 1994 WL 88234 (S.D. N.Y. 1994) (stating that

§ 2–614(2) did not apply to the failure of payment arrangements between contracting parties because those arrangements did not "unravel[ ] due to any government regulation").

It is important to recognize that § 2–614 does not completely excuse performance. Instead, it allows a party that satisfies its requirements to substitute a performance different from the one agreed to in the parties' contract. The Official Comment explains that unlike § 2–613 or § 2–615, which allow contract avoidance because of the failure of a basic assumption on which the contract was formed, § 2–614 provides for substitute performance of an incidental contractual obligation.

> This section appears between Section 2–613 on casualty to identified goods and [§ 2–615] on excuse by failure of presupposed conditions, both of which deal with excuse and complete avoidance of the contract where the occurrence or non-occurrence of a contingency which was a basic assumption of the contract makes the expected performance impossible. The distinction between the present section and those sections lies in whether the failure or impossibility of performance arises in connection with an incidental matter or goes to the very heart of the agreement. . . .
>
> There must, however, be a true commercial impracticability to excuse the agreed performance and justify substituted performance. When this is the case a reasonable substituted performance tendered by either

party should excuse him from strict compliance with contract terms which do not go to the essence of the agreement.

UCC § 2–614, Comment ¶ 1.

Bear in mind that § 2–614 is a " 'gap-filler' provision that applies only in the absence of the parties' specific agreement." Virginia Power Energy Marketing v. Apache Corp., 297 S.W.3d 397 (Tex. App. 2009). In *Virginia Power,* Apache agreed to sell natural gas to Virginia Power. The parties' contract contained a force majeure clause that, among other things, excused contract performance for various acts of God, including hurricanes. When Hurricane Katrina and then Hurricane Rita hit the Gulf Coast, Apache invoked the force majeure clause to excuse delivery of natural gas to the Tennessee L-500 delivery point provided for in the parties' agreement. Virginia Power, however, argued that § 2–614 required Apache to deliver the natural gas to an alternate delivery location. The court rejected Virginia Power's argument. Section 2–614 did not apply because it could not "vary the terms of the parties' express agreement." *Id.* at 404. The parties' agreement contained a force majeure clause that excused Apache's performance. Thus, Apache was not required to deliver to an alternate location.

c. Impracticability: § 2–615

The UCC's impracticability provision excuses a seller's failure to deliver or its delay in delivering goods if the seller's agreed performance "has been made impracticable by the occurrence of a contingency the non-occurrence of which was a basic assumption on which the contract was made." UCC § 2–615(a). Section 2–615 also provides that a seller's obligation to deliver or make timely delivery of goods is not a breach of contract if performance has been rendered impracticable by "compliance in good faith with any applicable foreign or domestic governmental regulation or order whether or not it later proves to be invalid." *Id.* The seller must notify the buyer in a timely fashion of the delay in delivery or non-delivery of the goods. UCC § 2–615(c). If the impracticability affects only a part of the seller's ability to perform, the seller "must allocate production and deliveries among his customers" but may include his own requirements for the goods as well as those of "regular customers not then under contract." UCC § 2–615(b). Allocation is proper so long as it is "fair and reasonable." *Id.*

The seller, in its agreement with the buyer, may assume greater liability for non-delivery or delay in delivery than is provided for by § 2–615. *See* UCC § 2–615. In other words, the seller may agree to limit the grounds for excuse that § 2–615 otherwise would make available. *See* UCC § 2–615, Comment ¶ 8 (stating that § 2–615 is "made subject to assumption of greater liability by agreement and such agreement is to be found not only in the expressed terms of the contract but in the circumstances surrounding the contracting, in trade usage and the like").

Section 2–615, then, covers two situations. The first is when performance has become impracticable because some event that the parties assumed would not occur did occur. The second is when performance has become impracticable due to good faith compliance with a governmental regulation or order. The central question in both situations is what *impracticable* means. The UCC does not define the term.

The Official Comment provides two examples. The first involves the failure of "a particular source of supply [that] is exclusive under the agreement" or where the circumstances show that a particular source of supply was "contemplated or assumed by the parties at the time of contracting." UCC § 2–615, Comment ¶ 5. The reason to excuse the seller in a case involving failure of an agreed source of supply is that "production by an agreed source is without more a basic assumption of the contract." *Id.* For example, in the pre-Code case of Thaddeus Davids Co. v. Hoffman-La Roche Chemical Works, 178 A.D. 855 (N.Y. App. Div. 1917), the parties entered into a contract for the purchase and sale of 1120 pounds of carbolic acid. Hoffman La-Roche, the seller, canceled the contract when European governments, after the outbreak of war, placed an embargo on the export of carbolic acid. The UCC drafters cited this case as an example of how the failure of a particular source of supply may serve to excuse performance under a contract.[1]

---

[1] The court, however, did not excuse the seller's performance. The contract contained a force majeure clause that allowed for cancellation for "[c]ontingencies beyond our control, fire, strike, accidents to our works or to our stock, or change in tariff." Applying the principle of *ejusdem generis,* the court concluded that an embargo was not like the other events—all

Comment ¶ 9 provides a second example. Suppose Farmer contracts with Buyer to "sell crops to be grown on designated land." UCC § 2–615, Comment ¶ 9. If the crops are destroyed through no fault of Farmer, Farmer may argue that his obligation to deliver the crops is excused "because of the failure of a basic assumption of the contract." *Id.* Farmer also may claim excuse based on destruction of identified goods under § 2–613. *Id.*

It may be simpler to define what does *not* constitute impracticability. Swings in market price do not make out a case for impracticability. After all, the entire point of entering into a contract is to lock in a price to avoid potential swings in the price of the goods bought and sold. There are two parties to the contract; avoiding a contract because the seller must sell goods whose price has increased markedly deprives the buyer of the good bargain it struck when it contracted with the seller. While excusing the seller from performing rescues the seller from a bad bargain, it often deprives the buyer of a good bargain. Thus, increased cost *alone* does not render performance impracticable.

> Increased cost alone does not excuse performance unless the rise in cost is due to some unforeseen contingency which alters the essential nature of the performance. Neither is a rise or a collapse in the market itself a

---

beyond the seller's control—that were enumerated in the contract. The drafters cited the case as *Davis Co v. Hoffman-La Roche Chemical Works,* rather than *Thaddeus Davids Co. v. Hoffman-La Roche Chemical Works.*

> justification, for that is exactly the type of business risk which business contracts made at a fixed price are intended to cover.

UCC § 2–615, Comment ¶ 4; *see* Publicker Industries, Inc. v. Union Carbide Corp., 1975 U.S. Dist. LEXIS 14305 (E.D. Pa. 1975) (holding that seller Union Carbide did not make out a case for impracticability due to "excessive cost increases" resulting from "allegedly unprecedented Arab price hikes" and stating that the court was unaware of "any cases where something less than a 100% percent [sic] cost increase has been held to make a seller's performance 'impracticable' ").

That does not mean, however, that a seller may never use increased cost as the basis for excuse under § 2–615. But the cost increase must be truly substantial and not result from the normal risks of a changing market.

> But a severe shortage of raw materials or of supplies due to a contingency such as war, embargo, local crop failure, unforeseen shutdown of major sources of supply or the like, which either causes a marked increase in cost or altogether prevents the seller from securing supplies necessary to his performance, is within the contemplation of [§ 2–615].

UCC § 2–615, Comment ¶ 4.

Notice use of the word "unforeseen" in the quotation above. Even an extraordinary price increase, resulting from a contingency such as a shutdown of major supply sources, does not excuse performance if the parties should have foreseen the contingency and provided for it in their contract. Thus, § 2–615 does not apply

> when the contingency in question is sufficiently foreshadowed at the time of contracting to be included among the business risks which are fairly to be regarded as part of the dickered terms, either consciously or as a matter of reasonable, commercial interpretation from the circumstances.

UCC § 2–615, Comment ¶ 8. For example, in Bende and Sons, Inc. v. Crown Recreation, Inc., 548 F. Supp. 1018 (E.D. N.Y. 1982), the seller argued that its failure to deliver 11,000 pairs of combat boots was excused because the boots were destroyed in a train derailment. The district court disagreed. The court explained that § 2–615 does not provide an excuse for performance when the "contingency that eventually occurred could have been foreseen as a real possibility that would affect performance." *Id.* at 1022. The court held that because "the derailment was not unforeseeable, there [was] no excuse for non-performance under § 2–615" unless the parties' agreement provided "specific, exculpatory language" covering such a contingency. *Id.*

Keep in mind that performance also may become impracticable because the seller must comply in good faith with a foreign or domestic governmental regulation. UCC § 2–615(a). The drafters intended courts to "disregard[ ] any technical distinctions between 'law', 'regulation', 'order' and the like." UCC § 2–615, Comment ¶ 10. For example, in Ab v. Harris

Corp, 1990 U.S. Dist. LEXIS 20006 (W.D. N.Y. 1990), Harris contracted to sell radio parts to Ab, which intended to deliver those parts to Iran. In late 1985, the U.S. Customs Service seized a shipment of radio parts from Harris that were destined for sale in Iran. Harris held a valid license to export all but a small fraction of the parts. Harris learned that the seizure was at the behest of the Department of Defense, which wanted to prevent the radio parts from reaching Iran. Ultimately, Harris entered into a compromise with U.S. government officials in which Harris agreed to withdraw from the Iranian market, which, in turn, led to Harris not fulfilling its contract with Ab. Harris claimed that § 2–615 excused its performance under the contract. Harris, however, had a license to export the parts; no formal rule or regulation prohibited the sale of the radio parts to Iran. Nonetheless, the court agreed with Harris, pointing to Comment ¶ 10's language about disregarding technical distinctions between laws, regulations, orders, and the like. The court explained that Harris "was not free to disregard the Government's 'informal' prohibition on the importation of Harris products to Iran . . . notwithstanding the fact that Harris's existing export licenses would have permitted the importation of all but a very few of the ordered parts." *Ab*, 1990 U.S. Dist. LEXIS 20006, at **8–9.

Even if a court later rules that the law or regulation is invalid, the test under § 2–615 is the "seller's good faith belief in the validity of the regulation." UCC § 2–615, Comment ¶ 10. The best evidence of the seller's good faith "is the general commercial acceptance of the regulation." *Id.* But government regulation does not excuse a seller's performance "unless it truly 'supervenes' in such a manner as to be beyond the seller's assumption of risk." *Id.*

The discussion thus far has focused on the seller's use of § 2–615 to excuse its performance under the contract. Does § 2–615 apply to buyers? The text of § 2–615 seems to suggest the answer is "no." Section 2–615 begins with the following language: "Except so far as a seller may have assumed a greater obligation." UCC § 2–615. But Official Comment ¶ 9 suggests that the UCC's impracticability section is available to buyers.

> [W]here the buyer's contract is in reasonable commercial understanding conditioned on a definite and specific venture or assumption as, for instance, a war procurement subcontract known to be based on a prime contract which is subject to termination or a supply contract for a particular construction venture, the reason of the present section may well apply and entitle the buyer to the exemption.

UCC § 2–615, Comment ¶ 9. Thus, some courts have held that while the text of § 2–615 is limited to sellers, Comment ¶ 9 makes § 2–615 applicable to buyers, as well. *See* Citizens Fidelity Bank & Trust Co. v. Kentucky Utilities Company, 1991 Ky. App. LEXIS 12 (Ky. Ct. App. 1991) (agreeing with "some authorities" that § 2–615 also applies to buyer but reversing the "trial court's finding of material unforeseen events excusing [buyer's] performance of the contract")

d. What Happens After Notice of Excuse? § 2–616

The seller that cannot deliver or must deliver late due to the impracticability of performance must seasonably notify the buyer of the delay in delivery or non-delivery. UCC § 2–615(c). If the seller intends to allocate production and deliveries because only part of its performance has been rendered impracticable, the seller also must inform the buyer of the "estimated quota" that will be made available to the buyer. *Id.*

When the buyer receives the seller's notice of a "material or indefinite delay" in delivery or an "allocation justified" under § 2–615, the buyer has two basic options. These options apply to any delivery affected or in the case of an installment contract to any delivery "where the prospective deficiency substantially impairs the value of the whole contract." UCC § 2–616(1); *see* UCC § 2–612. The first option allows the buyer to "terminate and thereby discharge any unexecuted portion of the contract." UCC § 2–616(1)(b). Termination may occur by virtue of the buyer's silence upon receipt of the seller's notice. If the seller provides the required notice of excuse to the buyer and the buyer does not "modify the contract within a reasonable time not exceeding thirty days the contract lapses with respect to any deliveries affected." UCC § 2–616(2); *see* UCC § 2–616, Comment: Purposes (stating that the buyer's "silence after receiving the seller's notice of excuse operates as such a termination"). The second option available to the buyer is to "modify the contract by agreeing to take [the buyer's] available quota in substitution." UCC § 2–616(1)(b). Consideration is not needed for such a modification. *See* UCC § 2–616, Comment: Purposes.

Unless the seller has assumed a greater obligation under § 2–615, the parties may not negate by agreement the provisions of § 2–616. *See* UCC § 2–616(3).

B. LEASES

This portion of the Chapter covers those provisions of Article 2A dealing with performance of the parties' lease agreement. It covers: (1) the perfect tender rule; (2) what constitutes acceptance versus rejection of goods by the lessee, and when the lessee has the right to cure a nonconforming delivery; (3) when the lessee may revoke acceptance of goods; (4) which party bears the risk of loss for damaged or destroyed goods; (5) when performance of the lease agreement is excused; and (6) irrevocable promises in certain finance leases.

1. PERFECT TENDER: § 2A–509 AND § 2A–510

The perfect tender rule also applies to non-installment lease agreements. If the goods fail to conform to the lease contract, the lessee may "reject or accept the goods or accept any commercial unit or units and reject the rest of the goods." UCC § 2A–509(1). If the agreement is an installment lease, the perfect tender rule does not apply. Instead, the rule is the same as it is for an installment sales contract, with changes to terminology, e.g., substituting the word "delivery" for the word "installment." *Compare* UCC § 2A–510(1) *with* UCC § 2–612(2); *see supra* § A.1.a of this Chapter. An installment lease contract is a lease agreement that "authorizes or requires the delivery of goods in separate lots to be separately accepted, even though the lease contract contains a clause 'each delivery is a separate lease' or its equivalent." UCC § 2A–103(1)(i).

2. ACCEPTANCE, REJECTION, AND CURE: § 2A–509, § 2A–513, § 2A–515, AND § 2A–516

Recall that once a buyer accepts goods, it no longer can reject them. UCC § 2–607(2); *see supra* § A.2 of this Chapter. The same principle holds for a lessee under a lease agreement. "A lessee's acceptance of goods precludes rejection of the goods accepted." UCC § 2A–516(2).

What constitutes acceptance? Acceptance may occur in one of three ways: (1) the lessee signifies to the lessor that it accepts the goods, even if non-conforming; (2) the lessee's actions signify that the lessee accepts the goods, even if non-conforming; or (3) the lessee fails to make an effective rejection. *See* UCC § 2A–515(1). In each case, acceptance occurs after the lessee has had "a reasonable opportunity to inspect the goods." *Id.* The lessee cannot delay the period for acceptance by failing to inspect the goods. The language is "reasonable opportunity" not "after the lessee inspects the goods."

What constitutes an acceptance of goods by a lessee differs from what constitutes an acceptance of goods by a buyer in two respects. First, while the buyer or the lessee may signify to the seller or the lessor that they accept the goods, notwithstanding any non-conformities, the lessee may "act[ ] with respect to the goods in a manner that signifies to the lessor or the supplier" that the lessee accepts the goods, even if non-conforming. UCC § 2A–515(1)(a). In other words, a lessee may signify acceptance not only by its oral or written communications, but also by its conduct. That is not the case for a sale of goods. Section 2–606(1)(a) uses the word "signify" but says nothing about the buyer's conduct signifying acceptance. *See* UCC § 2A–515, Comment: Changes (stating that "[t]he provisions of Section 2–606(1)(a) were substantially rewritten to provide that the lessee's conduct may signify acceptance").

Second, § 2–606(1)(c) provides that the buyer may accept the goods by doing "any act inconsistent with the seller's ownership." This language was not incorporated into § 2A–515 because it is "irrelevant given the lessee's possession and use of the leased goods." UCC § 2A–515, Comment: Changes.

As mentioned above, the lessee is afforded a reasonable opportunity to inspect the goods. What constitutes a "reasonable opportunity" is a question of fact. If the lessee does not signify by its words or actions that it accepts the goods, it nonetheless may accept by failing to reject the goods. "Rejection of goods is ineffective unless it is within a reasonable time after tender or delivery of the goods." UCC § 2A–

509(2). In addition, the lessee must seasonably notify the lessor that it is rejecting the goods. *See id*. Failure to provide seasonable notice renders the "rejection" ineffective, thereby amounting to an acceptance of the goods by the lessee. *See* UCC § 1–205 (stating that action is seasonable if "taken at or within the time agreed or, if no time is agreed, at or within a reasonable time").

If the lessee does reject the goods, the lessor or the supplier may cure the non-conforming delivery in the same two circumstances in which the seller of goods may cure under a contract for sale of goods. *See supra* § A.3 of this Chapter. The first is when the lessee rejects nonconforming goods and the "time for performance has not yet expired." UCC § 2A–513(1). The lessor or supplier must provide notice of its intent to cure and "then make a conforming delivery within the time provided in the lease contract." *Id.* The lessor or supplier also has the right to cure when the lessee rejects nonconforming goods that the lessor or supplier "had reasonable grounds to believe would be acceptable with or without money allowance." UCC § 2–513(2). The lessor or seller must provide notice of its intent to cure and then has a "further reasonable time to substitute a conforming tender." *Id.*

3. REVOCATION OF ACCEPTANCE: § 2A–517

Article 2A's rules on revocation of acceptance are modeled on § 2–608. *See supra* § A.4 of this Chapter. Thus, the lessee may revoke acceptance only if the good's nonconformity "substantially impairs its value to the lessee." UCC § 2A–517(1); *see supra* § A.4.a for a discussion of substantial impairment. In addition to substantial impairment, the lessee also must satisfy one of the following conditions to revoke its acceptance.

a. The lessee, other than a lessee under a finance lease, accepted on the "reasonable assumption" that the nonconformity would be cured but it has not been seasonably cured. UCC § 2A–517(1)(a).

b. The lessee accepted without discovering the nonconformity if its acceptance was "reasonably induced [ ] by the lessor's assurances." UCC § 2A–517(1)(b).

c. The lessee, other than a lessee under a finance lease, accepted without discovering the nonconformity if its acceptance was "reasonably induced . . . by the difficulty of discovery before acceptance." UCC § 2A–517(1)(b).

In order for a revocation of acceptance to be effective, the lessee must notify the lessor. UCC § 2A–517(4). In addition, revocation must occur "within a reasonable time after the lessee discovers or should have discovered the ground for it and before any substantial change in condition of the goods which is not caused by the nonconformity." *Id.*; *see supra* § A.4.b–c of this Chapter.

As the foregoing demonstrates, the lessee in a finance lease has a "limited right to revoke acceptance." UCC § 2A–517, Comment: Changes. For example, the finance lessee only may revoke if its "acceptance was without discovery of the nonconformity (with respect to the lease agreement, not the supply agreement) and was reasonably induced by the lessor's assurances". UCC § 2A–516, Comment ¶ 1; *see* UCC § 2A–517(1)(b).

Section 2A–517 also allows revocation of acceptance in two situations not expressly provided for by § 2–608. *See* UCC § 2A–517, Comment: Changes. The first allows certain lessees to revoke acceptance of goods based on a lease default that is *not* a delivery of non-conforming goods.

> Except in the case of a finance lease that is not a consumer lease, a lessee may revoke acceptance of a lot or commercial unit if the lessor defaults under the lease contract and the default substantially impairs the value of that lot or commercial unit to the lessee.

UCC § 2A–517(2). For example, suppose Small Biz leases equipment from Acme. The lease agreement requires Acme to service the equipment. Acme delivers the equipment on time, and it conforms to the lease agreement. But Acme fails to provide the necessary service and that failure substantially impairs the value of the equipment to Small Biz. Small Biz may revoke its acceptance of the equipment. *See* UCC § 2A–517, Comment ¶ 1. Of course, Small Biz still must satisfy the other requirements for revocation, e.g., notice. *See* UCC § 2A–517(4).

The second states that the parties to a lease may provide that a lessee may revoke its acceptance for defaults that may not rise to the level of substantial impairment. "If the lease agreement so provides, the lessee may revoke acceptance of a lot or commercial unit because of other defaults by the lessor." UCC § 2A–517(3). In other words, "the parties are free to contract" as to what constitutes a default that is "so material that the lessee can cancel the lease." UCC § 2A–517, Comment ¶ 2.

4. RISK OF LOSS: § 2A–219 AND § 2A–220

Like Article 2, Article 2A divides the risk-of-loss rules on the basis of whether there is a default, by either the lessor or the lessee, of the lease agreement. Section 2A–219 provides the rules on risk of loss when there is no lease default. The effect of default on the risk of loss is covered by § 2A–220.

a. Risk of Loss—No Default: § 2A–219

It is important to realize that subsection (1) of § 2A–219 provides the basic rules, absent agreement to the contrary, about which party to the lease agreement bears the risk of loss. Subsection (2) explains *when* the risk of loss shifts to the lessee *if* the risk of loss is to pass to the lessee.

If the lease is a finance lease, then the "risk of loss passes to the lessee." UCC § 2A–219(1). If the lease is *not* a finance lease, the risk of loss "is retained by the lessor and does not pass to the lessee." *Id.* The reason for this rule is that "the lessor owns the goods" and, thus, "the lessor should obtain any necessary insurance and, absent the lessee's fault, should bear the loss." 4C Anderson U.C.C. § 2A–219:3 (3d ed.).

Can the parties to the lease alter § 2A–219's allocation of the risk of loss and provide, for example, that the risk of loss in a non-finance lease, at some point, passes from the lessor to the lessee? Section 2A–219, unlike § 2–509, does not state that the risk-of-loss rules "are subject to contrary agreement of the parties." *Compare* § 2–509(4) *with* § 2A–219. The reason, however, is that the drafters considered it unnecessary. *See* UCC § 2A–219, Comment: Purposes (stating that the "provisions of subsection (4) of Section 2–509 are not incorporated as they are not necessary"). Unnecessary, because § 1–302 already provides that the absence of "the phrase 'unless otherwise agreed', or words of similar import, does not imply that the effect of other provisions may not be varied by agreement under this section." UCC § 1–302(c). In other words, § 1–302 already allows the parties to a lease to shift the risk of loss from the lessor to the lessee, even if § 2A–219 does not expressly so provide. *See* Addison Express, LLC v. Medway Air Ambulance, 2006 WL 1489385 (N.D. Tex. 2006) (analyzing question of whether parties could vary § 2A–219(1)'s rules on risk of loss and holding that the "more reasoned view" is that the parties to a non-finance commercial lease may agree to shift the risk of loss to the lessee).

If risk of loss is to pass to the lessee, the parties may provide in their agreement *when* that will happen. If the parties do not state in their agreement when risk of loss passes to the lessee, then the rules in subsection (2) govern. Thus, if the parties to a finance lease do not state when risk of loss passes to the lessee, then subsection (2) provides the applicable rules. Because risk of loss remains with the lessor in a non-finance lease, subsection (2) only applies if the parties to a non-finance lease agree to shift the risk of loss to the lessee but fail to specify *when* risk of loss passes. In other words, in a case involving a non-finance lease, subsection (2) is irrelevant if the parties do not vary by agreement the risk-of-loss rules of subsection (1).

Subsection (2) provides the time when risk of loss passes to the lessee when (1) the parties' contract requires shipment of the goods; (2) the goods are held by a bailee; or (3) the contract does not require shipment and there is no bailment of the goods, i.e., all other cases. If the lease agreement requires that the goods be shipped to the lessee and the agreement qualifies as a shipment contract, then "the risk of loss passes to the lessee when the goods are duly delivered to the carrier." UCC § 2A–219(2)(a)(i); *cf.* UCC § 2–509(1)(a). If the agreement is a destination contract, the risk of loss passes to the lessee when the goods are duly tendered at the destination "as to enable the lessee to take delivery." UCC § 2A–219(2)(a)(ii); *cf.* UCC § 2–509(1)(b).

Section 2A–219 has a single rule for when goods held by a bailee are to be delivered without moving them. *Compare* UCC § 2A–219(2)(b) *with* UCC § 2–509(2)(a)–(c); *see* UCC § 2A–219, Comment: Changes (stating that only part of § 2–509(2) was incorporated into § 2A–219(2)(b), "reflecting current practice in lease transactions"). In such a case, the risk of loss "passes to the lessee upon acknowledgment by the bailee of the lessee's right to possession of the goods." UCC § 2A–219(2)(b).

In all other cases—no shipment and no bailment—the risk-of-loss rules depend on whether the lessor, or supplier in a finance lease, is a merchant. If the lessor or supplier is a merchant, then the "risk of loss passes to the lessee on the lessee's receipt of the goods." UCC § 2A–219(2)(c). Receipt is defined as "taking physical possession" of goods. UCC § 2–103(1)(c); *see* UCC § 2A–103(3). "[O]therwise, the risk passes to the lessee on tender of delivery." UCC § 2A–219(2)(c).

b. Effect of Default on Risk of Loss: § 2–220

Section 2A–220 provides the risk-of-loss rules when there is a default of the lease agreement. The rules largely track those spelled out in cases involving breach of a contract for the sale of goods. *See* UCC § 2–510. Subsection (1) covers risk of loss when the lessor defaults. The rules in subsection (1) only apply if the "risk of loss is to pass to the lessee and the time of passage is not stated." UCC § 2A–220(1); *see supra* § B.4.a of this Chapter. In other words, § 2A–220(1)'s rules apply to finance leases, and to non-finance leases in which the parties agree to shift the risk of loss to the lessee. Subsection (2) addresses risk of loss if the lessee defaults and applies regardless of whether "risk of loss is to pass to the lessee." UCC § 2A–220(2).

If the lessee has the right to reject the goods because they fail to conform to the lease agreement, then "the risk of loss remains with the lessor, or, in the case of a finance lease, the supplier, until cure or acceptance." UCC § 2A–220(1)(a). If the lessee rightfully revokes its acceptance of the goods, then the lessee, "to the extent of any deficiency in his [or her] effective insurance coverage, may treat the risk of loss as having remained with the lessor from the beginning." UCC § 2A–220(1)(b). This risk-of-loss rule does not permit the *lessee in a finance lease* to "treat the risk of loss as having remained with the supplier from the beginning." UCC § 2A–220, Comment: Changes. The reason for this limitation is that there are "limited circumstances under which the lessee under a finance lease is allowed to revoke acceptance." *Id.*; *see supra* § B.3 of this Chapter.

Section 2A–220 also provides the rule for cases in which the lessee defaults.

> Whether or not risk of loss is to pass to the lessee, if the lessee as to conforming goods already identified to the lease contract repudiates or is otherwise in default under the lease contract, the lessor, or, in the case of a finance lease, the supplier, to the extent of any deficiency in his [or her] effective insurance coverage may treat the risk of loss as resting on the lessee for a commercially reasonable time.

UCC § 2A–220(2). Notice that this provision applies regardless of whether the risk of loss is to pass to the lessee. In other words, the lessee may be responsible for a deficiency in the lessor's or supplier's effective insurance coverage even if the lessor has the risk of loss. For example, in a non-finance lease, the lessor retains the risk of loss. *See* UCC § 2A–219(1). Thus, even in cases in which the parties to a non-finance lease do not agree to shift the risk of loss to the lessee, the lessee that defaults on the lease nonetheless may bear the risk of loss to the extent of a shortfall in the lessor's insurance coverage, e.g., a deductible. The lessee's liability is for any deficiency in the lessor's insurance coverage but only for a "commercially reasonable time." The rationale for the rule is that "the lessor or supplier needs a period of time to dispose of the wrongfully rejected goods, and the lessee should have the risk of loss only during this period." 3 Hawkland UCC Series § 2A–220:4.

c. Summary

When analyzing a problem involving risk of loss for a lease agreement, start by asking whether a default has occurred. If not, then § 2A–219 applies. If the agreement is a finance lease, then the risk of loss passes to the lessee. The parties to the finance lease may specify when risk of loss passes. If they fail to do so, the rules at § 2A–219(2)(a)–(c) provide the time when risk of loss passes to the lessee. In the case of a non-finance lease, the risk of loss remains on the lessor. Of course, the parties may agree to the contrary and specify when risk of loss passes to the lessee. If the parties agree that risk of loss will pass to the lessee but fail to specify when that will occur, then the rules at § 2A–219(2)(a)–(c) provide the relevant time.

What happens if the lessor or lessee defaults on the lease agreement? For finance leases or for non-finance leases in which the parties agree to shift the risk of loss to the lessee, § 2A–220(1) provides the risk-of-loss rules in the case of a default by the lessor. (Remember: absent a contrary agreement, the lessor retains the risk of loss in a non-finance lease.) If the lessee defaults, § 2A–220(2) provides the rule, which does not depend on whether the risk of loss is to pass to the lessee.

5. EXCUSE: § 2A–221, § 2A–404 THROUGH § 2A–406

The rules on excuse for leases are in two parts of Article 2A: in Part 2 on formation and construction of the lease contract—§ 2A–221 on casualty to identified goods—and in Part 4 on performance—§ 2A–404 through § 2A–406 on substituted performance and impracticability. By comparison, the excuse provisions for sales of goods are in consecutive sections of Part 6 (breach and excuse) of Article 2.

Section 2A–221 is modeled on § 2–613 and excuses performance in certain circumstances when identified goods required for performance of the lease agreement are damaged or destroyed. Section 2A–221 only applies if the damage to the goods occurs "without the fault of the lessee, the lessor or the supplier." UCC § 2A–221. Casualty to the goods must happen before delivery or before the risk of loss passes to the lessee either under the lease agreement or pursuant to § 2A–219. *See id.* If the goods are destroyed, i.e., the "loss is total," then the "lease contract is avoided." UCC § 2A–221(a). In a case in which "the loss is partial or the goods have so deteriorated as to no longer conform to the lease contract," the lessee may inspect the goods and either treat the lease as avoided or, with the exception of a non-consumer finance lease, accept the goods "with due allowance from the rent payable for the balance of the lease term." UCC § 2A–221(b). The drafters did not take a position on whether to credit the "due allowance" against the first or last rental payments *or* to allocate it *pro rata* to all rental payments. *See* UCC § 2A–221, Comment: Purpose.

Section 2A–404 requires that, if available, a "commercially reasonable substitute . . . must be tendered and accepted" when berthing or loading facilities "fail", an agreed kind of carrier "becomes unavailable," or the manner of delivery agreed upon by the parties "becomes commercially impracticable." UCC § 2A–404(1). The rule under subsection (1) applies only if the failure is not the fault of the lessee, the lessor, or the supplier. *See id.* Subsection (2) provides the rules for cases in which the "agreed means or manner of payment fails because of domestic or foreign governmental regulation." UCC § 2A–404(2). Section 2A–404 largely tracks Article 2's provision on substituted performance for sales of goods. *Cf.* UCC § 2–614; *see supra* § A.6.b of this Chapter.

Section 2A–405 contains the impracticability provision for lease contracts. While there are changes to terminology to cover leases as opposed to sales of goods, § 2A–405 largely tracks the language of § 2–615. *See supra* § A.6.c of this Chapter. To successfully claim excuse of performance under § 2A–405, the lessor or supplier must demonstrate that its performance under the lease contract "has been made impracticable by the occurrence of a contingency the nonoccurrence of which was a basic assumption on which the lease contract was made." UCC § 2A–405(a). Performance of the lease contract also may be rendered impracticable based on the lessor's or supplier's "compliance in good faith with any applicable foreign or domestic governmental regulation or order," even if such regulation or order later turns out to be invalid. *Id.* If only part of the lessor's or supplier's performance is rendered impracticable, the lessor or supplier must "allocate production and deliveries" among its customers. UCC § 2A–405(b). The lessor or supplier may include in its allocation its regular customers not then under contract and its own requirements for manufacture. *See id.* Any allocation that is "fair and reasonable" is acceptable. *Id.* Notice must be provided by the lessor to the lessee and in a finance lease by the supplier to both the lessor and the lessee of any delay in delivery or any nondelivery. *See* UCC § 2A–405(c). If the lessor or supplier must allocate production and deliveries, the notice must include the "estimated quota" available for the lessee. *See id.*

A lessee that receives a notification of excuse under § 2A–405 may either terminate the lease contract or, except in the case of a non-consumer finance lease, "modify the lease contract by accepting the available quota in substitution." UCC § 2A–406(1). Any modification is with "due allowance" from the remaining rent due for the deficiency in performance of the lessor's obligation under the lease agreement. UCC § 2A–406(1)(b). The lessee that modifies the lease pursuant to § 2A–406(1)(b) has no "further right against the lessor." *Id.* Bear in mind that the option of modifying the contract is not available in the case of a non-consumer finance lease. The reason is based on "the same policy that led to codification of provisions with respect to irrevocable promises. Section 2A–407." UCC § 2A–406, Comment: Changes; *see* the next section for discussion of irrevocable promises. If the lessee fails to modify the lease agreement within a reasonable time, not to exceed 30 days, after receiving the lessor's notice, then the "lease contract lapses with respect to any deliveries affected." UCC § 2A–406(2).

6. FINANCE LEASES—IRREVOCABLE PROMISES: § 2A–407

When the lessee in a non-consumer finance lease accepts the goods, its "promises under the lease contract become irrevocable and independent." UCC § 2A–407; *see supra* § B.2 of this Chapter on acceptance. Section 2A–407 is "self-executing" and does not require the parties to include any specific provision in their lease agreement. UCC § 2A–407, Comment ¶ 1. Section 2A–407 "extends the benefits of the classic 'hell or high water' clause" to non-consumer finance leases. *Id.* In other words, the lessee, once it accepts the goods, must pay rent come hell or high water, "even if the lessor's performance after the lessee's acceptance is not in accordance with the lease contract." UCC § 2A–407, Comment ¶ 2. Thus, the lessee's performance is not dependent on the lessor's performance of its lease obligations. Stated another way, the lessor's performance is not a constructive condition of the lessee's performance. *See* Kingston v. Preston, 2 Doug. 689, 99 Eng. Rep. 437 (K.B. 1773) (stating that "[t]here are three types of covenants": (1) "mutual and independ[e]nt"; (2) "conditions and depend[e]nt"; and (3) "mutual conditions to be performed at the same time").

In Hitachi Data Systems Credit Corp. v. Precision Discovery, Inc., 2019 WL 3802178 (S.D. N.Y 2019), the court held that the lessee was obligated to make rental payments on equipment even though the equipment had not been installed. Hitachi Data Systems (HDS) and Precision entered into an agreement under which Precision leased equipment for a two-year period from HDS with Hitachi Vantara Corporation or a third-party vendor supplying the equipment. The parties agreed that the lease "would be treated as a 'finance lease' under the UCC." *Id.* at *8. The equipment was not installed. Precision initially made rent payments but then stopped, at which point HDS sued Precision for breach of contract. Precision claimed that it had not accepted the equipment and, thus, its obligation to pay rent had not been triggered. Precision pointed to the lease agreement, which tied the obligation to pay rent to installation of the equipment. The court rejected Precision's argument, noting that Precision had "retained the equipment and made lease payments for multiple months." *Id.* at * 12. No evidence existed in the record to indicate that Precision told HDS it was rejecting the equipment. The court explained that Precision's failure to reject the equipment constituted an acceptance. *See* UCC § 2A–515(1)(b); *see also* § B.2 of this Chapter on acceptance. By accepting the equipment, Precision became obligated to make rent payments, regardless of HDS's performance and notwithstanding the fact that the equipment had not been installed.

The Official Comment to § 2A–407 provides another example. Suppose Acme Corporation, Bellona, Inc., and Calypso Company are parties to a finance lease of an expensive piece of equipment. (For an explanation of the arrangements among Acme, Bellona, and Calypso that resulted in a finance lease, *see* UCC § 2A–407, Comment ¶ 3.) The supplier is Calypso, the equipment manufacturer. Acme is the finance lessor and Bellona is the lessee. Calypso delivers the equipment to Bellona, and after Bellona tests the equipment, it accepts it. Bellona signs off on a certificate of acceptance, which it then sends to both Acme and Calypso. About a year later, the equipment malfunctions. What rights, if any, does Bellona have against Acme? *See* § 2A–407, Comment ¶¶ 3–5.

With limited exceptions, Bellona has no claim against Acme. When Bellona accepted the equipment, its promise to pay rent to Acme and perform its lease obligations became "irrevocable and independent." *See* UCC § 2A–407, Comment ¶ 5. Because this is a finance lease, Bellona looks to Calypso "to perform the essential covenants and warranties." UCC § 2A–407, Comment ¶ 1. Recall that the warranties of merchantability and fitness for a particular purpose are not implied in the lease agreement between the lessor (Acme) and lessee (Bellona) in a finance lease. *See* UCC § 2A–212, § 2A–213; *see also supra* Chapter 6, § B.1. There also is no warranty against infringement by a merchant lessor in a finance lease. *See* UCC § 2A–211(2). Of course, the lessor in a finance lease *may* make express warranties and the lessee may then hold the lessor to account for breach of such warranties. The lessee also may sue the lessor for fraud; basic principles of law and equity still apply. *See* Xerox Corp. v. JCTB Inc., 2018 WL 5776423 (W.D. N.Y. 2018) (stating that in New York, the obligations of the lessee in a non-consumer finance lease are " 'fully enforceable . . . in the absence of fraud' "), *aff'd* 787 F. App'x 43 (2d Cir. 2019). Absent such circumstances, however, Bellona must pursue Calypso for relief. *See* UCC § 2A–209(1) (finance lease lessee as beneficiary of supply contract).

If the lessee's promise becomes irrevocable and independent, then the promise not only is effective between the parties but also against third parties. *See* UCC § 2A–407(2)(a). "Thus, the finance lease can be transferred or assigned without disturbing enforceability." UCC § 2A–407, Comment ¶ 7. In addition, the lessee's irrevocable and independent promise cannot be canceled, terminated, modified, repudiated, excused, or substituted without the lessor's consent. UCC § 2A–407(2)(b); 2A–407, Comment ¶ 7.

What about consumer finance leases? The language of § 2A–407(1) and (2) is limited to non-consumer finance leases and, thus, does not apply to consumer finance leases. Thus, § 2A–407 does not operate to make the consumer lessee's promises irrevocable and independent upon accepting the goods. The drafters expressed concern about a consumer being obligated "to pay notwithstanding defective goods or the like." UCC § 2A–407, Comment ¶ 2. Suppose, however, that a consumer finance lease contains a "hell or high water" clause that operates like § 2A–407, thereby making the consumer lessee's promises under the lease agreement irrevocable and independent upon the consumer's acceptance of the goods? *See* UCC § 2A–407(3) (stating that § 2A–407 "does not affect the validity under any other law" of "hell or high water" clauses). The drafters left to the courts whether to enforce such "hell or high water" clauses based on "the facts of each case and other law which [§ 2A–407] does not affect." UCC § 2A–407, Comment ¶ 6.

CHAPTER 10

ANTICIPATORY REPUDIATION AND ADEQUATE ASSURANCE

A. SALES

1. ANTICIPATORY REPUDIATION AND RETRACTION: § 2–610 AND § 2–611

In your first-year Contracts course, you likely discussed the case of Hochster v. De La Tour, 118 Eng. Rep. 922 (Q.B. 1853). De La Tour hired Hochster, a courier, to accompany him on a three-month European tour to start on June 1, 1852. On May 11, however, De La Tour wrote to Hochster stating that he had changed his mind and no longer needed Hochster's services. De La Tour declined to compensate Hochster. Hochster then secured employment with Lord Ashburton on terms similar to those of his contract with De La Tour although his employment with Lord Ashburton did not begin until July 4, 1852.

Hochster sued De La Tour for breach of contract. Counsel for De La Tour argued that there could be no breach until June 1, and that by taking employment with Lord Ashburton Hochster had made it impossible for him to carry out the terms of the contract with De La Tour. The court rejected these arguments by De La Tour's counsel, noting that De La Tour had renounced the agreement. After renunciation, it was "much more rational" for Hochster to seek other employment to mitigate damages for breach of contract. Moreover, Hochster, the injured party, had the option of waiting until June 1 for performance or filing suit immediately.

> If it should be held that, upon a contract to do an act on a future day, a renunciation of the contract by one party dispenses with a condition to be performed in the meantime by the other, there seems to be no reason for requiring that other to wait till the day arrives before seeking his remedy by action: and the only ground on which the condition can be dispensed with seems to be, that the renunciation may be treated as a breach of the contract.

Hochster, 118 Eng. Rep. at 927–28. Thus, if one party to the contract repudiates the contract prior to the date for performance, the injured party may await performance or may immediately file suit for breach of contract. This basic rule is found in § 2–610 and applies when one party's anticipatory repudiation "substantially impair[s] the value of the contract to the other." UCC § 2–610.

Suppose Bailey and Sergeant make a contract for the purchase and sale of snorkels with delivery by Sergeant to occur on April 1. On March 10, Sergeant informs Bailey that Sergeant's business is in serious financial trouble and, therefore, Sergeant cannot and will not deliver snorkels to Bailey on April 1. The failure to deliver any goods to Bailey substantially impairs the value of the contract to him. What options are available to Bailey? He may await performance by Sergeant for a "commercially reasonable time." UCC § 2–610(a). Even if he informs Sergeant that he will await performance and urges

Sergeant to retract his repudiation, Bailey may still "resort to any remedy for breach." UCC § 2–610(b). Regardless of whether he decides to await performance or to resort to Article 2's remedies for breach, Bailey may "suspend his own performance." UCC § 2–610(c).

Be careful when analyzing a problem in which a party to the contract expresses reservations about performing. For example, suppose Seller says the following to Buyer: "We are experiencing problems with production and may be unable to deliver the goods, as agreed." Seller has not told Buyer that it will not deliver; rather, its statement provides Buyer with grounds for insecurity about Seller's performance. Rather than treating the statement as anticipatory repudiation, Buyer should demand adequate assurance of performance from Seller pursuant to § 2–609. *See infra* § A.2 of this Chapter. If Buyer fails to perform because it treats Seller's statement as anticipatory repudiation, then Buyer is in breach, not Seller.

In order to qualify as anticipatory repudiation, there must be "an overt communication of intention or an action which renders performance impossible or demonstrates a clear determination not to continue with performance." UCC § 2–610, Comment ¶ 1. Courts use various terms to describe the communication or behavior that constitutes anticipatory repudiation: definite, unequivocal, positive, absolute, unconditional. *See, e.g.*, BRC Rubber & Plastics, Inc. v. Continental Carbon Co., 981 F.3d 618 (7th Cir. 2020) (stating that "Indiana courts have said that anticipatory repudiation under § 2–610 must be positive, absolute, and unconditional"); Carnes Co. v. Stone Creek Mechanical, Inc., 412 F.3d 845 (7th Cir. 2005) (stating that "[i]n order to constitute an anticipatory repudiation of a contract, there must be a definite and unequivocal manifestation of intention on the part of the repudiator that he will not render the promised performance when the time fixed for it in the contract arrives"); Automated Cutting Technologies, Inc. v. BJS North America East, Inc., 2012 WL 2872823 (E.D. Ky. 2012) (stating that the "communication constituting anticipatory repudiation must be 'unequivocal' "). While the words vary, the idea is the same—the repudiating party must make clear its intention not to perform.

A seller, for example, may tell a buyer that it does not intend to perform. But a clear statement of non-performance is not the only way in which anticipatory repudiation may occur. A failure to provide adequate assurance of performance after a justified demand constitutes repudiation. UCC § 2–609(4); *see infra* § A.2 of this Chapter.

"Repudiation [also] can result from action which reasonably indicates a rejection of the continuing obligation." UCC § 2–610, Comment ¶ 2. For example, Scientific Machine & Welding, Inc. v. FlashParking, Inc., 641 S.W.3d 454 (Tex. App. 2021), involved a contract for the sale by Scientific to FlashParking of parking-payment kiosks. The parties' contract required that the kiosks be United Laboratories (UL) compliant. Scientific entered into a separate contract with MET Laboratories (METLabs) to certify that the kiosks were UL compliant. Without the UL compliance mark (MET Mark), the kiosks were not marketable.

Scientific failed an unannounced inspection by METLabs, which then refused to permit Scientific to use the MET Mark on the kiosks and required Scientific to sign a successor contract, as Scientific was not in compliance with its existing contract with METLabs. Scientific signed that contract but made various amendments, including striking a provision agreeing to unannounced factory inspections. METLabs refused to agree to Scientific's amendments. While Scientific told FlashParking that it wanted to figure out how to make the parties' contract work, it refused to sign the METLabs contract without the amendments it wanted, it failed to inform FlashParking of the steps it had taken to fix the problems identified by METLabs during its inspection, and it did not procure another company to provide the UL-compliance certification for the kiosks. FlashParking informed Scientific that Scientific had repudiated a "critical requirement" of the parties' contract—the certification of UL compliance—and terminated the contract. Quoting Comment ¶ 2—that rejection of a continuing obligation may constitute repudiation—the Texas Court of Appeals concluded that Scientific had "intentionally and unequivocally repudiated the FlashParking contract when it refused to execute" the METLabs contract in the form required by METLabs. *Scientific Machine*, 641 S.W.3d at 469.

The repudiating party can retract its repudiation up until the next performance is due "unless the aggrieved party has since the repudiation cancelled or materially changed his position or otherwise indicated that he considers the repudiation final." UCC § 2–611(1). For example, suppose Acme makes a contract to sell 100 anvils to Road Runner, Inc. (RRI) with delivery to occur on October 1. On September 5, Acme informs RRI that it will not deliver any anvils to RRI on October 1. Assume that Acme unequivocally states that it will not perform its contractual obligation to sell anvils to RRI. On September 6, RRI makes a contract to buy 100 anvils from Beep Company with delivery to occur on October 1. If Acme contacts RRI on September 9 to retract its repudiation, it is too late. RRI has materially changed position by making a cover contract with Beep Company. Section 2–611 does not require the aggrieved party, RRI, to inform the repudiating party of its change of position. All that is required is a material change of position.

The repudiating party may retract its repudiation by "any method which clearly indicates that the repudiating party intends to perform." UCC § 2–611(2). The repudiating party's rights under the contract are reinstated by a retraction. UCC § 2–611(3). Suppose in our example above, RRI did not make a contract with Beep Company on September 6 and did not otherwise cancel or indicate that it considered Acme's repudiation final. On September 9, Acme retracts its repudiation. By doing so, Acme reinstates its rights under the contract subject to any allowance to RRI for delay caused by Acme's repudiation. *See* UCC § 2–611(3). Acme's repudiation suffices to give RRI "reasonable grounds for insecurity [ ] to warrant a request for assurances as an essential condition of the retraction." UCC § 2–611, Comment ¶ 2. But Acme's retraction coupled with any assurances requested by RRI means that RRI must accept Acme's tender of the anvils on October 1. If RRI refuses to accept a conforming delivery, then RRI will be in breach of contract.

2. ADEQUATE ASSURANCE: § 2–609

Suppose Sherman Company agrees to sell 10 Wayback Machines to Peabody, Inc. with delivery to occur on August 15. On July 15, Sherman informs Peabody that it is experiencing problems obtaining the parts needed for the Wayback Machines and, thus, may be unable to deliver the machines on August 15. Peabody needs the machines because it entered into a contract to provide the machines for the Moose & Squirrel Trade Show at the end of August. Sherman's communication is not anticipatory repudiation; it is not an unequivocal refusal to perform. Therefore, Peabody may not resort to any remedy for breach. *See* UCC § 2–610(b).

But Peabody now has reason to be insecure about Sherman's performance under the contract. While Peabody may sue Sherman if Sherman fails to deliver on August 15, Peabody entered into a contract with Sherman not simply for a right to file and win a lawsuit in the event of nonperformance. Peabody made the contract with Sherman in order to plan for its business; it relied on Sherman's contractual promise to deliver the Wayback Machines in time for the trade show.

> [Section 2–609] rests on the recognition of the fact that the essential purpose of a contract between commercial men is actual performance and they do not bargain merely for a promise, or for a promise plus the right to win a lawsuit and that a continuing sense of reliance and security that the promised performance will be forthcoming when due, is an important feature of the bargain. If either the willingness or the ability of a party to perform declines materially between the time of contracting and the time for performance, the other party is threatened with the loss of a substantial part of what he has bargained for.

UCC § 2–609, Comment ¶ 1.

The solution to Peabody's dilemma—it cannot cover because Sherman's statement is not anticipatory repudiation—is Article 2's "significant and pragmatic innovation" in the form of § 2–609. BRC Rubber & Plastics, Inc. v. Continental Carbon Co., 981 F.3d 618 (7th Cir. 2020). Section 2–609 provides that "[w]hen reasonable grounds for insecurity arise with respect to the performance of either party the other may in writing demand adequate assurance of due performance." UCC § 2–609(1). The question, of course, is what constitutes "reasonable grounds for insecurity." In deciding whether reasonable grounds exist, a court must apply "commercial rather than legal standards." UCC § 2–609, Comment ¶ 3. Whether there are reasonable grounds generally is a question of fact to be determined based on all the circumstances. *See BRC Rubber,* 981 F.3d at 623.

The Official Comment to § 2–609 is useful for understanding what constitutes reasonable grounds for insecurity. "[A] ground for insecurity need not arise from or be directly related to the contract in question." UCC § 2–609, Comment ¶ 3. For example, suppose that over the past two months, Seller and Buyer have entered into three contracts, all of which provide for payment in full within 30 days of delivery of the goods. Seller delivered the goods for the first two contracts on January 15 and February 10. It now is March 15, and payment is past due on both contracts. The third contract for widgets provides for delivery of the widgets no later than May 1. While the prior contracts are "separate and legally distinct" from the current widget contract, Buyer's failure to pay for those goods within 30 days of delivery impairs Seller's expectation that Buyer will pay on time for the widgets, thereby giving Seller reasonable grounds for insecurity. *Id.*

Suppose that on March 1, Seller makes a contract to deliver widgets to Buyer on June 1. In late April, Buyer learns from a trustworthy source that Seller has delivered defective widgets to other buyers in the industry. Such information from a trustworthy source also would "normally give the buyer reasonable grounds for insecurity." *Id.*

Reasonable grounds for insecurity also exist in the case of an "assignment which delegates performance." UCC § 2–210(6); 2 Hawkland UCC

Series § 2–609:2 (stating that "Section 2–210(6) also provides that a delegation of duties under a contract creates reasonable grounds for insecurity"); *see supra* Chapter 5, § B. In such a case, the non-delegating party may demand adequate assurance of performance from the assignee. UCC § 2–210(6), Comment ¶ 6.

B. LEASES

1. ANTICIPATORY REPUDIATION, RETRACTION, AND ADEQUATE ASSURANCE: § 2A–401, § 2A–402 AND § 2A–403

Article 2A's rules on anticipatory repudiation, retraction of such repudiation, and adequate assurance of performance largely track those of Article 2. *See supra* § A of this Chapter. For example, suppose on March 1, Lessee enters into an equipment lease with Lessor with delivery of the equipment and first rental payment to occur on July 1. On May 15, Lessee informs Lessor that it is encountering financial problems and may not need to lease the equipment. Such a statement is too equivocal to constitute anticipatory repudiation. Instead, Lessor now has reasonable grounds for insecurity and "may demand in writing adequate assurance of due performance." UCC § 2A–401(2); *cf.* UCC § 2–609(1). If Lessee fails to provide adequate assurance of performance "within a reasonable time, not to exceed 30 days after receipt of a demand by the other party," then Lessee has repudiated the lease agreement. UCC § 2A–401(3); *cf.* UCC § 2–609(4). Commercial standards determine "the reasonableness of grounds for insecurity and the adequacy of any assurance offered" when the lessor and the lessee are both merchants. UCC § 2A–401(4); *cf.* UCC § 2–609(2).

Suppose that on May 15, Lessee had informed Lessor that due to its financial problems Lessee no longer could afford the leased equipment and that Lessee would refuse delivery of such equipment. This is an anticipatory repudiation by Lessee. UCC § 2A–402; *cf.* UCC § 2–610. Upon Lessee's anticipatory repudiation, Lessor may suspend its own performance under the lease agreement. UCC § 2A–402(c); *cf.* UCC § 2–610(c). In addition to suspending its own performance, Lessor may (1) wait for a commercially reasonable time for Lessee to retract its repudiation and perform; (2) demand adequate assurance of performance; or (3) resort to any remedy for default. UCC § 2A–402(a)–(c).

Lessee may retract its repudiation "by any method that clearly indicates" to Lessor that Lessee intends to perform the lease agreement and provides any assurance of performance demanded by Lessor. UCC § 2A–403(2); *cf.* UCC § 2–611(2). But any retraction must occur before Lessor has canceled the lease agreement, materially changed its position, or otherwise indicated that Lessor "considers the repudiation final." UCC § 2A–403(1); *cf.* UCC § 2–611(1). For example, suppose that on May 15, Lessee informs Lessor that it will refuse delivery of the equipment. On June 1, Lessor enters into an agreement to lease the equipment covered by its March 1 agreement with Lessee to another company. On June 10, Lessee retracts its repudiation. Lessee's

June 10 attempt to retract is ineffective because Lessor has materially changed position by contractually committing itself to lease the same equipment to another party.

But suppose Lessor was only discussing renting the equipment to another party when Lessee retracted its repudiation on June 10. Lessor did not contractually commit to lease the equipment to another party; thus, there is no material change of position. If Lessor neither cancelled the lease agreement nor otherwise indicated it considered Lessee's repudiation final, then Lessee's retraction is good. Lessee's retraction reinstates its rights under the lease agreement with "due excuse and allowance to [Lessor] for any delay occasioned by the repudiation." UCC § 2A–403(3); *cf.* UCC § 2–611(3). That means that Lessor must deliver the equipment to Lessee on July 1 and perform its obligations under the lease agreement. If Lessor fails to do so, it will be in breach of the lease.

CHAPTER 11

REMEDIES

A. SALES: INTRODUCTION

Part 7 of Article 2 covers remedies. Section 2–703 provides an index of the seller's remedies. Sections 2–706 through 2–709 contain the basic damage provisions in the event of the buyer's breach. The seller's incidental damages are provided for at § 2–710. Other seller remedies, such as those applicable at the time when the seller learns of the buyer's insolvency, are found at § 2–702 and § 2–705.

Buyer's remedies are indexed at § 2–711. Sections 2–712 through 2–714 contain the basic damage provisions when the seller breaches the contract. Section 2–715 covers the buyer's incidental and consequential damages. The buyer's rights to specific performance or to deduct its damages from the contract price are found at § 2–716 and § 2–717, respectively.

Section 2–718 addresses liquidated damages while § 2–719 covers modification or limitation of remedies. Section 2–723 provides the rules for determining market price for both the seller's and the buyer's market price damage formulae in cases in which an action based on anticipatory repudiation is tried prior to the contractual time for performance. *See* § 2–708(1) (seller market) and § 2–713 (buyer market). Finally, § 2–725 provides the statute of limitations for breach of contracts for sale of goods.

B. SELLER'S REMEDIES

When the buyer breaches, including a breach of the whole of an installment contract under § 2–612(3), the seller may:

(1) withhold delivery of the goods;

(2) stop delivery of goods in the possession of a carrier or bailee under § 2–705;

(3) identify to the contract goods unidentified at the time of breach under § 2–704;

(4) resell and sue for damages under § 2–706;

(5) sue for the difference between market and contract price under § 2–708(1);

(6) sue for damages under § 2–708(2) if seller is a lost volume seller;

(7) sue for the contract price under § 2–709; and

(8) cancel the contract.

UCC § 2–703. The "remedies are essentially cumulative" because the drafters of Article 2 "reject[ed] any doctrine of election of remedy as a fundamental policy." UCC § 2–703, Comment ¶ 1. Thus, whether the seller may pursue more than one remedy depends on the facts of the seller's case for breach. *See id.*

Section A of this Chapter is divided into two subsections. The first, below in § 1, covers Article 2's provisions on damages. The second, in § 2, addresses other seller remedies, such as the seller's right to stop delivery of the goods in transit upon discovery of the buyer's insolvency.

1. SELLER'S DAMAGES

Article 2 contains four basic damage provisions for sellers. Section 2–706 provides that the seller may recover the difference between the price at which it resold goods and the contract price. Section 2–708(1) provides that the seller may recover the difference between the market price and the contract price. If the seller is a lost volume seller, then § 2–708(2) applies and the seller may recover the profit lost due to the buyer's breach. Finally, the seller may recover the contract price, but only in three circumstances. *See* UCC § 2–709. All four damage provisions provide for the seller's recovery of its incidental damages. *See* UCC § 2–710. If a seller incurs consequential damages, it is unclear whether the seller may recover such damages because none of Article 2's formulae include consequential damages as part of the seller's recovery. This issue is addressed *infra* § B.1.e of this Chapter.

The following table provides a key to the abbreviations used in the various formulae for seller damages.

TABLE #3: SELLER DAMAGES: KEY TO ABBREVIATIONS

ES	Expenses Saved
FC	Fixed Costs (see Overhead)

ID	Incidental Damages
KP	Contract Price
Mkt	Market Price
OH	Overhead (see FC)
π	Profit
RP	Resale Price
VC	Variable Costs (or Direct Costs)

a. Resale: § 2–706

If the seller resells goods in good faith and in a commercially reasonable manner, it may recover damages for the difference between the contract price and the resale price *plus* any incidental damages incurred *minus* any expenses saved by virtue of the buyer's breach. UCC § 2–706(1). The seller will sue for resale when the resale price is *less than* the contract price. If the seller resells for *more* than the contract price, it is not "accountable to the buyer for any profit made on the resale." UCC § 2–706(6).

The language of § 2–706 gives the following formula for resale damages:

$$KP - RP + ID - ES$$

For example, suppose Sam Seller makes a contract with Bella Buyer in which Buyer agrees to purchase 100,000 widgets at a price of $1 per widget. Seller's facility is located in Detroit; the contract delivery term is "FOB Detroit". The contract requires delivery no later than March 1 to Buyer's facility in Gary,

Indiana. Seller delivers conforming widgets on time, but Buyer wrongfully rejects them. Seller resells the widgets at a public sale for $.85 per widget. Assume that the usual market for public sale is located 100 miles from Buyer's facility in Gary. Seller incurs $500 in transporting the widgets to the market for public sale. Damages are as follows:

$$\$100{,}000 - \$85{,}000 + \$500 - 0 = \$15{,}500$$

The contract price is $100,000: 100,000 widgets × $1 per widget. Resale is $85,000: 100,000 widgets × 85 cents per widget. Incidental damages include "any commercially reasonable charges, expenses, or commissions incurred . . . in the transportation . . . of goods after the buyer's breach, in connection with . . . resale of the goods." UCC § 2–710. The cost of transporting the widgets to the market for public sale is an incidental damage and recoverable by Seller. *See* UCC § 2–706, Comment ¶ 9. There are no expenses saved. The parties' agreement was a shipment contract ("FOB Detroit"), which means that Buyer bore the cost of transporting the goods to its facility in Gary. *See* UCC § 2–319(1)(a).

The resale may be by public or private sale. A public sale is a "sale by auction." UCC § 2–706, Comment ¶ 4. The seller must give the buyer "reasonable notice of the time and place" of a public resale, and the sale "must be made at a usual place or market for public sale if one is reasonably available." UCC § 2–706(4)(b). The purpose of notice is to afford the buyer the "opportunity to bid or to secure the attendance of other bidders." UCC § 2–706, Comment ¶ 8. Notice is not required in a case involving perishable goods or goods whose value are likely to "decline in value speedily." UCC § 2–706(4)(b). For a private resale, the seller also must give the buyer reasonable notice of its intent to resell. UCC § 2–706(3). But the seller is not required to provide the time and place of the private resale in its notification. UCC § 2–706, Comment ¶ 8. Failure to give notice deprives the seller of the right to recover its resale damages and "relegates him" to market price damages under § 2–708. *See* Sprague v. Sumitomo Forestry Co., 709 P.2d 1200 (Wash. 1985) (holding that seller could not recover damages for resale because seller's lawsuit for breach "was not an adequate substitute for the statutorily required notice of intent to resell" when the lawsuit gave "no notice of the remedy claimed other than damages").

In order to recover resale damages, the seller must resell in good faith and in a commercially reasonable manner. If the seller's conduct in reselling the goods is not in good faith or is not commercially reasonable, then the seller cannot recover resale damages and is "relegated" to market damages under § 2–708(1). UCC § 2–706, Comment ¶ 2; *see infra* § B.1.b of this Chapter. "[E]very aspect of the sale including the method, manner, time, place and terms must be commercially reasonable." UCC § 2–706, Comment ¶ 2. Whether the resale is commercially reasonable is a question for the trier of fact and depends on the circumstances of the particular case. *See* BAII Banking Corp. v. Atlantic Richfield Company, 1992 WL 209287 (S.D. N.Y. 1992) (denying buyer's motion to bar evidence of resale, which occurred more than two months after breach, because "whether the resale was commercially reasonable is a question of fact and [ ] evidence on that issue must be placed before the finder of fact at trial").

Suppose buyer breaches but seller does not resell the goods for a month. Is a month too long a time to wait, thereby resulting in a commercially unreasonable resale? The length of time between breach and resale "cannot be measured by any legal yardstick." UCC § 2–706, Comment ¶ 5. Whether the time is commercially reasonable "depends upon the nature of the goods, the condition of the market and the other circumstances of the case." UCC § 2–706, Comment 5; *see* Firwood Manufacturing Company, Inc. v. General Tire, Inc., 96 F.3d 163 (6th Cir. 1993) (stating that a three-year delay between buyer's breach and seller's resale, while not optimal, did not require the trial court jury to have found the resale commercially unreasonable when there was no market for the goods—machines costing over $30,000 apiece with "a very specialized use"—and where the seller "made a continuing good faith effort to locate other purchasers").

The same test of commercial reasonableness applies to the place of resale. Suppose buyer wrongfully rejects the goods upon delivery. Seller is not required to resell the goods at the buyer's location in order for the resale to be commercially reasonable. *See* UCC § 2–706, Comment ¶ 5 (rejecting requirement that seller "resell at the agreed place for delivery"). It is possible that for a public resale, the reasonably available usual place or market for a public sale is located "at a considerable distance from the place where the goods are located." UCC § 2–706, Comment ¶ 9. In such a case, the seller may transport the goods from the place of delivery and recover as incidental damages the cost of transporting the goods to the place or market for public sale. *Id.*

The seller's right to resale damages is not limited to breach of contract with regard to existing goods. *See* UCC § 2–706, Comment ¶ 7 (stating that "the goods need not be in existence to be resold"). Section 2–706 also provides that the seller may sue for resale damages for future goods. Suppose Acme Company and Omega, Inc. make a contract for widgets that Acme will manufacture and deliver to Omega. Before Acme begins producing the widgets, Omega repudiates the contract. Omega has anticipatorily repudiated the parties' contract. Acme then makes a contract to sell the widgets, which have not yet been produced, to Theta Corporation at a price lower than the price it charged Omega. *See* UCC § 2–706, Comment ¶ 7 (stating that in a case of anticipatory repudiation the seller may resell and "fix his damages by 'one or more contracts to sell' the quantity of conforming goods affected by the repudiation"); *but see* UCC § 2–706, Comment ¶ 9 (resale of unidentified goods as future goods at public sale). If the resale contract is commercially reasonable, then Acme may recover the difference between the contract price with Omega and the resale price with Theta as damages under § 2–706.

b. Market: § 2–708(1)

The seller also may sue for the difference between the market price and the contract price. The market price is the price at the time and place for tender. UCC § 2–708(1); *see* UCC § 2–503 (manner of seller's tender of delivery). Seller may recover the difference between contract and market price *plus* incidental damages *minus* expenses saved by virtue of the buyer's breach. UCC § 2–708(1).

The language of § 2–708(1) gives the following formula for resale damages:

$$KP - Mkt + ID - ES$$

Suppose that on March 1, Sam Seller makes a contract with Bella Buyer in which Buyer agrees to purchase 100,000 widgets at a price of $1 per widget. Buyer's facility is located in Gary, Indiana. The contract provides for delivery "FOB Gary" to Buyer's facility no later than May 1. Assume that the contract price does not include the $1,000 transportation cost. On April 15, Buyer informs Seller that Buyer will not accept the goods on May 1. This is anticipatory repudiation. On April 15, the market price for widgets is $1 per widget in Detroit, and $.95 in Gary. On May 1, the market price per widget is $.95 in Detroit, and $.90 in Gary. Damages are as follows:

$$\$100,000 - \$90,000 + \$0 - \$1,000 = \$9,000$$

The market price is the price in Gary on May 1, because § 2–708(1) calls for the market price at the time and place for tender. The time for tender is May 1 because that is the contract's date for delivery. In a case of anticipatory repudiation, the market price for sellers is generally *not* the price at the time when the seller learns of the repudiation. *Cf.* UCC § 2–713(1) (buyer's market price). The place for tender is Gary, because the contract provides for delivery F.O.B. Gary, making it a destination contract. In a destination contract, the seller bears the cost of transportation. *See* § 2–319(1)(b). Because Buyer breached, Seller does not incur the cost of transporting the goods, which is a savings of $1,000. (Note: In a case of anticipatory repudiation, if the lawsuit comes to trial *before* the time for performance, then the market price is the price "prevailing at the time when [the seller] learned of the repudiation." UCC § 2–723(1)).

Can the seller recover market price damages if it resells the goods? The answer to that question is not clear. In Peace River Seed Co-operative, Ltd. v. Proseeds Marketing, 322 P.3d 531 (Or. 2014), the Oregon Supreme Court surveyed the case law and commentary and set forth the arguments for and against allowing the seller who resells to recover market price damages. The *Peace River* court noted that "a number of courts" had adopted the view of Professors White and Summers that a seller who resells is not entitled to market price damages that exceed what the seller would recover based on § 2–706's resale formula. White and Summers point to the language of § 1–305, which provides that the objective of the UCC's remedy provisions is to put the aggrieved party "in as good a position as if the other party had fully performed." UCC § 1–305(a). This language from § 1–305 is a typical description of expectation damages. The *Peace River* court, however, explained that § 2–706 uses the word "may", not "shall", and, thus, does not mandate resale. The court also noted that Article 2 "rejects any doctrine of election of remedy as a fundamental policy." UCC § 2–703, Comment ¶ 1. Moreover, § 1–305 also provides that the UCC's remedy provisions are to be "liberally administered." UCC § 1–305(a). Thus, the *Peace River* court concluded that a seller has the right to "recover either market price damages or resale price damages, even if market price damages lead to a larger recovery." *Peace River*, 322 P.3d at 535.

Other courts have held to the contrary. In Tesoro Petroleum Corporation v. Holborn Oil Company, 547 N.Y.S.2d 1012 (N.Y. Sup. Ct. 1989), Tesoro contracted to sell approximately 10 million gallons of gasoline at $1.30 per gallon to Holborn Oil. When Holborn breached, Tesoro resold the gasoline for $1.10 per gallon. Tesoro argued that it was entitled to the difference between contract and market price when market price was $.80 a gallon. As the court noted, Tesoro would recover $3,000,000 more using market price versus resale price. (Resale price was $1.10 while market price was $.80 per gallon for a difference of $.30 per gallon over 10 million gallons.) The court agreed with White and Summers that resale damages were the proper measure of Tesoro's expectation.

> "[A] seller who resells goods reasonably identified to the broken contract for a price above the 2–708(1) market price should be

> limited to the difference between the contract price and his actual resale price. We believe that this is an exact measure of his expectation and that he should not recover more than that."

Id. at 1014 (quoting 1 White and Summers, Uniform Commercial Code 356 (Practitioner's 3d ed. 1988)). The court explained that awarding Tesoro an additional $3M over the resale damages amount would result in a windfall to the seller and "would be inconsistent with the policy of the Code as expressed in UCC 1–106 [now § 1–305]." *Id.* at 1016. Thus, the court held that Tesoro's damages were limited to the difference between contract price and resale price. *See also* Coast Trading Company v. Cudahy Company, 592 F.2d 1074 (9th Cir. 1979) (holding that seller's resale was commercially unreasonable but limiting seller's market price damages under § 2–708(1) "to the amount of damages that could be recovered under Section 2–706, that is, [seller's] actual losses" because awarding full market price damages would result in a windfall for seller).

c. Lost Volume Seller: § 2–708(2)

Suppose Acme makes a contract to sell Wiley Company 100 anvils at a cost of $100 per anvil. Acme expects to make a profit of $20 per anvil for a total profit of $2,000. Wiley breaches and Acme resells the anvils to Road Runner, Inc. (RRI) for $20 per anvil, which is the current market price. If Acme sues Wiley for breach, it will receive no damages because the difference between contract and resale price, or contract and market price, is $0.

But what if Acme had the capacity to produce anvils for *both* Wiley and RRI, and RRI would have purchased 100 anvils from Acme even if Wiley had not breached? Acme would have made a profit of $20 per anvil on 200, not 100, anvils. Thus, the "standard measure of damages is inadequate." UCC § 2–708, Comment ¶ 2. Acme is a lost volume seller because (1) its supply of anvils exceeds its demand; and (2) RRI would have purchased 100 anvils from Acme even if Wiley had not breached. *See, e.g.,* Unique Designs v. Pittard Machinery Company, 409 S.E.2d 241 (Ga. Ct. App. 1991) (stating that "[t]he whole concept of lost volume status is that the sale of the goods to the resale purchaser could have been made with other goods had there been no breach"). In such a case, § 2–708(2) provides the measure of damages.

> If the measure of damages provided in subsection (1) is inadequate to put the seller in as good a position as performance would have done then the measure of damages is the profit (including reasonable overhead) which the seller would have made from full performance by the buyer, together with any incidental damages provided in this Article (Section 2–710), due allowance for costs reasonably incurred and due credit for payments or proceeds of resale.

UCC § 2–708(2).

For the typical lost volume seller, including in the damages formula the last clause of § 2–708(2) (starting with the words "due allowance") results in a recovery that does not put the seller in the position it would have been had performance occurred. *See*

Unique Designs, 409 S.E. 2d at 244 (stating that "the overwhelming view of modern authority has concluded that the formula, if strictly applied, will not yield the correct recovery that a 'lost volume dealer' deserves"). Thus, courts award lost volume sellers their profit plus reasonable overhead and incidental damages, ignoring the final clause of § 2–708(2) in calculating damages. *Unique Designs,* 409 S.E. 2d at 244 (stating that seller's recovery for lost profits did not require deduction for the proceeds of its resale).[1]

The formula, then, for calculating the lost volume seller's damages is

$$\pi + \text{FC (Reasonable OH)} + \text{ID}$$

You may read court opinions that state the formula as follows:

$$\text{KP} - \text{VC (Direct Costs)} + \text{ID}$$

Either formula works to put the lost volume seller in the same position as if performance had occurred. Here is why. The seller prices its goods by taking account of its costs and what profit it wants to earn

---

[1] The formula in § 2–708(2) is not limited to lost volume sellers. It also applies to "jobbers" and "components sellers." 2 Hawkland UCC Series § 2–708:2. Suppose the buyer breaches when the seller has not completed manufacturing the goods, and the seller decides not to complete production under § 2–704(2). The seller has component parts that it resells for scrap. The seller must deduct from its recovery what it recoups as proceeds of reselling those component parts. For a good example and explanation of how § 2–708(2)'s formula works in such a case, *see* 2 Hawkland UCC Series § 2–708:2. Note: The discussion of § 2–708(2) in this Nutshell is limited to lost volume sellers.

on the sale. There are two types of costs: fixed costs and variable or direct costs. Fixed costs, e.g., cost of mortgage on the seller's plant, do not vary based on how many units of goods the seller produces. Variable or direct costs, e.g., raw materials used in production, do vary based on the number of units that the seller manufactures. Therefore, the following formula reflects what the seller includes in pricing its goods.

$$KP = \pi + FC + VC$$

If you subtract Variable Costs from both sides of the equation, you end up with the following:

$$KP - VC = \pi + FC$$

Because the seller is entitled to incidental damages under § 2–708, the final result is as follows:

$$KP - VC + ID = \pi + FC + ID$$

In the earlier example involving Wiley's breach of its contract with Acme, Acme earns $20 in profit per anvil. Each anvil is priced at $100. That means that Acme's costs are $80 per anvil. Suppose that $50 of that $80 are fixed costs while the remaining $30 are variable or direct costs. Assume that Acme incurs no incidental damages. Acme, as a lost volume seller, recovers $7,000 in damages under § 2–708(2).

$20 (profit) + $50 (fixed costs) + $0 (incidentals) = $70/anvil × 100 anvils = $7,000

Or

$100 (contract price) − $30 (variable costs) + $0 (incidentals) = $70/anvil × 100 anvils = $7,000

Therefore, either formula provides the proper measure of damages for the lost volume seller.

Students often wonder why the seller receives its fixed costs as part of its recovery as a lost volume seller. A simple example illustrates why. Suppose Seller has the capacity to make 10 units of Good X this year. Seller prices Good X at $10,000 per unit. It expects a profit of $3,000 per unit; $4,000 of its total $40,000 in fixed costs are allocated to each unit. Buyer A makes a contract with Seller to manufacture one unit of Good X. Assume Seller already has sold 8 units of Good X so Buyer A will purchase the 9th of 10 units that Seller manufactures this year. Before Seller begins production, however, Buyer A breaches. Seller makes a contract with Buyer B to buy the unit originally intended for Buyer A for $10,000. Assume that Buyer B would have purchased the 10th unit of Good X even if Buyer A had not breached its contract with Seller.

Seller is a lost volume seller. Buyer B would have purchased Good X even had Buyer A not breached, and Seller had the capacity to produce a 10th unit for Buyer B. Thus, had Buyer A not breached, Seller would have earned two profits of $3,000 each or $6,000. If Seller is limited to resale or market price damages, it gets only one profit or $3,000.

In addition, regardless of how much Seller produced, it had $40,000 in fixed costs to cover; it allocated $4,000 of that $40,000 fixed cost to each of the 10 units it expected to manufacture. Fixed costs are included in the contract price; contract price is profit plus costs. If Seller receives the contract price, which covers its profit and costs, *only* for the unit sold to Buyer B, then it does not recoup the fixed cost baked into the price for the unit that Buyer A contracted for. Fixed costs do not vary based on production. Seller must pay those costs whether it produces 1 or 10 units. If Seller sold 10 units, then it would recapture the $40,000 in fixed costs by virtue of its contract price. But if Seller receives only its profit of $3,000 for the breach by Buyer A, then the $4,000 in fixed costs allocated to unit #9 (the unit Buyer A contracted for) eats into Seller's profit. Instead of $4,000 in fixed costs per unit ($40,000 total/10 units), fixed costs are $4,444 per unit ($40,000 total/9 units). Thus, Seller's profit on each sale is reduced by the fixed cost not recovered for breach of the sale of unit #9. For this reason, the lost volume seller recovers not only its profit but also its fixed costs or overhead.

Suppose Seller and Buyer A contracted for purchase of the 10th unit of Good X. Buyer A breached, and Seller made a resale contract with Buyer B for the purchase of the 10th unit of Good X. In this scenario, Seller is *not* a lost volume seller, because it does not have the capacity to make an 11th unit of Good X. Seller's supply of Good X does not exceed its demand for Good X. Buyer B is simply replacing Buyer A as the purchaser of the 10th unit. In this case, § 2–706's resale formula would apply.

d. Action for the Price: § 2–709

In three and *only* three types of cases, the seller may recover the contract price together with any incidental damages incurred. UCC § 2–709, Comment ¶ 6 (stating that § 2–709 is "intended to be exhaustive in its enumeration of cases where an action for the price lies").

The first type of case is when the buyer has accepted the goods but failed to pay the price when it comes due. UCC § 2–709(1)(a). If the buyer rightfully revokes its acceptance of the goods, the seller is *not* entitled to the price.

> "Goods accepted" by the buyer under subsection (1)(a) include only goods as to which there has been no justified revocation of acceptance, for such a revocation means that there has been a default by the seller which bars his rights under this section.

UCC § 2–709, Comment ¶ 5. Thus, if the buyer's revocation is rightful, then the seller is in breach and the buyer remedies provisions of Article 2 apply. *See infra* § C of this Chapter.

The second type of case covered by § 2–709 is one in which the buyer fails to pay the price for "conforming goods lost or damaged within a commercially reasonable time after their risk of loss has passed to the buyer." UCC § 2–709(1)(a). For example, suppose Ajax Company agrees to sell 10,000 water flotation devices to Poseidon, Inc. with delivery to occur no later than June 1, F.O.B. Gary, Indiana. Ajax's plant is located in Gary, Indiana, and Poseidon's retail superstore is located in Portland, Oregon. Ajax puts the 10,000 devices into the hands of an appropriate carrier and promptly notifies

Poseidon of the shipment. *See* UCC § 2–503. While en route, the truck carrying the Ajax shipment is in an accident and all 10,000 flotation devices are destroyed. The contract was a shipment contract (FOB Gary) and, thus, the risk of loss passed to Poseidon when the flotation devices were delivered to the carrier. *See* UCC § 2–509(1)(a); UCC § 2–709, Comment ¶ 5 (stating that " '[g]oods lost or damaged' are covered by the section on risk of loss"). Thus, Ajax may recover the price from Poseidon. *See* Brewer v. J-Six Farms, L.P., 350 P.3d 420 (Okla. Civ. App. 2015) (stating that the "[t]he phrase 'within a commercially reasonable time,' as used in § 2–709(1)(b) clearly describes when the risk of loss passes to the buyer, and does not limit the ability of the seller to recover the contract price").

Finally, the seller may recover the price "of goods identified to the contract if the seller is unable after reasonable effort to resell them at a reasonable price or the circumstances reasonably indicate that such effort will be unavailing." UCC § 2–709(1)(b). In American Seating Company v. Archer Plastics, Inc., 2014 U.S. Dist. LEXIS 136007 (D. N.J. 2014), American Seating entered into a contract with Archer in which Archer agreed to pay for and take away approximately 45,000 stadium seats that had been disassembled and boxed up by Harriott, a subcontractor for American Seating that had removed the seats from the Camden Yards Baseball Stadium. Archer was in the business of selling sports team memorabilia, including used stadium seating. When the market for used seats collapsed, Archer breached its contract with American Seating.

American Seating resold more than 10,000 seats to another sports team and to a Florida county that purchased the seats for its stadium. Unable to sell the remaining seats, American Seating sold them for scrap or salvage value. American Seating sued Archer for recovery of the contract price.

Archer claimed that American Seating had not made "reasonable or diligent efforts to sell the seats" and, thus, was not entitled to recover the contract price. The court rejected this argument and found that American Seating had made "commercially reasonable efforts to sell the seats." The court noted that Archer failed to explain how American Seating, whose business was the sale of *new,* not used, seats, had acted unreasonably when Archer itself had found it impossible to sell the seats.

The court also found that sale of the seats for salvage value was commercially reasonable. The court noted that American Seating was in a "time bind" because it had to remove the old seating in order to finish its subcontracting work to install new seating at the stadium. The court rejected Archer's argument that American Seating should have stored the seats until resale could be arranged. The court concluded that the "only viable option" was to sell the seats for scrap value.

> Facing the choice of having to pay thousands of dollars to transport and store thousands of used seats for an indefinite time into the future, or saving these costs and earning some money by selling the seats for salvage, [American Seating]

> made the commercially reasonable choice to sell the seats for salvage.

American Seating, 2014 U.S. Dist. LEXIS at *28. The court held that American Seating had satisfied the requirements of § 2–709. American Seating's actions were commercially reasonable. It proved unable after reasonable efforts to resell all the seats at a reasonable price due to the collapse of the market for used seats. The sales for salvage value were commercially reasonable given the lack of a current market for the seats, the uncertainty of when the market would rebound, and the expense of storage. Thus, the court awarded American Seating the contract price after deducting for the amounts that (1) Archer had paid for the seats prior to breach, (2) American Seating had received from reselling more than 10,000 of the seats, and (3) American Seating had received from the sales for scrap value.

A seller who sues for the price must hold for the buyer goods identified to the contract and within the seller's control. UCC § 2–709(2). Prior to a court judgment for the price, if the seller is able to resell some (or all of the) goods, then the "net proceeds of any such resale must be credited to the buyer." UCC § 2–709(2). This is what happened in *American Seating*. The court deducted from the contract price the amounts that American obtained from reselling more than 10,000 seats to another company and a Florida county, and from sales of seats for scrap or salvage value. Any goods that the seller is unable to resell must be held for the buyer. UCC § 2–709(2). If a court holds that the seller is not entitled to the contract price, the seller "shall nevertheless be awarded damages for non-acceptance" under § 2–708. UCC § 2–709(3); *see* UCC § 2–709, Comment ¶ 7 (stating that the seller whose action for the price fails "may nonetheless have proved a case entitling him to damages for non-acceptance").

e. Consequential Damages?

None of the formulae for damages for sellers includes consequential damages. *See* § 2–706, § 2–708(1) & (2), § 2–709. Article 2's damages provisions for buyers do include consequential damages. *See* § 2–712, § 2–713, § 2–714; *see also* § C of this Chapter. As a practical matter, it is easy to see how a seller's breach might result in consequential damages for the buyer. Think about the commercial buyer who purchases goods for resale at its retail outlets. If the seller breaches, then that commercial buyer loses the profit expected from sales to third parties at retail.

Now consider the case of the buyer who breaches. The seller recovers the profit it expected from its sale to the buyer; that profit is captured in the various damage formulations in § 2–706, § 2–708, and § 2–709. But does the buyer's breach result in the typical seller losing profit from *third-party* sales or transactions? The answer generally is "no." The drafters of Amended Article 2, while including consequential damages as recoverable by the seller, noted that "[s]ellers rarely suffer compensable consequential damages." UCC revised § 2–710, Comment ¶ 1.

While uncommon, a seller nonetheless may suffer consequential damages. For example, in Stamtec, Inc. v. Anson Stamping Company, 346 F.3d 651 (6th Cir. 2003), Anson Stamping Company (ASCO) entered into a contract with Stamtec to deliver two mechanical presses. Stamtec then entered into a contract with its parent company Chin Fong to specially manufacture the presses. ASCO breached. When Stamtec subsequently entered into a contract with Precision Machine for two presses, Stamtec once again contracted with Chin Fong to manufacture the presses. Stamtec had not paid Chin Fong the purchase price for the ASCO presses but with the Precision order Chin Fong was able to use many of the parts produced for the ASCO presses. Thus, Chin Fong "forgave Stamtec's obligation to pay the purchase price for the ASCO presses and, instead, required Stamtec to pay a $272,000 salvage loss charge." *Id.* at 654. The Sixth Circuit held that this salvage loss charge constituted consequential damage.

If a seller suffers consequential damages, may it recover those damages from the buyer? Courts should liberally administer remedies such that "the aggrieved party may be put in as good a position as if the other party had fully performed." UCC § 1–305. If the buyer's breach results in consequential damages, then putting the seller in as good a position as if performance had occurred and the buyer had *not* breached should result in the seller recovering consequential damages, even though sellers rarely suffer such damages. But this language in § 1–305 is limited by the following phrase: "neither consequential or special damages nor penal damages may be had except as specifically provided in [the Uniform Commercial Code] or by other rule of law." UCC § 1–305; *see* UCC § 1–305, Comment ¶ 1 (stating that compensatory damages do not include "consequential or special damages, or penal damages"). None of the seller damages provisions include consequential damages. Thus, while § 1–305 provides for liberal administration of remedies it also clearly states that consequential damages are not recoverable unless specifically provided for by the relevant UCC provision. *See Stamtec,* 346 F.3d at 659 (stating that Tennessee UCC "preclude[d] the award of consequential damages except as provided by statute"); Firwood Manufacturing Company, Inc. v. General Tire, Inc., 96 F.3d 163 (6th Cir. 1996) (denying seller recovery of consequential damages because "sellers are entitled to incidental, but not consequential damages, under the U.C.C.") While Amended Article 2 includes in its damage formulae the recovery of consequential damages, no State has adopted the amendments.

2. SELLER'S OTHER REMEDIES

Article 2 also provides the seller with several non-damage remedies. Section 2–702 covers the seller's remedies, e.g., reclamation, when it discovers that the buyer is insolvent. Section 2–705 provides the rules for when the seller can stop delivery of the goods in transit.

a. Buyer's Insolvency: § 2–702

If the seller discovers that the buyer is insolvent, the seller may refuse to deliver goods to the buyer under the parties' contract unless the buyer pays in cash, including payment for all goods already delivered under the parties' contract. UCC § 2–702(1). The seller also may stop delivery of goods in transit. UCC § 2–702(1), § 2–705; *see infra* § B.2.b of this Chapter.

A buyer is insolvent if it (1) has generally stopped paying its debts in the ordinary course of business, except debts that are subject to bona fide dispute; (2) is unable to pay its debts at they become due; or (3) satisfies the Bankruptcy Code's definition of insolvency. UCC § 1–201(b)(23). The Bankruptcy Code's definition of insolvency for an individual or firm, other than a partnership, is a balance sheet test: if the buyer's liabilities exceed its non-exempt assets, then the buyer is insolvent. 11 U.S.C. § 101(32)(A).

Section 2–702 also allows the seller that has sold goods on credit to the buyer to reclaim those goods upon discovering that the buyer is insolvent.[2] "Reclamation is a limited in rem remedy that permits a seller to regain possession of goods delivered to an

---

[2] The Bankruptcy Code contains a reclamation provision, which "does not create a new, independent right to reclamation but merely affords the seller an opportunity, with certain limitations, to avail itself of any reclamation right it may have under nonbankruptcy law." Galey & Lord, Inc. v. Arley Corporation (*In re* Arlco, Inc.), 239 B.R. 261 (Bankr. S.D. N.Y. 1999). This Nutshell does not address the Bankruptcy Code's requirements for reclamation. *See* 11 U.S.C. § 546(c).

insolvent purchaser on credit." Whirlpool Corporation v. Wells Fargo, N.A. (*In re* hhgregg, Inc.), 949 F.3d 1039 (7th Cir. 2020). The rationale for this reclamation right is that "any receipt of goods on credit by an insolvent buyer amounts to a tacit business misrepresentation of solvency and therefore is fraudulent against the particular seller." UCC § 2–702, Comment ¶ 2. While the receipt by the insolvent buyer of goods is considered fraudulent, absent written misrepresentation of solvency by the buyer, the seller's right to reclaim the goods under § 2–702 is limited. In order to reclaim goods, the seller must make its reclamation demand within ten days of the buyer's receipt of the goods. While § 2–702 does not require that the demand be in writing, the short time frame necessarily limits the seller's reclamation right. UCC § 2–702(2); *cf.* UCC § 2–609(1) (stating that a party "may in *writing* demand adequate assurance of performance") (emphasis added). For example, Buyer and Seller enter into a contract for the purchase and sale of 10,000 widgets with delivery to occur at Buyer's retail store no later than March 1. The parties' contract provides for payment within 30 days of delivery. Seller delivers the widgets on March 1, and Buyer takes physical possession of the widgets on that date. *See* UCC § 2–103(1)(c) (defining "receipt"). Seller discovers Buyer's insolvency in early April when Buyer fails to pay for the March 1 delivery. Seller may not invoke its right to reclamation because more than 10 days have passed since Buyer received the widgets.

If Buyer had made a written representation of solvency to Seller within three months before March

1, then the 10-day limitation would not apply. *See* UCC § 2–702(2). Thus, suppose that on February 1, Buyer in the example above had stated in writing to Seller that it was solvent. The 10-day time frame would not apply, and upon discovery of Buyer's insolvency in early April, Seller could make a reclamation demand for the goods delivered to Buyer on March 1. Even this expanded right to reclaim, however, is limited. The seller's right to reclaim "is subject to the rights of a buyer in the ordinary course or other good faith purchaser" under Article 2. UCC § 2–702(3); *see* UCC § 2–403; *see also supra* Chapter 8, § A.2.

It is important to recognize that the UCC broadly defines the term "purchase" to include taking by pledge, lien, or security interest. UCC § 1–201(b)(29). Suppose BankOne extends a line of credit to Acme and Acme grants BankOne a security interest in all its inventory and accounts receivable, whether now owned or hereafter acquired. BankOne properly perfects its security interest. Samson Company subsequently sells goods to Acme on credit. Within 10 days of Acme receiving the goods, Samson discovers Acme's insolvency and makes a proper demand for reclamation of the goods. Is Samson's right to reclaim the goods subject to BankOne's perfected, floating lien on Acme's inventory? BankOne is a purchaser. *See* UCC § 1–201(b)(29) (taking by security interest). It gave value by extending credit to Acme. *See* UCC § 1–204. If BankOne acted in good faith, then Samson's right to reclaim the goods is subject to BankOne's superior rights as a good faith purchaser for value. *See* UCC § 1–201(b)(20) (good faith); *see also* Galey & Lord, Inc. v. Arley Corporation (*In re* Arlco, Inc.), 239 B.R. 261 (Bankr. S.D. N.Y. 1999) (stating that "[m]ost courts have treated 'a holder of a prior perfected, floating lien on inventory . . . as a good faith purchaser with rights superior to those of a reclaiming seller' " and rejecting the argument that a good faith purchaser for purposes of § 2–702 includes only a party acquiring its interest under Article 2 and not one acquiring a security interest under Article 9).

The seller that successfully reclaims goods "excludes all other remedies" with respect to the goods involved. UCC § 2–702(3). For example, suppose Seller successfully reclaims goods from Buyer. Seller re-sells the goods but for a price lower than the contract price with Buyer. Normally, Seller could sue Buyer for the difference between the contract and resale prices. *See* UCC § 2–706. But, by reclaiming the goods, Seller loses its ability to invoke any other Article 2 remedies with regard to the goods involved. The rationale for this rule is that reclamation "constitutes preferential treatment as against buyer's other creditors." UCC § 2–702, Comment ¶ 3. The cost to seller for obtaining this preferential treatment is the loss of any other Article 2 remedy. *See id.* (stating that because of this preferential treatment, § 2–702(3) "provides that such reclamation bars all [of seller's] other remedies as to the goods involved").

b. Stoppage of Delivery: § 2–705

As mentioned above, the seller, upon learning of the buyer's insolvency, may stop delivery of goods in transit or in the possession of a bailee. *See* UCC § 2–702(1), § 2–705(1). Section 2–705, however, expands the right of a seller to stop delivery to include situations in which the buyer repudiates or fails to make a payment due before delivery, or the seller has the right to withhold or reclaim the goods. *See* UCC § 2–705(1); UCC § 2–705, Comment ¶ 1 (noting expansion of the "remedy to cover situations, in addition to buyer's insolvency, specified in [subsection (1)]"). But, in cases in which the buyer is *not* insolvent, § 2–705 only allows the seller to "stop delivery of carload, truckload, planeload or larger shipments of express or freight." UCC § 2–705(1). Stopping delivery is a burden to carriers. Allowing sellers to stop delivery for even small shipments for reasons other than insolvency "might be a very heavy burden" for carriers; therefore, § 2–705 limits the right to stop delivery in cases other than insolvency to "carload, truckload, planeload, or other larger shipments." UCC § 2–705, Comment ¶ 1.

If the goods are in the possession of a bailee, then the seller must notify the bailee so as to "enable the bailee by reasonable diligence to prevent delivery of the goods." UCC § 2–705(3)(a). The bailee, after notification from the seller, must hold and deliver the goods according to the seller's instructions. *See* UCC § 2–705(3)(b). If the seller wrongfully stops delivery of goods, the seller is liable for breach and the bailee, even though obeying the seller's instructions, also may be liable to the buyer. *See* UCC § 2–705, Comment ¶ 1. Therefore, § 2–705(3)(b) gives the bailee a "right of indemnity as against the seller in such a case." *Id.*; *see* § 2–705(3)(b) (stating seller is liable to bailee for "any ensuing charges or damages").

C. BUYER'S REMEDIES

Section 2–711 provides an index of both the buyer's damage and non-damage remedies. Subsection (1) lists two basic damage remedies. When the seller fails to deliver the goods or repudiates, or the buyer rightfully rejects the goods or justifiably revokes acceptance of the goods, the buyer may cancel the contract and sue for cover or market price damages. UCC § 2–711(1)(a), (b). The buyer's right to cancel and sue for damages also applies to a breach of the whole of an installment contract. UCC § 2–711(1). Section 2–714 is not included in § 2–711, because § 2–714 is the damages provision applicable to *accepted* goods. Section 2–711(1) lists the damage remedies for cases in which the buyer rightfully *rejects* the goods or justifiably *revokes acceptance* of the goods. *See* UCC § 2–711, Comment ¶ 1. Article 2's damages provisions for buyers, unlike those for sellers, include the recovery of consequential damages. *See* UCC § 2–715.

Subsection (2) of § 2–711 lists the non-damage buyer remedies that permit the buyer to "reach[ ] the goods themselves." UCC § 2–711, Comment ¶ 1. If the seller repudiates or fails to deliver the goods, then the buyer may recover the goods if they have been identified to the contract or "in a proper case obtain specific performance or reply the goods." UCC § 2–711(2); *see* UCC § 2–716.

Finally, if the buyer rightfully rejects the goods or justifiably revokes acceptance of the goods, it has a security interest in goods in its possession or control for payments made to the seller on the contract price. *See* UCC § 2–711(3). The security interest also covers other reasonably incurred expenses, e.g., care and custody of the goods. *See* UCC § 2–711(3). The buyer may resell the goods in its control or possession using the procedures provided for resale under § 2–706. *See* UCC § 2–711(3).

The following table provides a key to the abbreviations used in the various formulae for buyer damages.

TABLE #4: BUYER DAMAGES: KEY TO ABBREVIATIONS

CD	Consequential Damages
Cover	Cover Price
ES	Expenses Saved
ID	Incidental Damages
KP	Contract Price
Mkt	Market Price
VGA	Value of Good Accepted
VGW	Value of Good as Warranted

1. BUYER'S DAMAGES

a. Cover: § 2–712

If the seller fails to deliver or repudiates, or the buyer rightfully rejects or justifiably revokes acceptance of the goods, the buyer may "cover" by purchasing or making a contract to purchase substitute goods. *See* UCC § 2–712(1). Cover is the buyer's counterpart to the right of the seller to resell. *See* UCC § 2–712, Comment ¶ 1.

The buyer's "cover" must be made in "good faith and without unreasonable delay." UCC § 2–712(1). Good faith is "honesty in fact and the observance of reasonable commercial standards of fair dealing." UCC § 1–201(b)(20). The words "without unreasonable delay" are not "intended to limit the time necessary for [the buyer] to look around and decide as to how he may best effect cover. The test here is similar to that generally used in [Article 2] as to reasonable time and seasonable action." UCC § 2–712, Comment ¶ 2. Whether action is reasonable "depends on the nature, purpose, and circumstances of that action." UCC § 1–205(a). If the parties' agreement provides no time period by which an action is to occur, then the action is seasonable if it is taken "within a reasonable time." UCC § 1–205(b). The delay is "determined from the date of breach" and the reasonableness of the delay is a question for the fact finder. Transammonia Export Corporation v. Conserv, Inc., 554 F.2d 719 (5th Cir. 1977).

For example, in Erie Casein Company v. Anric Corporation, 577 N.E.2d 892 (Ill. App. Ct. 1991), Erie

Casein, a buyer of casein for "food and feed ingredients", entered into three contracts in 1986 and 1987 with Anric, a wholesaler, for the purchase and sale of 575,000 pounds of New Zealand and Irish casein. Anric had difficulty fulfilling the contracts on a timely basis. In April 1987, the president of Anric told Erie Casein's vice president that it could not supply more New Zealand casein until late 1987, which was months after the delivery date provided for in the relevant contract. Erie Casein tried to find another supplier but did not make a cover contract for the New Zealand casein until August 1987. The cover contract price per pound was significantly higher than the original contract price per pound. Anric appealed the trial court's award of cover damages to Erie Casein, claiming that the buyer had failed to mitigate damages by timely effecting cover. The appellate court rejected Anric's argument and affirmed the trial court's findings. The court explained that notwithstanding Erie Casein's efforts to cover, a market shortage prevented the company from covering prior to August 1987. Given the circumstances, the delay between April and August in covering was not unreasonable and, thus, the court affirmed the trial court's award of cover damages.

The buyer need not buy identical goods in order to qualify for cover damages. The test is whether the goods are "commercially usable as reasonable substitutes under the circumstances of the particular case." UCC § 2–712, Comment ¶ 2. Moreover, the buyer may recover damages under § 2–712 even if it later is shown that the "method of cover used was not the cheapest or most effective." *Id.* The test is the commercial reasonableness at the time of cover, not what hindsight reveals.

But will a court award cover damages if the buyer upgrades to a better, more expensive good? It depends. In Nartron Corporation v. Amway Corporation, 1999 WL 33435058 (Mich. Ct. App. 1999), the court reversed the trial court's award of cover damages because the buyer Amway had failed to purchase an "equivalent substitute" product that was available, instead seeking cover damages for its purchase of a better performing product. Recognizing that the buyer need not purchase identical goods, the court explained that "[w]hen an equivalent product is available, a purchaser is not entitled to recover the full cost of cover for a product that is better than what was purchased." *Id.* at *2. Thus, whether the court will award cover damages to the buyer "depends in part on evidence suggesting that a more comparable substitute was not available." *Id.* at *3.

What about the buyer that self-covers—produces the goods itself or takes the goods from its own inventory? Will a court award such a buyer cover damages? The Fifth Circuit, in Dura-Wood Treating Company v. Century Forest Industries, Inc., 675 F.2d 745 (5th Cir. 1982), held that a buyer "may cover by manufacturing goods internally." Both the buyer Dura-Wood and the seller Century Forest were "in the business of treating cross-ties for industrial and commercial use." Dura-Wood entered into the contract with Century Forest when Dura-Wood recognized the need for additional cross-ties after having contracted to supply cross-ties to a third party. When Century Forest breached, Dura-Wood obtained price quotations from other companies but realized it could produce the cross-ties at a lower price itself. The Fifth Circuit concluded that Dura-Wood was entitled to cover damages.

> The purposes and presumptions of the Tex. Bus. & Com. Code can be, and are, fulfilled in those instances—such as in the instant case—when the buyer is already in the marketplace and can produce the goods at a price approximating or lower than the market price. It would defy reason and the Tex. Bus. & Com. Code's purposes of flexibility and adaptation to reasonable commercial practice to require a buyer to increase losses by covering through the purchase of goods from another seller, if it could produce the goods itself at a lower price.

Id. at 754.

In Chronister Oil Company v. Unocal Refining and Marketing, 34 F.3d 462 (7th Cir. 1994), however, the Seventh Circuit held that the buyer that covered by drawing on its own inventory of gasoline was not entitled to cover damages. The buyer Unocal sought cover damages equal to the difference between the contract price of 60.4 cents per gallon and the average cost of the inventory on which it drew, which was 63.14 cents per gallon. Had Unocal gone onto the market to purchase gasoline, it would have paid approximately 55 cents per gallon, thereby saving 5 cents per gallon as a result of the seller's breach. Thus, unlike the buyer in *Dura-Wood,* Unocal's self-cover was more expensive than purchasing the goods on the open market. This difference between the self-cover in *Dura-Wood* and *Chronister,* however, does not explain the Seventh Circuit's decision.

Judge Posner, writing for the Seventh Circuit panel, criticized the *Dura-Wood* decision, noting that the court had "shoehorned this kind of 'self-cover' into section 2–712." *Id.* at 465. Judge Posner explained that drawing on inventory is not a "purchase of or contract to purchase goods", as required by § 2–712. "You can't 'purchase,' whether in ordinary language or UCC speak (see § 1–201[(29)]), what you already own." *Id.* Moreover, doing "violence to the text" of § 2–712 was unnecessary, because § 2–713 provided a market price remedy. If it was reasonable for the buyer to produce the goods itself, then the difference between the market and contract prices would be an "appropriate measure" of damages. In fact, Judge Posner noted that this is what the court in *Dura-Wood* had done but had "merely cite[d] the wrong section." *Id.*

If a court awards cover damages, they are computed as follows:

$$\text{Cover} - \text{KP} + \text{ID} + \text{CD} - \text{ES}$$

UCC § 2–712(2). Notice that cover, the buyer counterpart to resale, provides for the recovery of consequential damages, unlike the resale formula for sellers. *See infra* § C.1.d of this Chapter for a discussion of consequential damages.

Suppose Acme and Wiley enter into a contract in which Acme agrees to sell 500 anvils for $700 per anvil to Wiley. It is a destination contract, so Acme bears the $5,000 cost of transport. Acme breaches and Wiley makes a reasonable cover contract with Road Runner for $750 per anvil. The contract with Road Runner is a shipment contract, which means that Wiley bears the $5,000 cost of shipment. (Assume transit charges are not included in the contract or cover prices.) Wiley's damages are $30,000.

$375,000 (Cover) − $350,000 (Contract) + $5,000
(Incidentals) + $0 (Consequentials)
− $0 (Expenses Saved)

Wiley now must pay for transportation of the goods, which is an incidental expense. Incidental damages include "any commercially reasonable charges, expenses or commissions in connection with effecting cover." UCC § 2–715(1). Wiley was able to sell all 500 anvils at retail, so it did not lose profit from retail sales and, thus, has no consequential damages. Wiley also did not save any expense by virtue of the breach.

Suppose Wiley cannot locate anvils similar to those that Acme agreed to sell to Wiley. Road Runner sells the Premium Anvil for $850 an anvil. Wiley enters into a contract for 500 Premium Anvils from Road Runner. There are no incidental expenses. Wiley is able to resell all 500 Premium Anvils but at a higher price than the regular anvils and, as a result, earns $150 in profit, rather than $100 in profit, from each retail sale. Assume that a court finds that the cover contract with Road Runner was reasonable, and that Wiley is entitled to cover damages. Its damages are $50,000. Why? Because you must deduct the extra profit that Wiley makes on resale from the damages it receives. The difference between cover and contract is \$75,000 (Cover of 500 × \$850 − Contract of 500 × \$700). But Wiley earned an additional \$25,000 in profit (\$50 more in profit per anvil × 500 anvils) from resale of the Premium Anvil. Remember: the goal is to put the buyer in as good a position as if the seller had performed. *See* UCC § 1–305.

b. Market Price: § 2–713

The buyer is not required to cover and instead may sue for the difference between market and contract price. UCC § 2–713, Comment ¶ 5 (stating that the market price damage remedy "applies only when and to the extent that the buyer has not covered"). The market price damage formula is as follows:

$$\text{Mkt} - \text{KP} + \text{ID} + \text{CD} - \text{ES}$$

UCC § 2–713(1). The seller's market price is the market price at the time for tender. *See* UCC § 2–708(1); *cf.* UCC § 2–723(1). The buyer's market price is the price at the time that the buyer learned of the breach. *See* UCC § 2–713(1). This difference matters in cases of anticipatory repudiation. For example, if Seller and Buyer make a contract for goods to be tendered on March 1, and Buyer anticipatorily repudiates on February 15, the market price for Seller under § 2–708(1) is the price on March 1, the time for tender. But suppose it is Seller who informs Buyer on February 15 that it will not deliver the goods on March 1. Seller's statement on February 15 is unequivocal and constitutes anticipatory repudiation. Using that date as the time when Buyer learns of the breach, the market price for Buyer is the price on February 15.

Seller's market price is determined by the price at the place of tender. UCC § 2–708(1). The same is true for the buyer *unless* the buyer rightfully rejects the goods after arrival or revokes its acceptance; in these cases, the market price is the price at the place of arrival. UCC § 2–713(2). The following examples illustrate how to determine which market price applies in computing market price damages.

Suppose that on May 1, Acme agreed to sell 500 anvils, at a price of $700 per anvil, to Wiley Company. Acme's plant is located in Detroit while Wiley's outlet is located in Cincinnati. The parties' contract provides for delivery of the anvils no later than June 15. The following chart provides the per-unit market price for anvils in Detroit and Cincinnati on various dates.

	Detroit	Cincinnati
May 1	$700	$705
May 31	$725	$730
June 10	$740	$745
June 12	$745	$750
June 15	$750	$755

Scenario #1: On May 31, Acme contacts Wiley to inform Wiley that Acme's plant is closing and, thus, Acme will not deliver anvils on June 15 (or any date) to Wiley. The delivery term in the parties' contract is

"F.O.B. Detroit." Assume that had Acme performed, it would have delivered the anvils to the carrier on June 10, and the anvils would have arrived in Cincinnati on June 12. Wiley learns of the breach on May 31; therefore, May 31 is the *time* for determining market price. *See* UCC § 2–713(1). This is not a case of rejection of the goods after arrival or revocation of acceptance; therefore, the *place* for determining market price is the *place for tender*. *See* UCC § 2–713(2). The delivery term "F.O.B. Detroit" means that the contract is a shipment contract. *See* § 2–319(1)(a). The place for tender, then, is Detroit. *See* § 2–503(2), § 2–504. The market price, then, is the price in Detroit on May 31, and Wiley is entitled to the $25 difference in market and contract prices ($725 versus $700) for 500 anvils.

Notice that when the goods arrive at the carrier and when they would have arrived at Wiley's outlet are irrelevant for market price damages for buyers. The reason is that the *time* for determining market price is the time when the buyer learns of the breach, not the time for tender, as in the case of the market price formula for sellers. *Compare* UCC § 2–708(1) *with* § 2–713(1).

Scenario #2: Same facts as in *Scenario #1*, except that the delivery term in the parties' contract is "F.O.B. Cincinnati." While the *time* for determining market price is still May 31, when the buyer learns of the breach, the *place for tender* changes because of the change in the delivery term. Therefore, market price is $730 per anvil, which is the market price in Cincinnati on May 31.

Scenario #3: The delivery term in the parties' contract is "F.O.B. Detroit." On June 10, Acme delivers the anvils to the carrier. They arrive at Wiley's outlet in Cincinnati on June 12 and upon inspection are found not to conform to the parties' contract. Wiley contacts Acme and rejects the shipment. (Assume that Acme does not invoke its right to cure.) June 12 is the *time* for determining market price because it is on June 12 that Wiley discovers the breach—the nonconforming goods. The place for tender does not apply because this scenario describes a case in which the goods are rejected after arrival. *See* UCC § 2–713(2). Cincinnati is the *place of arrival* and, therefore, the market price is $750, which is the price on June 12 in Cincinnati. Notice, once again, that the delivery term does not matter; the place for determining market price is the *place of arrival* in cases of "rejection after arrival or revocation of acceptance." UCC § 2–713(2).

If evidence of market price at the time and place provided for by § 2–713 is "not readily available," then the court is "granted reasonable leeway in receiving evidence of prices current in other comparable markets or at other times comparable to the one in question." UCC § 2–723, Comment: Purposes.

> [T]he price prevailing within any reasonable time before or after the time period described or at any other place which in commercial judgment or under usage of trade would serve as a reasonable substitute for the one described may be used, making proper allowance for the

> cost of transporting the goods to or from such other place.

UCC § 2–723(2). The court will not admit evidence of the prevailing market price at a time or place other than that described in § 2–713 "unless and until [the buyer] has given the other party such notice as the court finds sufficient to prevent unfair surprise." UCC § 2–723(3).

c. Accepted Goods: § 2–714

The damage formula at § 2–714 applies to cases in which the buyer accepts the goods. For example, suppose Seller delivers nonconforming goods to Buyer under the parties' contract. If Buyer rejects the goods after inspecting them, Buyer will cover and sue for damages under § 2–712 *or* sue for market price damages under § 2–713. But if Buyer accepts the goods and wants to sue for damages because the goods are nonconforming, then § 2–714 governs.

Section 2–714 provides for damages with regard to accepted goods in two situations. The first is a buyer's claim for damages resulting from breach of either express and/or implied warranties. *See* UCC § 2–714(2). The second involves a buyer's claim for damages for nonconforming goods that is not based on breach of warranty. *See* UCC § 2–714(1). In either case, the buyer must give notice to the seller of the breach within a reasonable time of discovering the breach. We turn first to that notice requirement.

1) Notice: § 2–607(3)

Section 2–714 provides that a buyer that accepts the goods and gives notice under § 2–607(3) may recover damages resulting from "any non-conformity of tender." UCC § 2–714(1). If the buyer that has accepted goods fails to give notice to the seller of the breach "within a reasonable time after he discovers or should have discovered any breach," then the buyer will be "barred from any remedy." UCC § 2–607(3)(a). For example, in JM McCormick Company, Inc. v. International Truck & Engine Corporation, 2008 WL 11375444 (S.D. Ind. 2008), International Truck learned in September of 2003 that chemicals used in the treated plywood supplied by McCormick caused corrosion in the floors of International Truck's buses. In January of 2005, McCormick filed suit against International Truck for breach of contract and International Truck counterclaimed. While International Truck amended its counterclaim in July 2005 to add claims for breach of implied warranties related to the quality of the plywood that McCormick had supplied, it failed to notify McCormick of the corrosion problem until December of 2005. The district court explained that giving notice is a "condition precedent" to recovery for breach of warranty and that the buyer must allege in its complaint that it had given notice to the seller. The court held that International Truck's breach of warranty claims were barred because it had failed to give notice prior to filing its breach of warranty claims and had not alleged in its counterclaim that it had provided notice to McCormick. *See also* Sta-Rite Industries, LLC v. Franklin Electric Company, 519

F. App'x 370 (6th Cir. 2013) (stating that compliance with § 2–607(3) requires the buyer to "provide reasonable notice to the seller before filing a lawsuit"); Huskey v. Colgate-Palmolive Co., 2020 WL 6342704 (E.D. Mo. 2020) (denying buyers leave to amend complaint because amendment was futile given the buyers' failure to allege that they had notified seller of the potential breach of warranty prior to filing their lawsuit).

The failure to give notice prior to filing suit may not be fatal if the seller already has actual knowledge of the defect on which the buyer bases its breach-of-warranty claims. For example, in Zakikhani v. Hyunai Motor Company, 2022 WL 1740034 (C.D. Cal. 2022), Hyundai and Kia moved to dismiss buyers' implied warranty claims, in part, for failing to notify Hyundai and Kia prior to litigation of problems with the anti-lock braking systems in buyers' vehicles that formed the basis of buyers' implied warranty claims. Buyers alleged that Hyundai and Kia had knowledge of the anti-lock braking system defect as early as 2012, which was years prior to the buyers filing suit. The court held that buyers' allegations of knowledge sufficed to deny Hyundai's and Kia's motion to dismiss the implied warranty claims on the basis of the UCC's notice requirements.

When assessing the buyer's compliance with § 2–607(3), keep in mind the reasons for the notice requirement. First, notifying the seller of the buyer's complaint "opens the way for normal settlement through negotiation." UCC § 2–607, Comment ¶ 4.

Second, providing the seller with notice gives the seller the chance to inspect the goods and investigate the buyer's claim at a time when the facts are fresh. Thus, the seller may minimize its damages and better defend itself should litigation occur. *See Sta-Rite,* 519 F. App'x at 376.

2) Damages for Breach of Warranty: § 2–714(2)

It is important to see the connection between the damages provision at § 2–714 and Article 2's warranty provisions. For example, suppose Merchant Seller delivers widgets to Merchant Buyer. Buyer accepts the shipment without inspecting the widgets. An inspection would have revealed that the widgets did not conform to the parties' contract and would not pass without objection in the widget trade. Buyer subsequently discovers the nonconformity but can no longer reject the goods nor revoke its acceptance. *See* UCC § 2–602, § 2–606, § 2–608. Yet, Seller has breached the implied warranty of merchantability by delivering widgets that cannot "pass without objection in the trade under the contract description." UCC § 2–314(2)(a). In such a case, Buyer may sue for damages caused by Seller's breach with regard to the accepted widgets.

In a case involving breach of warranty, § 2–714's formula for damages is as follows:

$$VGW - VGA + ID + CD$$

UCC § 2–714(2), (3). In many cases, the value of the good as warranted will be the contract price. *See, e.g.,* McCoolidge v. Oyvetsky, 874 N.W.2d 892 (Neb. 2016) (finding that purchase price of vehicle was "strong evidence of its value as warranted"); *see also* 2 Hawkland UCC Series § 2–714:2 (stating that value of goods as warranted is "often indicated by the contract price of the goods"). But what is the value of the good accepted? Let's look at a very simple example to work through § 2–714(2)'s damages language.

Suppose Bette purchases a high-end espresso machine for her home from *The Coffee Store*. The purchase price is $650. The machine arrives and Bette uses it for several weeks. One morning, however, the machine malfunctions and catches on fire. The machine is completely destroyed and unusable; assume it has no scrap value. The fire causes $1,000 in damage to Bette's kitchen counter. Bette sues for breach of the implied warranty of merchantability, arguing that the machine is not fit for its ordinary purpose, and seeks damages of $1,650 under § 2–714.

The value of the good as warranted is the contract price of $650. The machine is completely destroyed and unusable and has no scrap value. Thus, there is a good argument that the value of the good that Bette accepted is zero. Therefore, the difference in value between the good as warranted and as accepted is the purchase price of $650 ($650 – $0). There are no incidental damages, but the damage to Bette's countertop is consequential damage. "Consequential damages resulting from the seller's breach include . . . injury to person or property proximately resulting from any breach of warranty." UCC § 2–715(2)(b).

The espresso machine was not merchantable because it was unfit for the ordinary purpose of making coffee, and the machine malfunctioned, which was the proximate cause of the injury to Bette's property—her kitchen countertop.

Bette's example is simple. The value of the good as warranted is the contract price. If the good is completely destroyed and unusable, the value of the good as accepted is zero. In other words, the difference between the good as warranted and the good as accepted amounts to the purchase price of the good. *Cf.* Iron Dynamics v. Alstom Power, Inc., 2008 WL 2078621 (N.D. Ind. 2008) (stating that there "may be occasional cases where the measure of damages for the breach of a limited warranty is the purchase price, though that would not be the case where the goods have at least scrap value").

But what if the good is not destroyed but simply fails to work properly? What if the good is damaged but retains some value? What, then, is the value of the good as accepted? Section 2–714 provides that the measure of damages is the value at the "time and place of acceptance." UCC § 2–714(2); *see* UCC § 2–714, Comment ¶ 3 (stating that § 2–714(2) "departs from the measure of damages for non-delivery [§ 2–713(2)] in utilizing the place of acceptance rather than the place of tender"). Unlike market price, however, there is no established "market" for nonconforming goods, which makes this reference to time and place less than helpful in establishing the value of the goods as accepted.

Many courts use the cost of repair or replacement as evidence of the damages caused by the seller's breach of warranty. For example, the federal district court in IMI Norgren, Inc. v. D&D Tooling & Manufacturing, Inc., 247 F. Supp. 2d 966 (N.D. Ill. 2002) stated that in Illinois the measure of damages for breach of warranty when the seller has not fully performed or has defectively performed is the "cost of correcting the defective condition." *Id.* at 971.The court explained that damages under § 2–714(2) include the "costs of repair, replacement, and restoration." *Id.* In Holden Machinery v. Sundance Tractor & Mower (*In re* Fried Group), 218 B.R. 247 (Bankr. M.D. Ga. 1998), the bankruptcy court found at trial that evidence of the cost of repairs was "relevant and persuasive" in determining the difference between the value of the goods as warranted versus the value of the goods accepted. On the seller's motion for reconsideration, the court reaffirmed its earlier conclusion that the reasonable cost of repair was the "proper measure of damages for [seller's] breach of implied warranties." *Id.* at 249.

Some courts that allow evidence of the cost of repair or replacement to measure breach-of-warranty damages cite to the "special circumstances" exception in § 2–714(2). The measure of damages for breach of warranty is the diminution in value of the goods resulting from the breach "unless special circumstances show proximate damages of a different amount." UCC § 2–714(2). Thus, while the difference between the value of the goods as warranted and the value as accepted at the time and place of acceptance is "the usual, standard and reasonable method of ascertaining damages in the case of breach of warranty," this measure is "not intended as an exclusive measure." UCC § 2–714, Comment ¶ 3. For example, in New York v. Pullman, 662 F.2d 910 (2d Cir. 1981), the Second Circuit rejected the argument that current cost-of-replacement evidence was irrelevant to determining damages under § 2–714(2)'s "special circumstances" language. In *Pullman,* The New York City Transit Authority contracted to purchase 754 subway cars from Pullman. Pullman subcontracted with Rockwell International to design and manufacture dual undercarriages for the Pullman cars. The Transit Authority sued Pullman and Rockwell for breach of warranty based on defects in the cars and their undercarriages. Pullman argued that the measure of damages was the cost of retrofitting the dual undercarriages. The Transit Authority claimed that the proper measure of damages was the cost of replacing the defective dual undercarriages with standard, single frame undercarriages. The district court instructed the jury, in part, that it could find that the Transit Authority was entitled to cost-of-replacement damages, based on the circumstances of the case, including the Transit Authority's concern for passenger safety. The jury awarded the Transit Authority damages of $72 million—twice the amount that Pullman estimated for the cost of retrofitting the subway cars.

Pullman appealed the district court's decision in favor of the Transit Authority and argued, among other things, that the trial court had erred in allowing the jury to award damages based on the "special circumstances" language in § 2–714(2). The Second Circuit rejected Pullman's argument.

> Where special circumstance justify the use of a measure of damages other than that expressly provided by the statute "[a buyer] may recover for its direct damages in any manner that is reasonable." ... An appropriate measure of damages under that provision is the "actual cost" of a remedy that meets the ultimate requirements of the contract by converting non-conforming goods into goods which will perform as warranted—even if that remedy required replacing defective parts with parts substantially different than those provided under the contract, at a time later than delivery—as long as that remedy meets the ultimate requirements of the contract "at the lowest cost and with the least delay." ... Accordingly, the jury here was properly permitted to employ the "special circumstances" language to arrive at a measure of damages based on current replacement costs as the amount necessary to compensate [buyers] for breach of warranty.

Pullman, 662 F.2d at 918. The Second Circuit explained that evidence of current replacement cost "may properly be excluded" when there is no evidence of special circumstances. But the court noted that evidence of the cost of replacing the defective undercarriages was relevant to determining the buyers' actual damages. *See also* McCoolidge v. Oyvetsky, 874 N.W.2d 892 (Neb. 2016) (stating that "[c]ourts may invoke the 'special circumstances' exception in § 2–714(2) to award repair costs as damages").

In conclusion, evidence of the cost to repair or replace defective goods may be relevant to determine the damages to which a buyer is entitled for the seller's breach of warranty. Some courts consider such evidence when determining a good's diminution in value measure—the difference between the value of the goods as warranted versus the value of the goods as accepted. Other courts view such evidence as an alternative to § 2–714(2)'s standard diminution-in-value measure. Regardless, many courts use evidence of the cost to repair or replace defective goods to assess the buyer's damages for breach of warranty.

3) Damages for Any Nonconformity of Tender: § 2–714(1)

While § 2–714 provides remedies to the buyer in the case of breach of warranty, keep in mind that it applies not only to "breaches of warranty but also [to] any failure of the seller to perform according to his obligation under the contract." UCC § 2–714, Comment ¶ 2. The buyer may recover damages "in any manner which is reasonable" for "any non-conformity of tender the loss resulting in the ordinary course of events from the seller's breach." UCC § 2–714(1). In other words, if the seller delivers nonconforming goods that the buyer accepts but the nonconformity is not a breach of warranty or the seller disclaimed relevant warranties, the buyer still may sue for loss resulting from the seller's tender of nonconforming goods.

For example, in *In re* Lamica Corporation, 65 B.R. 849 (Bankr. S.D. N.Y. 1986), BHM Metal Products Company (BHM) contracted to sell metal frames and tubes to Lamica. Not only were the goods delivered late, they either were not painted properly or not painted at all, as required by the parties' agreement. Lamica had contracted to sell formica tabletops to a customer and needed the frames and tubes for that contract. Because BHM delivered late and Lamica's customer was threatening to impose liquidated damages, Lamica could not reject BHM's nonconforming parts. Instead, Lamica decided to touch up and paint the nonconforming goods itself, incurring more than $11,000 in expenses in doing so. In the bankruptcy case, Lamica objected to BHM's proof of claim and sought to reduce the amount owed to BHM by Lamica's costs to paint the nonconforming parts supplied by BHM.

The bankruptcy court ruled in Lamica's favor. The court began by noting that the term "nonconformity" in § 2–714(1) refers to "any failure of the seller to perform according to his obligations under the contract," not simply losses resulting from breach of warranty. UCC § 2–714, Comment ¶ 2. It then concluded that the cost to repair the nonconforming goods was "an appropriate measure of damages" because it satisfied the "ultimate requirements of the contract by converting non-conforming goods into goods" that complied with the parties' contract. *Lamica,* 65 B.R. at 855. Thus, Lamica's cost to touch up and paint the metal frames and tubes was deducted from the amount that Lamica owed BHM under the parties' agreement.

Section 2–714(1) also may apply to a case in which the seller has validly disclaimed warranties. In Morgan Buildings and Spas, Inc. v. Humane Society of Southeast Texas, 249 S.W.3d 480 (Tex. App. 2008), the Humane Society of Southeast Texas bought a steel frame building from Morgan to use to store animal feed and lawn equipment. The parties' agreement properly disclaimed warranties. But because the building was not secure, the Humane Society could not use it to store equipment, and rodents infested the stored animal food. The court rejected the idea that a buyer may only recover damages under § 2–714 for breach of warranty once it accepts the goods. It explained that § 2–714(1) provides for the recovery of damages for any nonconformity that results in loss to the buyer. Because Morgan had supplied a building that did not conform to the parties' agreement, Morgan had breached the contract. Therefore, the Humane Society was entitled to recover damages for that breach " 'as determined in any manner which is reasonable.' " *Id.* at 491 (quoting Texas Business and Commerce Code).

d. Consequential Damages: § 2–715

The damages provisions for buyers, unlike those for sellers, expressly provide for the recovery of consequential damages. *Compare* UCC § 2–710 *with* UCC § 2–715; *see* UCC § 1–305(a). Consequential damages include damages for injuries to "person[s] or property proximately resulting from any breach of warranty." UCC § 2–715(2)(b). A common type of consequential damage is lost profits from third-party sales. For example, Buyer makes a contract with Seller to purchase goods with a Fourth-of-July theme to sell in Buyer's retail store. Seller fails to deliver the goods. Buyer is unable to purchase the goods elsewhere in time to take advantage of the Fourth of July holiday. Lost profits from the sale of the Fourth-of-July themed goods are consequential damages.

In order to recover lost profits, the buyer must satisfy several requirements. Lost profits must be foreseeable and caused by the breach, and they cannot be speculative. The buyer cannot recover lost profits that it could have "prevented by cover or otherwise." UCC § 2–715(2)(a).

The buyer can recover consequential damages for "any loss resulting from general or particular requirements and needs of which the seller at the time of contracting had reason to know." *Id.* This is the foreseeability requirement. If the seller contracts to sell goods to a buyer that sells those goods at retail, then the seller has reason to know that its breach may result in the buyer suffering lost profits from those retail sales. *See* UCC § 2–715, Comment ¶ 6 (stating that in the case of a sale of goods to a buyer "in the business of reselling them, resale is one of the requirements of which the seller has reason to know"). The test for foreseeability is not whether the seller actually foresaw the losses but "whether the losses could reasonably have been foreseen."

Superwood Company v. Slam Brands, Inc., 2013 WL 6008489 (W.D. Wash. 2013).

Notice that foreseeability is measured as of the time of contracting, not at the time of breach. The reason is that foreseeability is about notice to the seller of its potential exposure for damages upon breach. "Such notice is critical because it ensures that the 'contracted for' price reflects the entire scope of the risk (i.e., the potential liability for breach) that the seller has agreed to bear." Mississippi Chemical Corporation v. Dresser-Rand Company, 287 F.3d 359 (5th Cir. 2002) (citing to Richard A. Posner, Economic Analysis of Law 141 (5th ed. 1998)).

The seller's breach also must have caused the buyer to lose the profits claimed as consequential damages. Suppose Buyer and Seller entered into a contract for the purchase and sale of an aerial lift. Buyer provides arborist services and intended to use the lift for tree trimming and cutting. Seller delivered the lift in early January 2021, but the lift malfunctioned. Seller attempted to repair the lift but was not successful until early July 2021. Rather than use the lift, Buyer decided to sell the lift after it was repaired and fully functional. Buyer sued Seller for breach of warranty and sought damages for its lost profits for all of calendar year 2021. Buyer argued that because of the malfunctioning lift it lost profits from tree-trimming contracts it could have made had the lift worked properly. While Buyer may be able to recover lost profits for January through early July 2021, it cannot recover lost profits for the period after the lift was repaired and fully functional. Buyer decided to sell the lift rather than use it. That decision, not the malfunctioning lift, caused any lost profits for the period after the lift was repaired and fully functional in early July 2021. *See* P.C. Hoag & Company v. Man Lift Manufacturing Company, 2018 WL 4298343 (D. N.H. 2018) (example modified from case facts).

Consequential damages in the form of lost profits also cannot be speculative. The buyer has the "burden of proving the extent of loss incurred by way of consequential damages" but is not required to prove its lost profits with "mathematical precision." UCC § 2–715, Comment ¶ 4.

Finally, the buyer cannot recover consequential damages that it could reasonably have "prevented by cover or otherwise." UCC § 2–715(2)(a). This is the mitigation principle. While a seller is responsible for the losses its breach causes, the buyer cannot simply sit back and run up losses that it could avoid. For example, in Irmscher Suppliers, Inc. v. Schuler, 909 N.E.2d 1040 (Ind. Ct. App. 2009), the appeals court reduced part of the damages awarded by the trial court because the buyers had failed to mitigate their damages. The Schulers purchased Pella casement windows for their home from Irmscher Supplies. The casement windows were equipped with "Rolscreens" to prevent bugs from entering the home when the windows were open. Gaps in the Rolscreens, however, resulted in large numbers of bugs getting into the Schulers' home during the spring and fall. The Schulers sued for breach of warranty and sought damages that included consequential damages for seven years of their time spent killing and cleaning up dead insects. The appeals court noted that three years after installation of the windows, Pella and Irmscher had offered to replace the Rolscreens with flat screens at no cost to the Schulers. The court explained that had the Schulers accepted the flat screens, they "could have minimized their damages due to the ingress of insects." *Id.* at 1052. Therefore, the court reduced the $8,428 in consequential damages awarded by the trial court for time spent killing and cleaning up after insects to $3,612, because the buyers could have mitigated their damages after three years by accepting the offer to replace the screens.

2. BUYER'S OTHER REMEDIES

a. Specific Performance: § 2–716(1) & (2)

A court may decree specific performance "where the goods are unique or in other proper circumstances." UCC § 2–716(1). The decree may include "terms and conditions as to payment of the price, damages, or other relief as the court may deem just." UCC § 2–716(2).

The drafters of Article 2 intended that courts take a "more liberal attitude" about granting a buyer specific performance of the contract. *See* UCC § 2–716, Comment ¶ 1. Thus, the phrase "other proper circumstances" expands the availability of specific performance beyond the narrower common law requirement of uniqueness. What constitutes "other proper circumstances"? Section 2–716 does not define the phrase, but the "inability to cover is strong evidence of 'other proper circumstances.'" UCC § 2–716, Comment ¶ 2.

The drafters also intended to broaden the meaning of the word "unique" with an "emphasis on the commercial feasibility of replacement." *Id.* In other words, whether the buyer can cover is important not only in determining whether "other proper circumstances" exist but also whether the goods are unique.

> The test of uniqueness under [§ 2–716] must be made in terms of the total situation which characterizes the contract. Output and requirements contracts involving a particular or peculiarly available source or market present today the typical commercial specific performance situation, as contrasted with contracts for the sale of heirlooms or priceless works of art which were usually involved in the older cases.

UCC § 2–716, Comment ¶ 2. For example, in Almetals, Inc. v. Wickeder Westfalenstahl, GmbH, 2008 WL 4791377 (E.D. Mich. 2008), Almetals and Wickeder entered into a seven-year contract in which Almetals was granted the exclusive right to sell Wickeder's clad metal in North America and required Wickeder to supply the clad metal. The parties' agreement included a Customer Order and Protection Clause that provided protection for an additional ten years for existing customers upon termination of the contract's seven-year term. Wickeder terminated the contract after seven years but altered payment terms that adversely affected Almetals with regard to existing customers, in violation of the contract's Customer Order and Protection Clause. Almetals' efforts to find other sources of the clad metal were unsuccessful.

The district court ruled that Wickeder breached when it altered the payment terms under the parties' agreement. The district court concluded that specific performance was the appropriate remedy.

> The UCC is consistent with the common law in which specific performance is well-recognized as an appropriate remedy where goods are unique or scarce. . . .
>
> Specific performance under UCC § 2–716 is the appropriate remedy because the varieties of clad metal supplied by Wickeder pursuant to the parties' requirements contract are unique and there are no known alternative sources of supply, but only speculation as to a possible alternative source for .2% of .3% of the product.

Almetals, 2008 WL 4791377, at **7, 8. Therefore, the court ordered specific performance by Wickeder of the terms of the parties' agreement for the duration of the Customer and Order Protection clause. *Cf.* INEOS Americas LLC v. Dow Chemical Company, 378 F. App'x 74 (2d Cir. 2010) (finding that district court did not err in denying buyer INEOS specific performance because it was able to make short-term contracts to cover its requirements for ethylene oxide that Dow had agreed to supply under the parties' long-term agreement and any damages flowing from

Dow's breach were "remediable with money damages" using Article 2's cover formula).

b. Replevin: § 2–716(3)

A court may order replevin of goods identified to the contract in two situations. The first is when the buyer is unable after reasonable effort to cover, or such effort would be "unavailing." UCC § 2–716(3). The focus on the ability to cover means that there is some overlap between the remedy of specific performance and that of replevin. 2 Hawkland UCC Series § 2–716:2. One difference, however, is that the buyer's right to replevin is only for goods identified to the contract. *See* UCC § 2–501. There is no such requirement for Article 2's specific performance remedy. *See* 2 Hawkland UCC Series § 2–716:2 (noting that "specific performance does not require the goods to be identified to the contract").

The second situation involves a case in which goods are shipped under reservation and "the buyer has tendered the amount of the security interest granted by Section 2–505." *Id.*; UCC § 2–716(3); *see* UCC § 2–505 (seller's shipment under reservation). In the case of consumer goods, the buyer's right to replevin "vests upon acquisition of a special property." UCC § 2–716(3). Such vesting occurs upon identification of the goods to the contract. *See* UCC § 2–716(3), Comment ¶ 3; *see also* UCC § 2–501. Bear in mind that a buyer seeking to replevy goods must comply with any state law requirements for replevin. 2 Hawkland UCC Series § 2–716:2 (explaining that "[m]ost states have statutes that govern the process of replevin . . . and Section 2–716(3) does not displace that state law process").

In *In re* Surplus Furniture Liquidators, 199 B.R. 136 (Bankr. M.D. N.C. 1995), customers who had purchased furniture pre-bankruptcy from debtor Surplus Furniture objected to sale of the furniture and sought various remedies, including specific performance of their contracts and replevin of the furniture. The customers had paid for the furniture that debtor had sold to them prior to bankruptcy. But before debtor made these furniture sales, it had granted a security interest to High Point Bank in its inventory as security for High Point's loans to the debtor. *Cf.* UCC § 2–716, Comment ¶ 5 (stating that a buyer that has a right of replevin takes free of a security interest "created by the seller if it attaches to the goods after the goods have been identified to the contract"). When the debtor defaulted on those loans, High Point took control of the inventory, which included the furniture claimed by the objecting customers. The debtor sought bankruptcy court approval for sale of some of its furniture inventory then in possession of High Point Bank. Pre-bankruptcy customers of the debtor objected to the sale, claiming that they were entitled to recover possession of the furniture for which they already had paid.

The bankruptcy court first denied the customers' request for specific performance of the contracts for their furniture. The court explained that not only were the goods not unique, "other proper circumstances" did not exist. The court noted that the objecting customers easily could cover by purchasing the furniture from other retailers. The bankruptcy court also held that the remedy of replevin was not available to the objecting customers. Once again, the court explained that cover was available and noted that the objecting customers presented no evidence that they had made reasonable efforts to cover but had been unable to do so. Therefore, the court overruled the customers' various objections and ordered that the sale proceed, although it did require the debtor to provide ten days' written notice to the objecting customers of the time and place set for the sale.

c. Security Interest in Goods and Resale: § 2–711(3)

Suppose Buyer and Seller entered into a contract for the purchase and sale of a machine for a total contract price of $20,000. Seller delivered the machine in a timely fashion. Buyer inspected and accepted the machine and paid Seller the purchase price. Approximately a month after delivery, the machine began to malfunction. Buyer contacted Seller but no cure was forthcoming. Buyer then contacted Seller to revoke its acceptance. Assuming Buyer's revocation was justified, Buyer has a security interest in the machine for the $20,000 it paid and for any reasonable expenses it incurred for "inspection, receipt, transportation, care and custody" of the machine. UCC § 2–711(3). Buyer also may resell the machine so long as it complies with § 2–706's requirements for resale. *See id.* Suppose Buyer resells the machine for $22,000. May Buyer keep the

$2,000 in profit it made from the resale? No. Unlike the seller that resells, the buyer that resells under § 2–711(3) "is limited to retaining only the amount of the price paid and the costs involved in the inspection and handling of the goods." UCC § 2–711, Comment ¶ 2; *cf.* UCC § 2–706(6) (stating that "seller is not accountable to the buyer for any profit made on resale").

The buyer that resells, however, must comply with the requirements of § 2–706. Deaton, Inc. v. Aeroglide Corporation, 657 P.2d 109 (N.M. 1982) involved the purchase and sale of Mini Dumps. (A Mini Dump works as a small dump truck when it is installed on the bed of a pickup truck.) Aeroglide sold the Mini Dumps to Deaton, but Deaton rightfully rejected them because they failed to operate properly. Upon rejecting the Mini Dumps, Deaton wrote to Aeroglide demanding payment of approximately $23,500, its cash outlay plus costs for storage and materials, and asked Aeroglide to pick up the Mini Dumps. Aeroglide offered to pay Deaton almost $22,000 for the Mini Dumps but Deaton insisted on a full refund of the purchase price and costs. Deaton and Aeroglide were unable to settle, and Deaton filed suit for breach of contract. About two years later, Deaton sold the Mini Dumps for $9,200 in a private sale.

The New Mexico Supreme Court held that because Deaton had rightfully rejected the Mini Dumps, it had a security interest in the goods for "the entire amount spent for the units" and, therefore, was not required to return them for $22,000 rather than the full $23,500 owed. The court rejected Aeroglide's contention that because Deaton had held the goods and resold them after rejection, Deaton had acted in a manner inconsistent with Aeroglide's ownership in violation of § 2–602(2). The court explained that the security interest provided by § 2–711(3) entitled Deaton to hold and resell the goods and, therefore, could not constitute a violation of § 2–602(2). The court also explained that Deaton's security interest in the Mini Dumps entitled it to resell the goods, so long as the resale was commercially reasonable.

The New Mexico Supreme Court, however, held that Deaton had failed to comply with the requirements of § 2–706. First, Deaton failed to provide Aeroglide with reasonable notice of its intention to resell at a private sale. *See* UCC § 2–706(3). Second, Deaton waited two years before selling the Mini Dumps, during which time the condition of the goods further deteriorated. Moreover, Deaton did not try to sell the units; it only resold once another buyer approached it two years after Aeroglide had delivered the Mini Dumps. The New Mexico Supreme Court noted that "excessive delay" can render a resale commercially unreasonable and reversed the trial court's award of damages for the unrecovered purchase price and shipping costs. Thus, the only portion of the trial court's damage award that survived on appeal was approximately $3,500 in incidental expenses for "inspection, receipt, transportation, care and custody" of the goods, pursuant to § 2–711(3).

d. Buyer's Right to the Goods: § 2–502

A buyer that has paid some or all of the purchase price of identified goods has the right to recover those goods from the seller under certain circumstances. UCC § 2–502. The buyer's right "vests upon acquisition of a special property, which occurs upon identification of the goods to the contract." UCC § 2–502, Comment ¶ 3; *see* UCC § 2–501 (identification). If the buyer has not paid the entire purchase price, it must be ready to tender to the seller the remainder of the purchase price of the goods. UCC § 2–502(1). The buyer's right to recover the goods applies even if the seller has not yet shipped the goods. But the buyer has the right to recover only goods that conform to the contract. UCC § 2–502(3). The purpose of this limitation is to prevent the "possibility of unjust enrichment" of the buyer by allowing the buyer to recover goods that are "greatly superior in quality or quantity to that called for by the contract for sale." UCC § 2–502, Comment ¶ 4. (Recall that the word "non-conforming" does not mean defective. *See supra* Chapter 9, § A.3.b.)

The buyer's right of recovery applies in two situations. For goods purchased for personal, family, or household purposes, the buyer has the right to recover the goods from a seller that repudiates or does not deliver the goods as the contract requires. UCC § 2–502(1)(a). In all other cases, the buyer has such right if "the seller becomes insolvent within ten days after receipt of the first installment" on the price of the goods. UCC § 2–502(1)(b).

The buyer's right to act upon the seller's insolvency raises tricky questions. Does it apply to a case in which the seller becomes insolvent *before* the buyer pays, in whole or in part, for the goods? Section 2–502 states that the buyer may recover identified goods if the "seller becomes insolvent within 10 days *after* receipt of the first installment on their price." UCC § 2–502(1)(b) (emphasis added). Suppose Seller becomes insolvent on March 10. On March 18, Buyer enters into a contract with Seller to buy equipment to be delivered on April 1. Buyer makes an initial payment on the equipment on March 18. Buyer's payment is *within* 10 days of Seller becoming insolvent, but Seller's insolvency comes *before* not *after* receipt of Buyer's initial payment on the equipment. *See* 2 Hawkland UCC Series § 2–502:2 (stating that "[t]he wording of Section 2–502 has the unfortunate effect of precluding the buyer's right if the seller was insolvent before the buyer made its first pre-payment").

How does the buyer prove *when* the seller becomes insolvent? The buyer in *In re* Surplus Furniture Liquidators, Inc., 199 B.R. 136 (Bankr. M.D. N.C. 1995) faced this problem. In *Surplus Furniture*, customers of a bankrupt furniture dealer objected, on various grounds, to the sale of furniture in the debtor's bankruptcy case.[3] Leigh Dutton, one of the

---

[3] *Surplus Furniture* was decided in 1995, prior to the amendments that added the "personal, family, or household" subsection to § 2–502(1), which explains why a case involving furniture for a customer's home was decided under the 10-day insolvency test. *See* 2 Hawkland UCC Series § 2–502:1 (stating that the revisions to Article 9 added the "consumer" buyer

objecting customers, argued that she had the right to recover her furniture under § 2–502. On June 3, 1995, Dutton paid the debtor by check for her furniture; her bank honored the check on June 8. On June 7, High Point Bank, which had a security interest in debtor's furniture inventory, took possession of that inventory. Dutton argued that High Point's taking possession of the furniture on June 7 meant that debtor was not paying its debts in the ordinary course of business and, thus, was insolvent. *See* UCC § 1–201(b)(23)(A). June 7 was within 10 days of June 3, when the debtor received Dutton's check for the furniture.

The bankruptcy court rejected Dutton's argument, stating that § 2–502 requires that the debtor *become* insolvent within 10 days after receipt of payment. The court explained that even if the evidence sufficed to show that the debtor was unable to pay its debts in the ordinary course of business after June 7, that evidence did not suffice to "support a reasonable inference that Debtor *first* became unable to do so on June 7, 1995." *Surplus Furniture,* 199 B.R. at 141 (emphasis in original). The bankruptcy court noted that the evidence suggested that the debtor had serious cash flow issues several months before June 7. In other words, while the debtor may have *been* insolvent on June 7, Dutton failed to provide sufficient evidence that the debtor/seller "*became* insolvent within ten days after either June 3 or June 8, 1995." *Id.* Therefore, Dutton's failure to prove

---

language to § 2–502(1)(a)); *see also* 2000 N.C. Sess. Laws 2000–169, § 11 (amending N.C. GEN. STAT. § 25–2–502).

when debtor became insolvent doomed her claim for recovery under § 2–502.

D. LESSOR'S REMEDIES

1. OVERVIEW

The lessor remedy provisions of Article 2A are set forth in § 2A–523 through § 2A–532. Section 2A–523 provides an overview of lessor remedies with subsection (1) setting forth the specific actions that the lessor may take upon a lessee's default. If the lessee wrongfully rejects or wrongfully revokes its acceptance of the goods, fails to make a payment when due, or repudiates, the lessor may:

a. Cancel the lease (§ 2A–505(1));

b. Identify goods to the lease contract (§ 2A–524);

c. Withhold delivery of the goods (§ 2A–525) or stop delivery of goods in transit (§ 2A–526);

d. Re-lease the goods to another party and sue for damages (§ 2A–527);

e. Sue for damages based on the difference between market rent and the lease contract rent (§ 2A–528(1));

f. In a proper case, sue for damages as a lost volume lessor (§ 2A–528(2));

g. Bring an action to recover the rent (§ 2A–529); and

h. Exercise any rights or pursue any remedies provided by the lease agreement.

UCC § 2A–523(1). The drafters rejected the doctrine of election of remedies. UCC § 2A–523, Comment ¶ 1. "Multiple remedies are barred only if the effect is to put the lessor in a better position than it would have been in had the lessee fully performed under the lease." UCC § 2A–523, Comment ¶ 4.

The damages that a lessor may recover upon the lessee's default are explored in greater detail in § 2 below. Section 3 discusses the lessor's non-monetary remedies.

2. LESSOR'S DAMAGES

The ensuing pages examine Article 2A's damage remedy provisions in the event of a default by the lessee. The following is a key to the abbreviations used in the various formulae for lessor damages.

TABLE #5: LESSOR DAMAGES: KEY TO ABBREVIATIONS

AUR	Accrued Unpaid Rent
ES	Expenses Saved
ID	Incidental Damages
Mkt	Market Rent
New	New Lease Rent
Old	Original Lease Rent

PV	Present Value
RLT	Remaining Lease Term

a. Re-Lease of the Goods: § 2A–527

Suppose Acme Builders needs equipment to fulfill a contract it has signed with a local town. In December of 2021, Acme enters into a two-year lease with Big Machines Company (BMC) for the necessary equipment. The lease begins on January 1, 2022, and sets a monthly rental of $10,000. Acme pays the rent due for January through October on time but fails to pay November's rent. BMC notifies Acme that it is in default, and BMC re-takes possession of the equipment without a breach of the peace. *See* UCC § 2A–525(2), (3). BMC receives no rental from Acme for November or December, but enters into a one-year lease, starting on January 1, 2023, for the same equipment with We Build It (WBI). (The one-year lease with WBI corresponds to the second year of the original Acme lease.) Unfortunately for BMC, WBI negotiated a more favorable monthly rental of $9,000 for the equipment. Otherwise, the terms of the WBI and the Acme leases are the same.

Assume that BMC acted in good faith and in a commercially reasonable manner, and a court determines that the two leases are substantially similar. *See* UCC § 2A–527(2). Thus, BMC may recover damages in an amount equal to:

> (i) accrued and unpaid rent as of the date of the commencement of the term of the new lease agreement, (ii) the present value, as of the same

> date, of the total rent for the then remaining lease term of the original lease agreement minus the present value, as of the same date, of the rent under the new lease agreement applicable to that period of the new lease term which is comparable to the then remaining term of the original lease agreement, and (iii) any incidental damages allowed under Section 2A–530, less expenses saved in consequence of the lessee's default.

UCC § 2A–527(2). The unwieldy statutory language above produces the following formula:

AUR + ([PV of Old for RLT] – [PV of New for RLT]) + ID – ES

The accrued unpaid rent as of the start of the new lease with WBI equals $20,000: unpaid rent of $10,000 for November and December. The remaining lease term or RLT is one year. The remaining lease term runs from the date of the new lease, which is January 1, 2023, in our example. The total rent due for the remaining term of Acme's lease is 120,000: $10,000 per month for 12 months. But the formula requires you to take the present value of that figure. For the next year, WBI will pay $108,000 in rent to BMC: $9,000 per month × 12 months. Once again, the formula requires you to take the present value of that figure. Incidental damages include "commercially reasonable charges, expenses, or commissions incurred in stopping delivery", in the post-default transport, care, or custody of the goods, in connection with the goods' return or disposition, or "otherwise resulting from the default." UCC § 2A–530. There are no such expenses in this hypothetical and there also are no expenses saved.

Inputting figures from our example above produces the following:

$20,000 + ([PV of $120,000] –
[PV of $108,000]) + $0 – $0

What if BMC re-leased the equipment to WBI for two years, starting on January 1, 2023? A court still may conclude that the two leases are substantially similar even though the replacement lease extends beyond the time remaining on the original lease. *See* UCC § 2A–527, Comment ¶ 7. The issue is whether the lease terms are "commercially comparable," and the court can "fairly apportion a part of the rental payments under the new lease to that part of the term of the new lease which is comparable to the remaining lease term under the original lease." *Id.* Assume that a court finds that the lease terms are commercially comparable. Is fair apportionment possible? Rent is paid on a monthly basis. The first year of the BMC/WBI lease corresponds exactly to the second year and remaining term of the BMC/Acme lease. Therefore, if a court determines that the two leases are substantially similar, then the calculation above would be the same if BMC re-leased the equipment for two years, not one, to WBI.

Suppose the one-year lease agreement with WBI requires BMC to insure the equipment while the lease with Acme required Acme to provide the insurance? Are the two leases substantially similar? If they are not, then the lessor may not recover damages under § 2A–527. Instead, the lessor will sue for the difference between the lease agreement rent and market rent under § 2A–528. *See infra* § D.2.b of this Chapter. But a court still may find that the two leases are substantially similar if this difference between the two leases "can be easily valued". UCC § 2A–527, Comment ¶ 5. Assume that equipment insurance is easy to obtain, and BMC insures the equipment for $5,000; the insurance company bills on an annual basis. If the insurance premium on the equipment can be easily valued, then the court can deduct $5,000 from the amount of rent WBI owes BMC before calculating the difference in rental between the two leases. *See id.* For an example in which the difference may not be easily valued, *see* UCC § 2A–527, Comment ¶ 6.

Determining whether the new and original leases are substantially similar requires the court to look at both transactions as a whole and apply commercial judgment. There is no bright-line test. Instead, a court must examine various elements of the new lease, including "options to purchase or release", "representations, warranties and covenants" by the lessor "as well as those to be provided by the lessee to the lessor", any services that the lessor or lessee must provide, and any other factors that "allocate cost and risk between the lessor and the lessee and thus affect the amount of rent to be paid." UCC § 2A–527, Comment ¶ 5.

One final note before moving onto Article 2A's market rent formula. What if a lessor makes a profit when it re-leases the goods after the original lessee's default? As with the seller who resells for a profit, the lessor that re-leases for profit "is not accountable to the lessee for any profit made." UCC § 2A–527(5); *cf.* UCC § 2–706(6).

b. Market Rent: § 2A–528(1)

The market rent measure of damages applies in two situations. The first is when the re-lease measure of damages under § 2A–527(2) does not apply, for whatever reason. UCC § 2A–528, Comment ¶ 1; *see* § 2A–527(3). The second is when the lessor "elects to retain the goods (whether undelivered, returned by the lessee, or repossessed by the lessor after acceptance and default by the lessee)." UCC § 2A–528, Comment ¶ 1. The lessor's damages for the lessee's default in these cases is as follows:

> (i) accrued and unpaid rent as of the date of default if the lessee has never taken possession of the goods, or, if the lessee has taken possession of the goods, as of the date the lessor repossesses the goods or an earlier date on which the lessee makes a tender of the goods to the lessor, (ii) the present value as of the date determined under clause (i) of the total rent for the then remaining lease term of the original lease agreement minus the present value as of the same date of the market rent at the place where the goods are located computed for the same lease term, and (iii) any incidental damages allowed under Section 2A–530, less expenses saved in consequence of the lessee's default.

UCC § 2A–528(1). The unwieldy statutory language above produces the following formula:

AUR + ([PV of Old for RLT] –
[PV of Mkt for RLT]) + ID – ES

While the formula looks similar to the formula for damages upon re-lease of the goods under § 2A–527(2), notice that the amount for AUR varies, depending on whether the lessee ever took possession of the goods. If the lessee never took possession, then accrued but unpaid rent runs up to the date of default. But, if the lessee took possession of the goods, then the accrued but unpaid rent runs up to the date that the lessor repossessed the goods *or* an earlier date on which the lessee tendered the goods back to the lessor. The RLT runs from the date used to calculate AUR. The place for determining market rent is the place where the goods are located. UCC § 2A–528(1); *see* UCC § 2A–507 (time and place for determining proof of market rent).

Suppose that in August of 2022, Acme enters into a two-year agreement to lease equipment from BMC. (Both Acme and BMC are located in Detroit.) Rent for the equipment is $10,000 per month. The lease begins January 1, 2023. After signing the lease with BMC, Acme begins encountering financial problems. In November of 2022, Acme contacts BMC and says that it cannot afford to lease the equipment. Assume that Acme's statement is an anticipatory repudiation. *See* UCC § 2A–402; *see also supra* Chapter 10, § B.1. BMC treats Acme's statement as a default under the lease and resorts to its remedies under Article 2A. *See* UCC § 2A–402(c). Because

Acme never took possession of the equipment and does not owe any rent until January 1, 2023, there is no accrued but unpaid rent. Assume that in November of 2022, market rent in Detroit, where the equipment is located, is $9,700 per month. The time for determining market rent is the date of default, which is in November of 2022. While BMC is able to re-lease the equipment, assume that the new lease and the original lease are not substantially similar. *See* § 2A–527(3), § 2A–528(1). There are no incidental damages and no expenses saved. *See* UCC § 2A–530. BMC will seek the following damages from Acme:

$0 + ([PV of $240,000] − [PV of $232,800]) + $0 − $0

Suppose Acme and BMC enter into the same two-year lease, but Acme takes possession of the equipment on January 1, 2023, and pays rent for the month of January. Acme fails to pay rent for February or March, and BMC then repossesses the equipment without a breach of the peace. The accrued but unpaid rent runs up to the date of repossession because Acme took possession of the equipment and there was no tender by Acme to BMC of the equipment. To simplify the analysis, assume that accrued but unpaid rent as of the date of repossession is $20,000 or two months' rent. Market rent is determined as of the date of repossession; assume that market rent is $9,500 on this date in Detroit, where both parties and the goods are located. There are 21 months remaining on the lease: 24 months − 3 months of January through March. Thus, the present value figures are for that 21-month period, not the full 24 months of the lease. BMC is able to re-lease the equipment, but the new lease is not substantially similar to the original lease with Acme. Thus, BMC will seek the following amount in damages under § 2A–528(1):

$20,000 + ([PV of $210,000] – [PV of $199,500]) + $0 – $0

c. The Lost Volume Lessor: § 2A–528(2)

Suppose Clean Whiz, Inc. (CWI) owns a large inventory of coin-operated laundry equipment that it leases to apartment complexes. Green & White (GW) is a large student apartment complex on State University's campus. On February 1, 2019, GW enters into a five-year lease for 10 washers and 10 dryers from CWI. Rent is due on the first of each month. GW pays rent on time for 36 months but then decides it is cheaper to simply purchase machines. GW disconnects the CWI machines and in January of 2022 contacts CWI to pick up the machines. CWI takes possession of the machines and stores them in its warehouse. *See* Jetz Service Co. v. Salina Properties, 865 P.2d 1051 (Kan. Ct. App. 1993) (discussion of lost volume lessor in context of contract for services involving lease of coin-operated laundry machines).

CWI sues GW for damages for breach of its lease contract. GW argues that CWI incurred no damage because there was no accrued but unpaid rent at the time that CWI repossessed the machines and market rental for the machines is the same as the rent due under GW's lease with CWI. Thus, damages under § 2A–528(1) are zero, according to GW. CWI, however, proves that it has more inventory of machines than it can lease at any given time. It argues that it is a lost volume lessor. Just because CWI can re-lease the equipment to another lessee at the same rental does not mean that CWI suffered no damage. For example, if GW had not breached, CWI would earn profit from its lease with GW. If CWI entered into a five-year lease with another lessee for 20 machines, it would earn profit from that lease, as well. If GW's breach deprives CWI of profit from GW's full performance of its lease contract, the second lease's profit does not *substitute* for the profit lost on the remaining term of the GW lease. CWI would earn two profits for two five-year leases if GW had not breached. Therefore, CWI is entitled to the present value of the profit, including reasonable overhead, that was lost for the remaining two years on GW's lease plus any incidental expenses incurred. UCC § 2A–528(2).

d. Action for the Rent: § 2A–529

The lessor also may bring an action for the rent, which is similar, although not identical to § 2–709's action for the price in contracts for the sale of goods. The lessor may recover the rent from the lessee in three situations.

The first situation covers "goods accepted by the lessee and not repossessed by or tendered to the lessor." UCC § 2A–529(1)(a). The drafters of Article 2A rejected the idea that the lessor could bring an action for the rent simply because the lessee once had accepted the goods. Thus, if the lessee tenders the goods back to the lessor but the lessor refuses to accept the tender, then the lessor will not recover under an action for the rent. Instead, the lessor's damages are limited to those it would have incurred had it accepted the tender back of the goods from the lessee. The drafters considered it more efficient for the lessor, not the lessee, to dispose of the goods, e.g., by re-lease, upon default by the lessee.

> In a lease, the lessee always has a residual interest in the goods which the lessor usually realizes upon at the end of a lease term by either sale or a new lease. Therefore, it is not a substantial imposition on the lessor to require it to take back and dispose of the goods if the lessee chooses to tender them back before the end of the lease term: the lessor will merely do earlier what it would have done anyway, sell or relet the goods. Further, the lessee will frequently encounter substantial difficulties if the lessee attempts to sublet the goods for the remainder of the lease term. In contrast to the buyer who owns the entire interest in goods and can easily dispose of them, the lessee is selling only the right to use the goods under the terms of the lease and the sublessee must assume a relationship with the lessor. In that situation, it is usually more efficient to eliminate the original lessee as a middleman by allowing the lessee to return the goods to the lessor who can then redispose of them.

UCC § 2A–529, Comment ¶ 1.

The lessor also may recover the rent for "conforming goods lost or damaged within a commercially reasonable time after risk of loss passes to the lessee (Section 2A–219)." UCC § 2A–529(1)(a). The final situation in which the lessor may recover the rent is if the lessor is unable to dispose of goods identified to the contract at a reasonable price after reasonable effort or the circumstances indicate that any such effort will be unavailing. *See* UCC § 2A–529(1)(b).

The measure of damages for the rent is as follows:

$$AUR + PV \text{ of Rent for } RLT + ID - ES$$

UCC § 2A–529(1). The AUR is the accrued but unpaid rent up to the date of entry of judgment in favor of the lessor. The present value calculation takes the present value as of the date that judgment is entered of the rent then remaining on the lease term.

A lessor suing for the rent under § 2A–529 must hold for the lessee goods identified to the lease contract and in the lessor's control for the remainder of the lease term. UCC § 2A–529(2). If the lessee pays the judgment for rent to the lessor, then the lessee is entitled to use and possess the goods "not then disposed of for the remaining lease term and in accordance with the lease agreement." UCC § 2A–529(4). A partial satisfaction of the judgment for rent does not entitle the lessee to use and possess the goods. *See* UCC § 2A–529, Comment ¶ 4.

What if the lessor files suit for the rent but disposes, e.g., by re-lease, of the goods before entry of judgment? If the lessor disposes of the goods after the end of the lease, then the lessor may recover a judgment for the rent under § 2A–529. In such a case, the lessor did not dispose of the goods during the lease term; it held the goods for the lessee. But, if the lessor disposes of the goods before the end of the lease term, then either § 2A–527 or § 2A–528 provides the measure of the lessor's damages for the buyer's default. UCC § 2A–529(3); UCC § 2A–529, Comment ¶ 3. In such a case, if the lessor's suit for the rent proceeds to judgment, then the lessee is not liable for any amount by which damages provided for by the judgment exceed the amount to which the lessor would be entitled under § 2A–527 or § 2A–528. *See* UCC § 2A–529(3) (stating that the lessor must "cause an appropriate credit to be provided against a judgment for damages to the extent" that judgment damages exceed damages under § 2A–527 or § 2A–528).

e. Residual Interest

By definition, a lease is an agreement in which the lessor has a reversionary interest in the goods. Unlike a buyer of goods, a lessee does not own the goods that it leases. Thus, the lessor has a right to the good's residual interest and may sue for damages to that interest.

> In addition to any other recovery permitted by [Article 2A] or other law, the lessor may recover from the lessee an amount that will fully compensate the lessor for any loss of or damage

> to the lessor's residual interest in the goods caused by the default of the lessee.

UCC § 2A–532. For example, the lessee may return the goods in a damaged condition at the end of the lease. The damage to the goods adversely affects the lessor's residual interest. *See* UCC § 2A–532, Comment: Purposes. Even if the goods are not in a damaged condition, they may not be in the condition required by the lease agreement. For example, suppose you sign a three-year lease for a car. The lease agreement provides that you cannot put more than 36,000 miles on the vehicle, and that you will be charged 15 cents per mile for every mile in excess of 36,000. This type of provision recognizes that the lessor has a residual interest in the vehicle. If you return the car and the odometer reads 40,000 miles, you have not damaged the car, but you have adversely affected the lessor's residual interest in the vehicle. In this case, the lessor has a contractual provision protecting its residual interest, but the logic of § 2A–532 is the same: the lessor has a residual interest in the goods that the lessee's conduct may adversely affect.

3. LESSOR'S OTHER REMEDIES

The Official Comment to § 2A–523 provides a hypothetical that is slightly modified here to explain the non-monetary remedies provided by Article 2A. *See* UCC § 2A–523, Comment ¶¶ 5 through 9; *see also* UCC § 2A–523(1)(b)–(d).

Suppose *Summer Fun* (SF) is located on an island in a desirable resort village. SF rents out various kinds of equipment to tourists and village residents during the summer months. SF decides to expand its business and rent bicycles. It contacts *Wheelz, Inc.* (WI), which is in the business of selling and leasing bicycles of all descriptions. SF only operates during the summer and does not want to buy bikes; it wants to lease them for several months. SF agrees to lease 60 bikes from WI. There is one master lease that provides for staggered deliveries and terms for the bikes. The first delivery of 20 bikes is due June 1; the lease term for these bikes is four months. The second 20-bike delivery is due on July 1; the lease term is three months for these bikes. The final delivery is due on August 1, and the lease term for these 20 bikes is two months.

WI does not have sufficient inventory to fulfill the lease for 60 bikes, so it enters into a contract with *Bicyclette Corporation* (BC), WI's principal manufacturer, to produce the 60 bikes that are the subject of the WI/SF lease agreement. The contract between WI and BC provides for delivery of the bikes to SF's business on the island, according to the delivery schedule provided in the WI/SF lease agreement.

SF receives the first shipment of 20 bikes on June 1. SF inspects the shipment and accepts it. Weather on the island is unseasonably cold and damp, and demand for bicycles is low. SF fails to pay rent on June 15, as required by the lease agreement, and WI sends SF a notice of default, as provided for in the lease. Because the agreement is an installment lease, WI consults with its attorney who informs the company that SF's failure to pay on June 15 is a default as to the whole contract. *See* UCC § 2A–510(2). What can WI do?

With respect to the 20 bikes at SF's business, WI can take possession of those bikes. *See* UCC § 2A–525(2). WI can do so without going to court so long as it can take possession of the 20 bikes without breaching the peace. *See* UCC § 2A–525(3).

What about the other 40 bikes? Assume that BC has produced the 20 bikes due for delivery no later than July 1, and those bikes are on a truck that has not yet reached the ferry to the island. WI notifies BC to instruct the carrier to stop delivery of the 20 bikes to SF and instead deliver the 20 bikes to WI's place of business. *See* UCC § 2A–526(1).

Assume further that BC has not completed manufacture of the remaining 20 bikes. If this fact scenario only involved a lease agreement between WI and SF, WI could exercise its commercial judgment and decide not to continue manufacturing the remaining 20 bikes intended for lease to SF. But WI has a binding contract to buy bikes from BC. If WI told BC to discontinue production, BC would have the right to damages, if any, under Article 2 for WI's breach of its sales contract with BC. Assume, then, that WI simply instructs BC to deliver the remaining 20 bikes when completed to WI's place of business. *See* UCC § 2A–524(2).

As for WI's right to recover damages from SF, *see supra* § D.2 of this Chapter; *see also* UCC § 2A–523,

Comment ¶¶ 12 through 17 (discussing various damage remedies for hypothetical).

E. LESSEE'S REMEDIES

1. OVERVIEW

If the lessor fails to deliver conforming goods, repudiates the lease agreement, or the lessee rightfully rejects the goods or justifiably revokes its acceptance, the lessee may cancel the contract pursuant to § 2A–505(1). UCC § 2A–508(1)(a). The lessee may cover and recover damages for the difference in rent between the original lease and the cover lease or sue for the difference between the lease rent and the market rent. UCC § 2A–508(1)(c); *see* UCC § 2A–518, § 2A–519. The lessee also may recover rent or security already paid that is "just under the circumstances." UCC § 2A–508(1)(b). For example, suppose Lessor delivers the goods and Lessee immediately rejects the goods due to a defect discovered. Assume Lessee has already paid Lessor the first month's rent for the goods. In such a case, Lessee should receive from Lessor that first month's rental payment. But suppose Lessee has a 36-month equipment lease with Lessor. After 12 months, Lessor materially breaches the agreement by not performing its contractual obligation to maintain the equipment. What is just in such a case? While Lessor breached, Lessee used the equipment for a year. Thus, returning 12 months of rental payments to Lessee does not take account of the value Lessee obtained from use of the equipment during those 12 months. Thus, a just result may be return of a small part or perhaps none of the rental payments already made. UCC § 2A–508, Comment ¶ 2 (example from Comment modified).

These remedies—cancellation, cover or market damages, and recovery of rent—are cumulative. The lessee may pursue one or more of them so long as the lessee is not put in a better position than it would have occupied had the lessor fully performed. *See* UCC § 2A–508, Comment ¶ 2 (stating that Article 2A "rejects any general doctrine of election of remedy"). Of course, the lessee also may "exercise any rights or pursue any other remedies provided in the lease contract." UCC § 2A–508(1)(d).

In addition, if the lessor does not deliver the goods or repudiates the lease agreement, the lessee may recover the goods in certain cases, if they have been identified to the contract, or obtain specific performance or replevy the goods in "a proper case." UCC § 2A–508(2); *see* UCC § 2A–521, § 2A–522. For a case in which the lessee has accepted the goods and not revoked its acceptance, the lessee may recover damages for breach of warranty. UCC § 2A–508(4); *see* UCC § 2A–519(4).

Section 2A–508 provides no special rules for finance leases. The reason is that in most finance leases, after accepting the goods the lessee has "no rights or remedies against the lessor." UCC § 2A–508, Comment ¶ 10. Instead, the lessee looks to the supplier for performance. *See* UCC § 2A–209 (lessee under finance lease as beneficiary of supply contract).

2. LESSEE'S DAMAGES

Before diving into the specific provisions on lessee damages, notice that the various damage formulae all include recovery of consequential damages. Recall that the damage formulae for lessors do *not* include recovery of consequential damages. *See supra* § D.2 of this Chapter.

Consequential damages for which the lessee may recover include "any loss resulting from general or particular requirements and needs of which the lessor at the time of contracting had reason to know." UCC § 2A–520(2)(a). The lessor's breach must proximately cause the loss. UCC § 2A–520(2)(b). Damages cannot be speculative, and the lessee cannot recover consequential damages that it could have avoided by cover or otherwise. UCC § 2A–520(2)(a); *see* § C.1.d of this Chapter for a discussion of the requirements to recover consequential damages in sales contracts.

The ensuing pages explore the damage remedy provisions of Article 2A for cases involving a default by the lessor. The following is a key to the abbreviations used in the various formulae for lessee damages.

TABLE #6: LESSEE DAMAGES: KEY TO ABBREVIATIONS

CD	Consequential Damages
ES	Expenses Saved

ID	Incidental Damages
Mkt	Market Rent
New	New Lease Rent
Old	Original Lease Rent
PV	Present Value
RLT	Remaining Lease Term
VGA	Value of Good Accepted
VGW	Value of Good as Warranted

a. Cover: § 2A–518

If the lessor fails to deliver conforming goods or repudiates the contract, or the lessee rightfully rejects the goods or justifiably revokes its acceptance, the lessee may cover. UCC § 2A–518(1). To recover damages for cover under § 2A–518, the lessee must satisfy three criteria. First, cover must be by lease agreement. *See* UCC § 2A–518, Comment ¶ 2. Thus, if the lessee decides not to lease, but to buy the good, the cover damage formula at § 2A–518(2) does not apply. If the lessee's cover is "by purchase or otherwise," then the lessee may recover damages from the lessor "as if the lessee had elected not to cover and Section 2A–519 governs." UCC § 2A–518(3).

Second, the lessee must act in good faith and in a commercially reasonable manner when effecting cover. *See* UCC § 2A–518(2); *see also* UCC § 2A–518, Comment ¶ 2.

Finally, the cover lease must be substantially similar to the original lease contract. *See id.* This determination is made on a case-by-case basis and includes an examination of the terms of the new lease agreement. *See* UCC § 2A–518, Comment ¶ 3 (stating that drafters decided "not to draft with specificity", thinking it "unwise to seek to establish certainty at the cost of fairness"). Factors to consider in determining whether the original and cover leases are substantially similar are comparable to those discussed earlier for the lessor's re-lease of goods. *See supra* § D.2.a of this Chapter; *see also* UCC § 2A–518, Comment ¶ 5. The court also should examine the goods that are the subject of the new lease agreement. *See* UCC § 2A–518, Comment ¶ 4. For example, suppose Lessee leases computer equipment from Lessor, but Lessor defaults. Lessee enters into a lease with Lessor 2 for computer equipment, but this equipment consists of newer models. Is this cover? It may be, depending on the facts at the time of breach. If Lessee could not obtain equipment like the original, then the new lease, albeit of newer models of equipment, may qualify as cover. *See* UCC § 2A–518, Comment ¶ 4 (example drawn from Comment).

If the new lease qualifies as cover, then the lessee may recover damages in an amount equal to

> (i) the present value, as of the date of the commencement of the term of the new lease agreement, of the rent under the new lease agreement applicable to that period of the new lease term which is comparable to the then

> remaining term of the original lease agreement minus the present value as of the same date of the total rent for the then remaining lease term of the original lease agreement, and (ii) any incidental or consequential damages, less expenses saved in consequence of the lessor's breach.

UCC § 2A–518(2). The statutory language translates into the following formula:

(PV of New for RLT) − (PV of Old for RLT) + ID + CD − ES

The present value is computed as of the date that the new lease commences. The RLT is the term remaining on the original lease; that same time period is used when computing present value of the payments under the new lease. For example, suppose that on February 1, Acme signs an agreement to lease equipment for two years from Zephyr Corporation. Monthly rental is $5,000. The lease provides that Zephyr must deliver the equipment no later than May 1. On April 5, Zephyr informs Acme that Zephyr will not deliver the equipment, as required by the parties' lease agreement. *See* UCC § 2A–402. On April 16, Acme signs a two-year lease, starting on May 1, with Mammoth, Inc. for the equipment but the monthly rental is $5,500. In addition, the Mammoth/Acme lease requires Acme to pay for transportation of the goods ($1,000). Zephyr paid for transit under the Zephyr/Acme lease. Assume that Acme searched in good faith for a replacement lease but had to pay extra because it needed the equipment by May 1. If a court determines that the two leases are substantially similar, then Acme will recover the following amount in damages:

(PV of [$5,500 × 24 months]) – (PV of [$5,000 × 24 months]) + $1,000 + $0 – $0

If the two leases are not substantially similar, then the lessee may recover market rent damages under § 2A–519. UCC § 2A–518(3).

What if the term of the cover lease extends beyond the term of the original lease? If the terms of the two leases are comparable and the court can fairly apportion rental payments, then the court may determine that the two leases are substantially similar. *See* UCC § 2A–518, Comment ¶ 7 (stating that two leases may be substantially similar even though the term of the new lease extends beyond the term of the old lease). Suppose Acme enters into a one-year lease of equipment from Zephyr, Inc. The lease term runs from February 1 through January 31 of the following year. Zephyr delivers the equipment to Acme. Acme inspects the goods and rightfully rejects the equipment as non-conforming. Acme notifies Zephyr of the rejection; Zephyr does not cure. *See* § 2A–509(2), § 2A–513. Acme covers by leasing the same equipment from Mammoth on terms similar to those in its lease with Zephyr. What is different, however, is that the Mammoth one-year lease runs from February 15 through February 14 of the following year. Notwithstanding the different beginning and ending dates, a court still may determine that the two leases are substantially similar. Cover damages may be "the entire difference between the costs under the two leases" if the terms of the two leases are comparable. UCC § 2A–518, Comment ¶ 7 (example of cover lease beginning on January 15 and original lease beginning on January 2).

b. Market: § 2A–519(1) & (2)

If the lessee covers but a court determines that the lessee did not satisfy the requirements of § 2A–518 or if cover is "by purchase or otherwise," then the lessee may recover market rent damages under § 2A–519. UCC § 2A–519(1). Moreover, the lessee is not required to cover; instead, it may sue for market rent damages. *See* UCC § 2A–519, Comment ¶ 1 (stating that the market rent measure of damages applies "if the lessee does not cover or if the cover does not qualify under Section 2A–518"). The measure of damages is as follows:

> the present value, as of the date of default, of the then market rent minus the present value as of the same date of the original rent, computed for the remaining lease term of the original lease agreement, together with incidental and consequential damages, less expenses saved in consequence of the lessor's default.

UCC § 2A–519(1). The statutory language above translates into the following formula:

[PV of Mkt for RLT] − [PV of Old for RLT] + ID + CD − ES

The *time* for determining market rent is the date of default. Bear in mind that the date of default is *not* necessarily the same as the date of an event of default. UCC § 2A–519(1), Comment ¶ 2. The reason is that the parties' agreement may provide a grace period after an event of default during which the defaulting party may cure or fix the default. *See id.* (stating that an event of default only becomes a default after expiration of any grace period and compliance with Article 2A's and the lease's notice requirements).

The *place* for determining market rent varies depending on the facts. If the lessor delivers the goods and the lessee either rejects them or revokes its acceptance, then the place of arrival is the place for determining market rent. UCC § 2A–519(2). Otherwise, market rent is determined as of the place for tender. *Id.*

Suppose Acme enters into an agreement to lease equipment for two years from Zephyr. Monthly rental is $5,000. The parties' agreement provides for delivery of the equipment no later than February 1. The delivery term is "F.O.B. Detroit"; Zephyr's facility is located in Detroit, Michigan. Acme is located in Toledo, Ohio. On January 5, Zephyr tells Acme that it will not deliver the equipment. Zephyr's statement is an anticipatory repudiation, which gives Acme the right to immediately resort to any remedy for breach or to await Zephyr's performance for a commercially reasonable time. *See* UCC § 2A–402. The date of default in a case of anticipatory repudiation "should be determined at the best moment for the lessee between the time the lessee learned of the repudiation and the outside limit of the commercially reasonable time to act." 3 Hawkland UCC Series § 2A–519:2. Assume that a court determines that January 5—the date that Acme learned of the repudiation—is the date of default. Market rent, then, is the rent on January 5 in Detroit, the place of tender. Because the remaining lease term is two years, damages are the difference between the present value, as of January 5, of market rent for two years minus the present value, also as of January 5, of rent under the parties' lease for two years, plus any incidental and consequential damages minus any expenses saved.

Suppose Zephyr delivered the equipment, as agreed, on February 1. Acme rightfully rejected the equipment as non-conforming and notified Zephyr on February 1 of its rejection. Market rent would be the rent on February 1 in Toledo. Because Acme rejected the goods after delivery, Toledo, which is the place of arrival, is the place for determining market rent. The time for delivery is February 1, so Zephyr cannot use § 2A–513(1) as a basis for cure. Assume that Zephyr did not have reasonable grounds to believe its nonconforming tender would be acceptable to Acme. *See* UCC § 2A–513(2). Therefore, February 1, when Acme notified Zephyr that the equipment did not conform to the lease agreement and that Acme was rejecting the delivery is the date of default. *See* 5 Anderson U.C.C. § 2A–519:9 (3d ed.) (stating that while Article 2A does not define "date of default," § 2A–519(1) lists the various lessor defaults, including the lessee's "rightful and effective rejection").

What if market rent for the time or place provided by § 2A–519 is not "readily available"? In that case, market rent "prevailing within any reasonable time before or after the time described or at any other place . . .which in commercial judgment or under usage of trade would serve as a reasonable substitute for the one described may be used." UCC § 2A–507(2). If market rent for a different place than that provided by § 2A–519 is used, "proper allowance" must be made for transportation of the goods to or from that other place. *Id.* If the lessee plans to offer evidence of market rent for a time or place different from that provided by § 2A–519, it must give the lessor sufficient notice to "prevent unfair surprise." UCC § 2A–507(3). Market reports about the rent or value of leased goods, e.g., in official publications or trade journals, are admissible in evidence if an issue arises as to the "prevailing rent or value of any goods regularly leased in any established market." UCC § 2A–507(4).

c. Breach of Warranty and Other Defaults: § 2A–519(3) & (4)

Suppose Acme enters into a one-year lease of equipment from Zephyr. Acme is located in Toledo and Zephyr has its place of business in Detroit. Assume that Zephyr did not disclaim the implied warranties. Zephyr delivers the equipment on February 1, the date for delivery under the parties' agreement. Acme inspects and accepts the equipment that same day. Several months later, however, Acme complains to Zephyr that the equipment is not operating properly. Assume that Acme does not satisfy the requirements to revoke its acceptance of the equipment. *See* UCC § 2A–517. What can Acme do?

If the equipment is not fit for its ordinary purpose, Acme can sue for breach of the implied warranty of merchantability. *See* UCC § 2A–212. (It also can sue for breach of any express warranties. *See* UCC § 2A–210).

> [T]he measure of damages for breach of warranty is the present value at the time and place of acceptance of the difference between the value of the use of the goods accepted and the value if they had been as warranted for the lease term, unless special circumstances show proximate damages of a different amount, together with incidental and consequential damages, less expenses saved in consequence of the lessor's default or breach of warranty.

UCC § 2A–519(4). The formula for determining damages is as follows:

$$PV\ (VGW - VGA) + ID + CD - ES$$

See UCC § 2A–519, Comment ¶ 5 (stating that the measure of damage for breach of warranty "in essence is the present value of the difference between the value of the goods accepted and of the goods if they had been as warranted"). The present value is done as of the time and place of acceptance. For the Acme/Zephyr example above, the time is February 1, the date when Acme accepted the goods. The place is Toledo, because Acme accepted the goods after they were delivered to Acme's place of business in Toledo.

Suppose Acme and Zephyr enter into the same lease agreement as described immediately above. Under the agreement's terms, Zephyr is obligated to maintain the equipment during the one-year lease term. Zephyr delivers on time, and Acme inspects and accepts the equipment. Acme makes its monthly rental payments, but Zephyr fails to maintain the equipment. Acme cannot revoke its acceptance. *See* UCC § 2A–517. Moreover, Zephyr's failure to maintain the equipment is not a breach of warranty. Nonetheless, Zephyr has defaulted on one of its lease obligations. *See* UCC § 2A–519, Comment ¶ 4 (giving the lessor's failure to "comply with an obligation to maintain the leased goods" as an example of a breach to which § 2A–519(3) would apply). The lessor's default, even though not a breach of warranty, gives the lessee that has accepted goods and given the notification required by § 2A–516(3) the right to recover damages. *See* UCC § 2A–519(3). The measure of damage is "the loss resulting in the ordinary course of events from the lessor's default as determined in any manner that is reasonable together with incidental and consequential damages, less expenses saved in consequence of the lessor's default." *Id.* Therefore, Acme may sue Zephyr for damages stemming from its failure to maintain the leased equipment.

3. LESSEE'S OTHER REMEDIES

Article 2A's provisions on the lessee's right to specific performance, to replevy identified goods, and to recover goods upon the lessor's insolvency are similar to their Article 2 analogues. Differences are largely the result of adapting the Article 2A provisions to "reflect leasing practices and terminology." UCC § 2A–521, Comment: Changes; UCC § 2A–522, Comment: Changes. Therefore, you should consult the Official Comments to § 2–716 and § 2–502 to understand the meaning of § 2A–521 and § 2A–522, respectively. *See* UCC § 2A–101, Comment: Relationship of Article 2A to Other Articles (stating that for provisions of Article 2 that are "carried over" to Article 2A, the Article 2 Official Comments are "incorporated by reference in Article 2A" and case law interpreting an Article 2 provision is "persuasive but not binding on a court when deciding a similar issue with respect to leases").

Section 2A–521 on specific performance and replevin is modeled on § 2–716. The court may grant the lessee specific performance of the lease agreement "if the goods are unique or in other proper circumstances." UCC § 2A–521(1); *see supra* § C.2.a of this Chapter for meaning of "unique" and "other proper circumstances." The specific performance decree may include terms and conditions about payment of the rent, damages, or "other relief that the court deems just." UCC § 2A–521(2).

If the lessee is unable to cover after making reasonable efforts to do so or the "circumstances reasonably indicate" that the lessee's efforts will be unsuccessful, then the lessee has "a right of replevin, detinue, sequestration, claim and delivery, or the like for goods identified to the lease contract." UCC § 2A–521(3); *see* UCC § 2A–217 (identification). The Article 2 counterpart to § 2A–521(3) mentions only replevin.

See UCC § 2–716(3). The other causes of action provided for in § 2A–521(3), however, are similar to replevin. *See* UCC § 2A–521, Comment: Changes (noting expansion of "the reference to the right of replevin in subsection (3) to include other similar rights of the lessee"). For example, claim and delivery is a legal action to recover personal property "wrongfully taken and detained"; it is a "modification of the common-law action of replevin." BLACK'S LAW DICTIONARY 128 (5th ed.). Detinue is a cause of action to recover personal property that is "unjustly detained." *Id.* at 235.

Under certain circumstances, a lessee also has the right to recover goods identified to the contract if the lessor becomes insolvent. UCC § 2A–522; *see* UCC § 2–716, Comment ¶ 3 (stating that in addition to the remedy of replevin, a buyer has the right to recover identified goods if the seller becomes insolvent). Section 2A–522 provides that the lessee that has paid some or all of the rent and security under a lease agreement and that makes and keeps good a "tender of any unpaid portion of the rent and security" may recover identified goods if the lessor becomes insolvent within 10 days after the first installment of rent and security is received. UCC § 2A–522(1). This insolvency provision raises difficult questions, as discussed earlier in this Chapter under Buyer's Other Remedies. *See supra* § C.2.d of this Chapter. One difference between § 2A–522 and § 2–502 is that the Article 2A provision does not include a right of recovery for goods leased for "personal, family, or household" purposes. *Compare* UCC § 2A–522(1) *with* UCC § 2–502(1)(a).

F. LIQUIDATED DAMAGES

1. SALES: § 2–718

Section 2–718 covers both liquidated damages clauses and the buyer's right to restitution of monies paid to the seller in excess of either statutory liquidated damages or a contractual liquidated damages provision. The criteria for determining the validity of a contractual liquidated damages clause are found at § 2–718(1). Subsection (2) provides for the buyer's right to restitution of monies paid that exceed the amount to which the seller is entitled under a valid liquidated damages clause in the parties' agreement. If the parties' agreement does not contain such a clause, subsection (2) not only contains a formula for statutory liquidated damages but also provides the buyer with a right of restitution for any monies paid to the seller in excess of the statutory liquidated damages formula. The buyer's right to restitution, however, is subject to the seller's right to offset any damages to which the seller is entitled under Article 2 by virtue of the buyer's breach. UCC § 2–718(3).

a. Validity of Liquidated Damages Clause: § 2–718(1)

Section 2–718(1) requires that the amount of liquidated damages be reasonable in light of (1) "the anticipated or actual harm caused by the breach", (2) "the difficulties" of proving loss from the breach, and (3) "the inconvenience or nonfeasibility of otherwise obtaining an adequate remedy." UCC § 2–718(1).

There is limited case law on the validity of liquidated damages clauses in contracts for the sales of goods. But the Restatement provides much needed guidance.

The Restatement's test for determining the enforceability of a liquidated damages clause is quite similar to § 2–718(1)'s test. Section 356 of the Restatement states that liquidated damages must be "reasonable in light of the anticipated or actual loss caused by the breach and the difficulties of proof of loss." RESTATEMENT (SECOND) OF CONTRACTS § 356(1). In fact, § 356 was "redrafted to harmonize with Uniform Commercial Code § 2–718(1)." RESTATEMENT (SECOND) OF CONTRACTS § 356, Reporter's Notes. Thus, the only difference between the Restatement's and the UCC's test is the final requirement. The Restatement omits the "inconvenience or nonfeasibility" requirement, viewing it as duplicative of § 2–718(1)'s requirement of the difficulties of proof of loss. *See id.* (stating that § 2–718(1)'s "reference to 'the inconvenience or nonfeasibility of otherwise obtaining an adequate remedy' has been omitted as already being expressed by the language of Subsection (1)"); Anderson, 2 Damages Under UCC § 13:11 (stating that the Restatement omitted the "inconvenience" factor as "redundant" because a party unable to prove loss "has little chance of obtaining an adequate remedy"). Given the paucity of opinions on § 2–718(1), this section of the Nutshell draws also from the examples and commentary of the Restatement to explain the requirements for a valid liquidated damages clause.

Read any judicial opinion on liquidated damages and you will see a statement to the effect that a liquidated damages clause that operates as a penalty is not enforceable. Section 2–718, in fact, states that a clause setting "unreasonably large liquidated damages is void as a penalty." UCC § 2–718(1). The Restatement provides that a clause "fixing unreasonably large liquidated damages is unenforceable on grounds of public policy." RESTATEMENT (SECOND) OF CONTRACTS § 356(1). The reason for disallowing a penalty provision is that contract remedies are intended to be compensatory, not punitive. *See* RESTATEMENT (SECOND) OF CONTRACTS § 356, Comment ¶ a. Stating that a clause is a penalty and, thus, unenforceable, however, is nothing more than a legal conclusion. The question is *how* to determine whether a clause is a penalty or is a valid fixing of liquidated damages. The test is one of reasonableness.

Both the UCC's and the Restatement's tests examine the reasonableness of the amount of liquidated damages in light of the *anticipated or actual* harm caused by the breach. *See* UCC § 2–718(1); RESTATEMENT (SECOND) OF CONTRACTS § 356(1). This anticipated-or-actual harm test differs from the test at common law. At common law, the amount of damages set by a liquidated damages clause had to be reasonable in light of the harm *anticipated* at the time of contracting that would result from a breach of the parties' agreement.

Notice that both the UCC's and the Restatement's tests are stated in the disjunctive—anticipated *or* actual harm. For example, suppose Acme agrees to build a grandstand for Benson's racetrack for $1,000,000 with the work to be completed by April 1. The parties' agreement provides for liquidated damages of $1,000 per day for each day of delay in completing the racetrack. Acme does not complete the work until April 10. If $1,000 was a reasonable estimate of the anticipated loss and actual damages are hard to prove, then the liquidated damages clause is valid and enforceable. *See* RESTATEMENT (SECOND) OF CONTRACTS § 356, Illustration 3. In this illustration, because damages are reasonable in terms of anticipated loss, the test is satisfied even though actual loss is incapable of proof.

But what happens if the nonbreaching party suffers no loss at all, i.e., its damages are zero? In this type of case, some courts alter the statutory language to require that the liquidated damages be reasonable in light of anticipated *and* actual harm. For example, in Garden Ridge, L.P. v. Advance International, Inc., 403 S.W.3d 432 (Tex. App. 2013), the parties entered into a contract for the purchase and sale of large, inflatable snowmen. Advance, the seller, delivered inflatable snowmen that did not wave, as the buyer Garden Ridge had ordered and, thus, did not conform to the parties' agreement. Nonetheless, at trial, a Garden Ridge vice president testified that Garden Ridge earned the same amount of profit from sales of the nonconforming snowmen as it would have earned from sales of the conforming snowmen. In other words, the buyer suffered no loss.

The majority stated the "anticipated or actual harm" requirement from § 2–718(1) as follows.

> Most importantly, the UCC reasonableness test explicitly refers to actual harm, providing that one way a liquidated-damages provision can be invalidated is where the stipulated amount proves *unreasonable* in light of "the anticipated or actual harm caused by the breach."

Garden Ridge, 403 S.W.3d at 440 (emphasis added). While the court cited to the Texas equivalent of § 2–718(1), it changed the phrase "reasonable in light of the anticipated or actual harm" in the statute to "unreasonable in light of the anticipated or actual harm." Thus, in effect, the court changed the "or" in the statute to an "and." In his concurrence, Judge Frost pointed out that the majority's interpretation was "contrary to the plain meaning of the statutory text, under which the liquidated-damages amount may be reasonable based upon either anticipated harm or actual harm caused by the breach." *Garden Ridge,* 403 S.W.3d at 448 (Frost, J., concurring).

The *Garden Ridge* majority clearly was concerned with enforcing a liquidated damages clause in a case in which actual damages were zero. If damages are compensatory, what justification exists for payment of liquidated damages when no damages are incurred? The court, however, could have reached the same conclusion—the clause was not enforceable—by recognizing the connection between the actual-or-anticipated-harm test and the difficulty-of-proof-of-loss requirement, as does the Restatement.

> [T]wo factors combine in determining whether an amount of money fixed as damages is so unreasonably large as to be a penalty. The first factor is the anticipated or actual loss caused by the breach. . . . The second factor is the difficulty of proof of loss. . . . A determination whether the amount fixed is a penalty turns on a combination of these two factors. If the difficulty of proof of loss is great, considerable latitude is allowed in the approximation of anticipated or actual harm. If, on the other hand, the difficulty of proof of loss is slight, less latitude is allowed in that approximation. If, to take an extreme case, it is clear that no loss at all has occurred, a provision fixing a substantial sum as damages is unenforceable. See Illustration 4.

RESTATEMENT (SECOND) OF CONTRACTS § 356, Comment ¶ b. Suppose Acme agrees to build a grandstand for Benson's racetrack for $1,000,000 with the work to be completed by April 1. The parties' agreement provides for liquidated damages of $1,000 per day for each day of delay in completing the racetrack. Acme does not complete the work until April 10. But Benson was delayed a month in getting permission to operate the racetrack. As a result, Benson incurred no loss due to Acme's delay. Because Benson's loss is not difficult to prove, the liquidated damages clause is not enforceable on "grounds of public policy." RESTATEMENT (SECOND) OF CONTRACTS § 356, Illustration 4.

In other words, in cases, such as *Garden Ridge,* there is no need to manipulate the language of § 2–718 to invalidate a liquidated damages clause. A liquidated damages clause must be reasonable not only in light of actual or anticipated harm but also in light of the difficulties of proving loss. If the nonbreaching party suffered no loss and, thus, it is not difficult to prove damages (or the absence of damage), then the liquidated damages clause is not reasonable and should not be enforced.

> If there is no difficulty, if damages can be readily proved, then the clause should not be enforced because it approximates a loss that did not occur. The court would then avoid allowing a liquidated damages clause to operate as a penalty. Although the parties did agree to the amount liquidated, their intent was to approximate damages that simply did not occur. In such circumstances, there is no rational basis for giving effect to their mistaken assumption. The proper result can easily be reached by reading Section 2–718(1) in its entirety so that the "difficulties of proof of loss" factor for reasonableness is given equal importance to that of "anticipated or actual harm."

Anderson, 2 Damages Under UCC § 13:9.

While there is disagreement over the time *when* to measure the difficulty of proving loss, the Restatement looks at *actual* damages, as Illustration 4's racetrack example indicates, not damages *anticipated* at the time of contracting. In other words, the difficulty of proof of loss is measured at the time of breach, when actual damages, if any, occur, not at the time of contracting. A noted commentator contends that this result "seems unarguably to be the better position and the one that would be reached by most courts". Anderson, 2 Damages Under UCC § 13:10; *see* Monsanto Co. v. McFarling, 363 F.3d 1336 (Fed. Cir. 2004) (stating that difficulty of proof of loss is measured at the time the breach is discovered, not the time of contracting).

One final question that neither the comments to Restatement § 356 nor to UCC § 2–718 answer is which party bears the burden of proof. Does the party challenging the validity of the liquidated damages clause have the burden of proving it is unenforceable or does the party claiming that the clause is valid have the burden of proving its validity? As a noted commentator explains, "[t]he burden of going forward with proof of any unreasonableness should fall on the party attacking enforcement". Anderson, 2 Damages Under UCC § 13:10. Many courts agree. For example, in Wahlcometroflex, Inc. v. Westar Energy, Inc., 773 F.3d 223 (10th Cir. 2014), the Tenth Circuit explained that the party challenging a liquidated damages clause has the burden of proving it is a penalty. *See also* Designee LLC v. Honda Aircraft Co. LLC, 2020 WL 3428930 (Ariz. Ct. App. 2020) (party challenging provision has burden of "establishing it is unenforceable"); Triton 88 v. Star Electric LLC, 411 S.W.3d 42 (Tex. App. 2013) (stating that party claiming liquidated damages clause was not enforceable has burden of proof); *but see* Wildwood Industries, Inc. v. Genuine Machine Design, Inc., 587 F. Supp.2d 1035 (N.D. Ind. 2008) (stating that the case law placed the "burden of proving reasonableness of a liquidated damages amount on the party seeking to enforce the liquidated damages provision").

b. Buyer's Right to Restitution and Seller's Offset: § 2–718(2)–(4)

If the seller justifiably refuses to deliver the goods when the buyer breaches, the buyer nonetheless is entitled to restitution of any amount of money already paid to the seller that exceeds the amount (1) to which the seller is entitled under a valid liquidated damages clause or (2) provided by § 2–718's statutory liquidated damages provision. UCC § 2–718(2). If the seller received payment in goods, then the reasonable value of those goods or the proceeds of resale of the goods constitute payment by the buyer for purposes of subsection (2)'s right of restitution. UCC § 2–718(4). The buyer's right to restitution, however, is subject to offset to the extent that the seller establishes a right to recover damages under Article 2 other than under a liquidated damages clause. UCC § 2–718(3)(a). The buyer's right to restitution also is subject to offset to the extent that the seller establishes direct or indirect benefits received by the buyer by virtue of the parties' contract. UCC § 2–718(3)(b).

The following examples illustrate how the buyer's right to restitution and the seller's offset operate in practice, and the problem posed by some of the statutory language.

Suppose Phoenix Company and Samson, Inc. enter into a valid, written contract in which Samson agrees to sell Machine X to Phoenix for $35,000. Samson requires Phoenix to deposit $3,500 of the purchase price prior to beginning manufacture of Machine X. Phoenix pays Samson $3,500. Phoenix subsequently breaches and Samson refuses to deliver the machine. Assume Samson does not incur damages by virtue of Phoenix's breach of contract. Also assume that the parties' contract does not contain a liquidated damages clause. Phoenix's right to restitution, then, is controlled by § 2–718's statutory liquidated damages formula. That formula provides that the buyer is entitled to restitution of any amount by which the buyer's payments exceed the *smaller* of 20% of the good's total purchase price *or* $500. UCC § 2–718(2)(b). Twenty percent of the purchase price is $7,000, which means that Samson can retain the smaller amount of $500 as statutory liquidated damages. Phoenix is entitled to restitution of $3,000 ($3,500 deposit – $500).

Same facts, except that the parties' contract contains a clause providing for liquidated damages of $3,500 in the event of breach. Assume that the liquidated damages clause is reasonable and, thus, enforceable. In this case, Phoenix is entitled to restitution of any amount that its payments exceed the amount to which Samson is entitled under the contract's liquidated damages provision. Samson is entitled to $3,500 under the liquidated damages clause, which is equal to Phoenix's deposit. Therefore, Phoenix receives nothing back from Samson because Phoenix's payments do not exceed the amount of liquidated damages. *See* UCC § 2–718(2)(a).

What happens if the seller incurs damages from the buyer's breach? Suppose Phoenix and Samson enter into the same contract for the purchase and sale of Machine X and the contract, once again, contains no liquidated damages clause. Phoenix pays $3,500 towards the purchase price and subsequently breaches, and Samson justifiably withholds delivery of Machine X. Samson resells the Machine X intended for Phoenix to Babcock Company for $35,000. Assume that Samson is a lost volume seller and but for Phoenix's breach would have sold Machine X to Phoenix and another Machine X to Babson. Samson makes a profit of $3,000 on each Machine X. Samson keeps $500, the smaller amount under the statutory liquidated damages provision and it appears that Phoenix is entitled to restitution of the remaining deposit ($3,000). UCC § 2–718(2)(b). But the buyer's right to restitution is offset to the extent that the seller establishes actual damages. Samson has actual damages of $3,000 in lost profit due to Phoenix's breach. Therefore, Samson keeps the entire deposit: $500 (statutory liquidated damages) + $3,000 (seller offset for actual damages).

The preceding example raises the question: why should the non-breaching party receive more in damages than it actually incurred? Samson lost profit of $3,000 but a literal reading of § 2–718(2) and (3) results in Samson keeping Phoenix's entire deposit, thereby receiving $500 more in damages than it actually incurred. In Neri v. Retail Marine Corporation, 334 N.Y.S.2d 165 (N.Y. 1972), the breaching buyer had deposited $4,250 with the seller. The seller proved damages as a lost volume seller of

$3,253. The court held that the buyer was entitled to restitution of the difference between the $4,250 deposit and the seller's actual damages of $3,253. The court discussed the buyer's right of restitution under § 2–718(2)(b) but without discussion did *not* reduce the amount of the buyer's restitution by an additional $500—the statutory liquidated damages amount. In other words, the court offset the buyer's right to restitution by the seller's actual damages.

Applying the *Neri* result to our example, Phoenix's right to restitution should be offset to the amount of Samson's actual damages. Thus, Samson keeps $3,000 of the $3,500, because $3,000 is its actual damage. Phoenix is entitled to $500 of its deposit back from Samson. The literal language of § 2–718(2) and (3) does not produce this result but it nonetheless makes sense because the purpose of contract damages is to compensate the non-breaching party for its loss. *See* UCC § 1–305(a).

There is virtually no case law on these issues. The above examples are intended to provide some guidance on how to interpret the language of § 2–718(2) and (3).

2. LEASES: § 2A–504

Section 2A–504 is a substantially revised version of § 2–718. The need for a more flexible standard than that provided by § 2–718 underlay the changes.

> Many leasing transactions are predicated on the parties' ability to agree to an appropriate amount of damages or formula for damages in

> the event of default or other act or omission. The rule with respect to sales of goods (Section 2–718) may not be sufficiently flexible to accommodate this practice. Thus, consistent with the common law emphasis upon freedom to contract with respect to bailments for hire, this section has created a revised rule that allows greater flexibility with respect to leases of goods.

UCC § 2A–504, Comment: Purposes.

a. Validity of Liquidated Damages Clause: § 2A–504(1) & (2)

The parties to a lease may liquidate damages for default or for "any other act or omission, including indemnity for loss or diminution of anticipated tax benefits or loss or damage to lessor's residual interest." UCC § 2A–504(1). Damages may be liquidated "only at an amount or by a formula that is reasonable in light of the then anticipated harm caused by the default or other act or omission." *Id.* Subsection (1) of § 2A–504 differs significantly from subsection (1) of § 2–718. *See* UCC § 2A–504, Comment: Purposes (stating that § 2A–504(1) is a "significantly modified version of the provisions of Section 2–718(1)").

First, § 2A–504(1) requires that liquidated damages be reasonable in light of the harm anticipated at the time of contracting. Section 2–718(1), by comparison, tests reasonableness in light of the anticipated or actual harm caused by the breach. Nonetheless, the extent of actual harm is one factor that many courts examine in deciding what losses the parties to a lease could reasonably anticipate at the time of contracting. *See* 3 Hawkland UCC Series § 2A–504:2. But a court should not invalidate a liquidated damages clause merely because the clause's estimate of loss turns out to be inaccurate. *See* 3 Hawkland UCC Series § 2A–504:1 (because "actual harm is not an explicit factor, a clause should not be overturned based purely on hindsight"). The test is one of reasonableness in light of the harm anticipated at the time of contracting.

Second, the parties to a lease may provide for liquidated damages based on a formula. By comparison, § 2–718(1) does not expressly provide for "liquidation by a formula." UCC § 2A–504, Comment: Purposes. The Official Comments to § 2A–504 give several examples of formulae used in leasing practice. One common formula for the lessor's damages is as follows, in which LP stands for lease payments:

> Past due LP + Accelerated future LP + Lessor's estimated residual interest − Net proceeds of disposition by sale or re-lease

See UCC § 2A–504, Comment: Purposes. Added to the lessor's damages are "[t]ax indemnities, costs, interest and attorney's fees." *Id.* The parties also may agree to liquidate damages by fixing a "number of periodic payments," e.g., stating that liquidated damages equal 3 months rental. *See id.* Another common method of liquidating damages in a lease is for the parties to stipulate to loss or damage schedules. *See id.*

A third difference between the sales and the lease provisions on liquidated damages is that § 2–718(1) provides for liquidated damages in the event of breach. Section 2A–504(1) covers not only default by either party, but also "any other act or omission", thereby expanding the reasons why the parties to a lease may provide for liquidated damages. Thus, § 2A–504(1) is "a further expansion of Section 2–718(1)." UCC § 2A–504, Comment: Purposes.

Fourth, § 2A–504(1) includes neither the "difficulty of loss" nor the "inconvenience or nonfeasibility of otherwise obtaining an adequate remedy" requirements of § 2–718(1). The reason for not carrying forward these two requirements from § 2–718(1) to § 2A–504(1)? "The ability to liquidate damages is critical to modern leasing practice; given the parties' freedom of contract at common law, the policy behind retaining these two additional requirements here was thought to be outweighed." UCC § 2A–504, Comment: Purposes.

Fifth, § 2A–504(1) does not provide that a clause fixing an unreasonably large amount of liquidated damages is a penalty, as does the final sentence of § 2–718(1). The reason for the difference is that the parties' lease agreement may liquidate damages for "indemnity for loss or diminution of anticipated tax benefits." UCC § 2A–504(1). "The impact of local, state and federal tax laws on a leasing transaction can result in an amount payable with respect to the tax indemnity many times greater than the original purchase price of the goods." UCC § 2A–504, Comment: Purposes. The drafters intended to free the parties to negotiate a formula for damages "restrained by the rule of reasonableness." *Id.*

Finally, § 2A–504(2) is a modification of the language of § 2–719(2) on remedy limitations. Section 2–719(2) provides that if circumstances cause a limited or exclusive remedy to fail of its essential purpose, then the parties may avail themselves of the remedy provisions of Article 2. *See infra* § G.1 of this Chapter. Section 2A–504(2) states that if a liquidated damages clause is an "exclusive or limited remedy" and circumstances cause it to fail of its essential purpose, then the remedy provisions of Article 2A are available to the parties. Subsection (2) also states that the parties may avail themselves of Article 2A's remedy provisions if the lease's liquidated damages clause fails to comply with the requirements of subsection (1) of § 2A–504.

b. Lessee's Right to Restitution and Lessor's Offset: § 2A–504(3) & (4)

As does the buyer in a contract for the sale of goods, the lessee under a lease contract has a right to restitution in certain cases. If the lessor justifiably withholds or stops delivery because the lessee has defaulted on the lease or is insolvent, the lessee is entitled to restitution of monies paid to the lessor in excess of the amount of damages provided either by a valid liquidated damages clause or if there is no valid liquidated damages clause by § 2A–504's statutory liquidated damages formula. *See* UCC § 2A–504(3).

The formula for statutory liquidated damages for consumer leases is similar to that for contracts for the sale of goods: the lessee is entitled to restitution of any amount in excess of the *lesser* of $500 or 20% of the present value of the remaining rent owed. *See* UCC § 2A–504(3)(b). For all other leases in which there is no valid liquidated damages clause, the lessee is entitled to restitution of any monies paid to the lessor that exceed 20% of the then present value of the rent remaining on the lease. *See id.* The $500 limitation was dropped for non-consumer leases "as unrealistically low with respect to a lease other than a consumer lease." UCC § 2A–504, Comment: Purposes.

Suppose that on March 1, Barney Company enters into a two-year lease with Slate, Inc. to rent equipment for $1,000 per month. The lease begins on April 1. The lease does not contain a liquidated damages clause. At the signing of the lease, Barney pays $1,000 for first month's rent. Assume that before April 1, Barney defaults and Slate justifiably withholds delivery of the equipment. Does Barney get its $1,000 back?

The short answer is "no." For a commercial lease, the lessee has a right to restitution for any amount by which the sum of its payments *exceeds* 20% of the then present value of the total rent the lessee is obligated to pay for the rest of the lease term. Barney is obligated under the lease to pay $1,000 per month for 24 months. Ignoring the present value calculation, 20% of $24,000 is $4,800. Barney paid only $1,000 to Slate. Therefore, Barney has no right of restitution and Slate keeps the $1,000.

Keep in mind that the lessee's right to restitution is subject to offset to the extent that the lessor establishes a right to recover damages, other than pursuant to a valid liquidated damages clause. *See* UCC § 2A–504(4). Thus, the calculation above is based on the assumption that Slate incurred no actual damages. Suppose, however, that Barney had paid $5,000 at the time of signing the lease. Ignoring the present value calculation, Barney would be entitled to restitution of $200: $5,000 paid − $4,800 (20% of remaining rent owed). Now, suppose Slate re-rented the equipment for two years but at a lower yearly rental. In such a case, Barney's recovery of $200 as restitution would be offset (decreased) to the extent of damages that Slate incurred due to Barney's default.

A final word of caution. Section 2A–504(3) speaks in terms of the *lessee's right to restitution,* not the *lessor's right to statutory liquidated damages*. For example, suppose Barney had paid nothing to Slate at the time that Barney signed the lease. Assume that Slate, upon Barney's default, was able to re-lease the equipment but at a lower yearly rental. Barney has no right to restitution in this case, because it has paid nothing to Slate. Therefore, § 2A–504(3)(b) simply does not apply. Slate may recover damages from Barney under § 2A–527 based on its re-lease of the equipment, but it is not entitled to 20% of the present value of the rent that Barney was obligated to pay for two years under the parties' lease agreement.

G. LIMITATION OF REMEDIES

1. SALES: § 2–719

The parties to a contract for the sale of goods may limit the remedies available, or the amount of damages recoverable, for breach. *See* UCC § 2–719(1). While the parties' contract may provide for an exclusive remedy for breach, such an exclusive or limited remedy is not enforceable if it fails of its essential purpose. *See* UCC § 2–719(1)(b), (2). The parties also may limit or exclude consequential damages unless such a limitation or exclusion is unconscionable. *See* UCC § 2–719(3). A limitation of consequential damages for personal injury in a contract for consumer goods is prima facie unconscionable. *See id.*

a. Remedy Limitations: § 2–719(1)

The parties to a contract for the sale of goods may provide remedies in addition to or in substitution of those provided by Article 2. *See* UCC § 2–719(1)(a). While the parties' agreement may provide for remedies in addition to those provided by Article 2, the far more common situation involves a seller's effort to limit the buyer's remedies for breach. Section 2–719 expressly provides that the parties' contract may limit the "buyer's remedies to return of the goods and repayment of the price or to repair and replacement of non-conforming goods or parts." UCC § 2–719(1)(a). Moreover, a seller may provide that the limited remedy is the buyer's sole remedy, but the agreement must clearly state that the remedy is exclusive.

Suppose Acme, Inc. purchases a machine for its factory from Machinex Corporation. Machinex provides a limited warranty on the equipment, and the parties' agreement clearly states that the exclusive remedy for any breach of warranty is repair or replacement of the equipment. The machine malfunctions and, as a result, Acme is unable to fulfill an order with another firm, thereby resulting in lost profit from that order of $50,000. Acme sues Machinex for damages. The $50,000 in lost profit is consequential damage. Notice that even if the parties' agreement did not contain a disclaimer of consequential damages, limiting Acme's remedy to repair or replacement of the machine effectively eliminates its right to recover consequential damages. *See, e.g.*, Prairie River Home Care Inc. v. Procura, LLC, 2019 WL 3021253 (D. Minn. 2019) (stating that an exclusive remedy provision, if valid, excluded recovery of consequential damages). The remedy limitation is clearly stated in the agreement and, thus, Acme cannot recover damages from Machinex for breach of warranty.

As the seller, it is important to state that a remedy is exclusive. *See* Anderson, 2 Damages Under UCC § 12:5 (stating that "[i]n short, a remedy limitation which is not made exclusive is not worth the paper on which it is printed"). The drafters intended those contractual clauses prescribing remedies to be "cumulative rather than exclusive." UCC § 2–719, Comment ¶ 2. If the intent is to make a remedy exclusive, that intent "must be clearly expressed." *Id.* For example, in Lowe v. Smith, 2016 WL 5210874 (Tenn. Ct. App. 2016), Lowe, the owner of a convenience store, sold his business to the Smiths. (The trial court held that the sale fell within the scope of Article 2 and the parties did not dispute that finding on appeal.) The contract provided that a breach by the Smiths of the agreement would render the sale "null and void" with the business reverting to Lowe. The trial court, however, did not enforce this provision of the parties' agreement and instead awarded money damages. On appeal, the Tennessee Court of Appeals affirmed the trial court's judgment. The Appeals Court noted that even though the contract specified the remedy, nothing in the contract "specifically state[d] that the remedy provided [was] intended to be the sole remedy available in the event of breach . . . [and] [t]hus, other remedies under the UCC [were] available in the event of breach." *Lowe,* 2016 WL 5210874, at *13.

Finally, bear in mind that while a liquidated damages clause in a contract is "by definition a form of remedy limitation", § 2–719 does not apply to such clauses. Anderson, 2 Damages Under UCC § 12:3. Instead, § 2–718 applies. In fact, § 2–719 specifically states that it is subject to § 2–718 on liquidated damages. *See* UCC § 2–719(1). Therefore, if a fact pattern involves a liquidated damages clause, turn to the standards set forth at § 2–718, not § 2–719.

b. Failure of Essential Purpose: § 2–719(2)

Suppose the parties' agreement provides that the buyer's exclusive remedy for breach by the seller is repair or replacement of nonconforming goods. The exclusive remedy provision is conspicuous and clearly expressed. If the buyer wants to recover damages from the seller, is the buyer simply out of luck in this situation? Not necessarily. The buyer can argue that the exclusive remedy fails of its essential purpose. "Where circumstances cause an exclusive or limited remedy to fail of its essential purpose, remedy may be had as provided in this Act." UCC § 2–719(2). The UCC, however, does not define the term "essential purpose." What does it mean to argue that a remedy has failed of its essential purpose? Consider the following example.

> Assume the seller expressly warrants its product to be the standard of the industry, that it will pass with only applause in the trade and that it is gloriously fit for all the buyer's particular purposes. Assume further, however, that in the event the product fails to measure up to expectations, the contract expressly and conspicuously limits the buyer's remedy to a personally signed letter of apology and condolence on embossed stationery from the president of the seller corporation.

Anderson, 2 Damages Under UCC § 12:4. The problem is that this exclusive "remedy" is no remedy at all. The drafters made clear that "it is of the very essence of a sales contract that at least minimum adequate remedies be available." UCC § 2–719,

Comment ¶ 1. A letter of apology on embossed letterhead is not, at a minimum, "a fair quantum of remedy for breach" of the seller's contractual obligations. UCC § 2–719, Comment ¶ 1.

The example above is easy because the facts are so extreme. The real question is this: In the real world of contracting, what amounts to a failure of essential purpose? A court may determine that a limited remedy fails of its essential purpose if the seller's product contains a latent defect that the buyer cannot discover within the time frame provided by the seller's limited remedy. For example, in U.S. Aprons, Inc. v. R-Five, Inc, 2010 WL 489540 (D. Neb. 2010), U.S. Aprons entered into a contract to supply disaster-relief vests to Hanover, which had contracted to supply the vests to the American Red Cross. U.S. Aprons ordered both red and white fabric from R-Five for the vests. The contract between U.S. Aprons and R-Five provided that U.S. Aprons had to bring any claims within 30 days or before the fabric was cut. When the red and white fabric was cut and sewn together, it yellowed. U.S. Aprons sued R-Five for breach of contract and breach of express and implied warranties. R-Five argued that the limited remedy provision in the parties' agreement barred any claims by U.S. Aprons for breach of contract or breach of warranty with regard to the cut fabric. The district court disagreed. The court explained that the defect in the dyed fabric—the yellowing—only occurred after the fabric was cut and sewn together. Enforcing the contractual clause barring claims after the fabric was cut "would completely deprive U.S. Aprons of any remedy for breach." *Id.* at *5. The court denied R-Five's motion for summary judgment and concluded that the contract's language had to "yield to the 'general remedy provisions' of the U.C.C., which allow a buyer a reasonable amount of time to notify the seller of the breach after he discovers or should have discovered, the product defect. U.C.C. § 2–607(3)(a)." *Id.*

In Prairie River Home Care, Inc. v. Procura, LLC, 2019 WL 3021253 (D. Minn. 2019), Prairie River purchased software and support services from Procura. The parties' agreement limited Procura's liability for breach to the total fees that Prairie River had paid to Procura within the twelve-month period prior to any claim initiated by Prairie River. Procura delivered the software to Prairie River on time, but the software was only incorporated into Prairie River's computer system eight to ten months after the parties had entered into their agreement. Prairie River only discovered the latent defects after incorporating the software into its computer system. The district court, ruling on Procura's motion to dismiss, concluded that Prairie River had alleged facts sufficient to demonstrate that Procura's limited remedy failed of its essential purpose.

> The defects were not only latent, but of such a nature that Prairie River could not discover them until after it had spent considerable time, money, and other resources integrating the Software into its systems. Moreover, Procura repeatedly assured Prairie River that it could fix the problems with the Software, leaving Prairie River with no way of knowing that new problems

> would arise with each update and attempted fix. By the time Prairie River determined it could not operate with the Software and abandoned it, more than twelve months had passed since it had paid Procura, which—under the limitation on remedies provision in the contract—would leave Prairie River with no remedy whatsoever. Considering all the circumstances, the Court finds that Prairie River has alleged facts sufficient to show that the limitation of remedy fails of its essential purpose.

Id. at **23–24.

Be careful not to conclude that a limited remedy fails of its essential purpose simply because the defect is latent. If the buyer discovers the defect within the time period provided by the limited remedy but fails to take advantage of the limited remedy, that remedy does not fail of its essential purpose. If the buyer does notify the seller within the relevant time period, but the seller assures the buyer that it will cure but fails to cure, a court may determine that the remedy does fail of its essential purpose.

c. Consequential Damages: § 2–719(3)

The parties' contract may disclaim consequential damages so long as the disclaimer is conscionable. *See* UCC § 2–719(3). Consequential damages disclaimers benefit sellers because buyers, not sellers, are entitled to recover such damages. *See supra* Chapter 11 § B.1.e, § C.1.d. A disclaimer of consequential damages for injury to the person in a contract for consumer goods is prima facie unconscionable. *See* UCC § 2–719(3). As discussed earlier in this Nutshell, an unconscionability analysis typically has a procedural and a substantive component. *See supra* Chapter 7, § A. As a noted UCC treatise explains, however, the timing of the unconscionability analysis under § 2–719(3) differs from that under § 2–302.

> [W]hether a provision of a contract is unconscionable is typically determined at the time the contract is formed. Section 2–719(3) provides a limited exception to that timing principle directed to clauses excluding recovery of consequential damages. The official comment notes that if such clauses "operate" in an unconscionable manner the exclusion of consequential damages is unenforceable.

2 Hawkland UCC Series § 2–719:2; *see, e.g.*, Tokyo Ohka Kogyo America, Inc. v. Huntsman Propylene Oxide, LLC, 35 F. Supp.3d 1316 (D. Ore. 201) (stating that in a § 2–719(3) unconscionability analysis, the court "is not limited to evaluating the provision at the time the contract was made, but must consider how the provision operated and evaluate the provision after the contract has been breached").

What happens if the parties' contract contains an exclusive remedy provision and a limitation on consequential damages, and the court determines that the exclusive remedy fails of its essential purpose? The Official Comment to § 2–719 provides that if an exclusive remedy fails of its essential purpose, the buyer may avail itself of the remedies provided by Article 2. *See* UCC § 2–719, Comment ¶ 1. Does that mean that the buyer may recover consequential damages if an exclusive remedy fails of its essential purpose, even if the parties' agreement disclaimed such damages? The courts are split on the question, but many courts hold that the buyer may recover consequential damages in such a case, notwithstanding a disclaimer of consequential damages in the parties' agreement. Some courts, however, will enforce a consequential damages limitation in such a case, in particular if the disclaimer is in a clause separate from the exclusive remedy provision, so long as the disclaimer of consequential damages is conscionable. Finally, other courts look to whether the "exclusive remedy and damage exclusions are 'separable elements of risk allocation' or 'inseparable parts of a unitary package of risk-allocation' " and, therefore, "take a case-by-case approach." *Tokyo Ohka Kogyo,* 35 F. Supp. 3d at 1331–31 (discussing the various approaches taken by courts).

Bear in mind that a seller may disclaim warranties altogether, thereby affecting the buyer's ability to recover damages, including consequential damages. *See* 2 Hawkland UCC Series § 2–719:3 (stating that sellers "can effectively limit their liability by disclaiming warranties—eliminating the basis for damages rather than the damages themselves"). For example, suppose Bette Buyer purchases a dehumidifier from *No Sweat Company* (NSC). The contract contains a limited 90-day warranty on the dehumidifier and properly disclaims all implied warranties after the 90-day period (to comply with

Magnuson-Moss). Six months after the purchase, the dehumidifier malfunctions, catches on fire, and damages the flooring around the dehumidifier. Assume that the dehumidifier is not fit for its ordinary purpose. Bette wants to sue NSC for breach of warranty to recover for the defective dehumidifier and the floor repair; the repair cost for the floor is consequential damage. Here is the problem. Bette cannot sue for breach of express warranty because the malfunction occurred after expiration of the express warranty. Bette cannot sue for breach of the implied warranty of merchantability or fitness for a particular purpose because NSC properly disclaimed all implied warranties. If Bette cannot sue for breach of warranty, then she cannot recover damages from NSC for breach of warranty, including consequential damages.

The drafters of Article 2 intended this result. The Official Comment notes that any limitation or exclusion of consequential damages must be conscionable. But it also provides that the "seller in all cases is free to disclaim warranties in the manner provided in Section 2–316." UCC § 2–719, Comment ¶ 3.

2. LEASES: § 2A–503

The parties to a lease may agree to "rights and remedies for default in addition to or in substitution for those provided" by Article 2A. UCC § 2A–503(1). The parties also "may limit or alter the measure of damages recoverable" for breach. *Id.* A lease, just like a sales contract, must expressly state that the parties intend a remedy to be exclusive. UCC § 2A–503(2). Section 2A–503, like § 2–719, provides that the remedies provisions of Article 2A are available if an exclusive remedy fails of its essential purpose. *Id.* Unlike § 2–719(2), however, § 2A–503(2) also states that Article 2A remedies are available if a "provision for an exclusive remedy is unconscionable." *Id.* The drafters of § 2A–503 sought to make clear what is only implicit in § 2–719(2): the UCC's other remedies are available if a court determines that an exclusive remedy is unconscionable. UCC § 2A–503, Comment ¶ 2.

The parties to a lease, just like the parties to a contract for the sale of goods, may limit, alter, or exclude consequential damages "unless the limitation, alteration, or exclusion is unconscionable." UCC § 2A–503(3). In the case of consumer goods, however, a disclaimer of consequential damages for personal injury is prima facie unconscionable. *Id.*

Subsection (4) of § 2A–503 has no counterpart in § 2–719. It is a "revision of the provisions of Section 2–701." UCC § 2A–503, Comment ¶ 4. Basically, subsection (4) provides that Article 2A does not impair the operation of other law with regard to the rights and remedies that the parties have upon default of collateral or ancillary obligations. The Official Comment provides two examples of such ancillary or collateral obligations. In the case of the lessor, an example would be the lessor's obligation to a secured creditor that provided the lessor with the funds to leverage the lease transaction. UCC § 2A–

503, Comment ¶ 4. Article 9 would govern the rights of the secured creditor upon default of the agreement between that creditor and the lessor; Article 2A would not impair the secured creditor's rights and remedies under Article 9. An example of such an obligation by the lessee would be the lessee's promise, as the seller, to the lessor/buyer in a sale-leaseback transaction. *Id.* Because of the "lessee's position as seller in a sale-leaseback transaction, . . . U.C.C. Article 2 and not U.C.C. Article 2A would govern" the lessee's collateral promise. 3 Hawkland UCC Series § 2A–503:9.

INDEX

References are to Pages